FROM THE WEST END

TO LIL PAKISTAN PART 1

Lucile Kil

Dear Momma,

It's been seven months since we last spoke but it seems like yesterday. Today is your birthday. This is my gift to you. The devil is a lie! I did it momma! Happy Birthday! Now, you can rest in peace, Artie C. Your fight has been won. Ours has just begun. We will miss you for eternity.

"THE CORNER OF LUCILE AND HOLDERNESS"

This is a book based on the story of my life, describing the brutal unsolved deaths of several neighborhood drug dealers during the height of the crack cocaine epidemic in the late 80's and early 90s. Most of the murders are unsolved cold cases, all carried out by the same Muslim assassin and ironically the self-proclaimed bodyguard of Jamil -. Formerly known as H. Rap, a radical black leader in the 60s. He was also a member of the Black Panther Party. Jamil was the most powerful man in the Atlanta and West End neighborhood. Allegedly he controlled all the Muslims that he moved in his Muslim community during the time of the killings.

This is my story, and I am the only living person who can tell it. It's the story of the dead, my dead homies, and how and why they died. It's the truth about the West End. We are about to take a ride on the Westside from zones 1-3-4-5- some of 6, and a stop and shop in zone 2. I'm from the 4th zone, Lucile Ave. and Holderness St. It was the heartbeat for drugs in Atlanta's West End, right next to the Muslims Den. How did two worlds so different, so close, co-exist for so long?

"Hello" I could barely hear Tamika's voice before the recording came in.

"This call is from a federal prison. To accept dial 9...... Beep,"

"Hey baby," Tamika answered. I could barely hear her.

"Speak up baby. What, you got a nigga over there in your ear? Tell me you love me and that's still my pussy". I said, trying to make it sound like a joke, but at this point in my life, I don't know what to think. I'm still in Federal custody, without bond. It's been one month and ten days. Something isn't right with this case. Why wouldn't they give me a bond? I'm not in for murder, just dope and guns! Niggas go to jail for that shit every day in the hood. The only way you don't get a bond is if you are on papers but I'm clean, no probation. That's what this call is about, bond hearing number 3. The 4th of July was a couple days ago, so court has been slow.

"Baby please! I can wait, but can your wife?" Tameka could talk shit, but she wasn't a shit talker. She had to be feeling some kinda way. I switched my gears.

"You're right baby fuck that shit, you talk to the lawyer?" I asked, praying for the best, hoping for nothing less.

"Nawl, I ain't talk to nobody. I don't know shit bout nothing!" she snapped;

Wow! She went from zero to a hundred too quick. My hair stood on the back of my neck. Something was wrong with this bitch, she's acting like she's spooked.

"Ok ok let's try this again. How was your day, Ms. Brown?" She paused, then said.

"My day was sadder than the last Rodney, I'm so tired, I need to sleep. You need to call home." Her voice, weak like a child.

"I called, and no one is home", I answered. She made a small gasp.

"So you haven't talked to anyone all day?" she asked. Why is she crying? I almost snapped from Rodney to Kil.

"Digg this bit.....This call is from a federal institution you have 5 minutes left for this call". Hope she didn't hear me call her a bitch.

"Listen, baby. You heard that I got five minutes left on this call, and my phone money is low, I ain't even heard from Lee. You need to serve this shit to me straight, stop the chase. I know you know something ain't right? Somebody threaten you? Give me the business, don't leave me in the blind bitch." I begged her. It was a long silence, over 2 minutes. Then she dropped a bomb on me.

"Listen baby, I love you. People saying a lot of shit around here, but I don't repeat most of it to you. But this morning Lil Red knocked on my window and told me to tell you they found another body. This one in your car. I thought you knew baby, that's why I didn't know what to say when you called. I'm so sorry baby, I'm so so sorry." She cried every word out, but what the fuck is she saying?

"I knew bout what? You sorry bout what? What the fuck bitch? Hello hello." The phone went dead.

"IN THE BEGINNING

OF THE END"

In the beginning of the End we all were friends, mothers, fathers, sisters, brothers, cousins, and then came the Muslims.

My government name is Rodney. My street name is Kil. I've lived in the West End of Atlanta my entire life. I was born in 1971 to Artie and Walter, the youngest of four. My oldest sister Kim is nine years my elder, second born Karen is 8 years my elder and my brother Walter is 5 years my elder. My earliest memories of life were when we all lived in a two-bedroom shack on Baldwin Place, right behind the Harris Holmes projects. It's hard to believe that I could be so poor and not even know it, but if poor is all you see, poor is all you know. Everything back then now seems like an old black and white movie. That's how I picture it in my mind. No color, and it's always winter time. I mainly remember when we lived on Baldwin Place, I was around four or five years old. We moved around a lot in my early years but never left the West End. I attended damn near all of the Elementary schools in the area; M. Agnes Jones, Dean Russell, Ragsdale, and J C Harris where I was promoted to high school. My father was an alcoholic and my mother wasn't far behind and raised hell with him on the weekend. I witnessed a lot of violence at a very young age but despite it all; I was still an enthusiastic kid. I was blessed to grow up with a father that I loved but feared. I loved my mother too, but everybody had a mother. You were truly blessed to have a father that lived in the same house with you. My father was a good man. He was an Air Force veteran and most of all he had a strong belief in education. Alcohol was his only downfall. I loved him all the same, and I could feel his love in every word he ever spoke to me. My father knew something about everything, and he shared so many things with me that I'm just starting to understand now.

I was around 7 years old when we moved from Baldwin Place to Lucile Ave. My father said it was because he didn't want us growing up in the projects. I did not understand what he meant and didn't care. I was going wherever my father went. Daddy was my world, I loved my mother too, but it was different. To be honest, I can remember as far back as 2, but only because my dog Tiger ate my rabbit and then tried to eat me, after I stabbed him with some scissors for killing Bunny. All my other memories are of me and my father. My siblings were jealous of me because I was the baby. I hate to admit that I don't think my mother liked me very much back then. I was the spoiled one and I let it be known. When we moved to Lucile, my eyes opened like a puppy. Lucile was walking distance from Baldwin Place. My entire life had been within walking distance and it would be that way for a while.

We moved into a house that really wasn't a house. It was a garage that had been converted into a house located behind a house. My father did his best to provide, and he had a way of making us feel happy at the worst of times. The house had three rooms. So, Walter and I had our room and Kim and Karen had theirs. The house was brick but painted white. The yard was a big gravel driveway, but like daddy said, at least it's big. The best part for me was the big park about a half block away, named the West End Park. It had a laundromat across the street, so when my sister went to wash clothes, I got to play at the park. Sometimes daddy and I would go to the Laundromat together. On this day, daddy and I were headed to the laundromat.

"Boy, you better keep up before I leave yo ass". Father said; as we walked down the steep hill beside the park. My father was a big man, 6'3 and 260 pounds. He had what seemed to me all the clothes we owed on his back. It made him look like a walking mountain. I'm small and skinny, maybe 7 or 8 years old. I had the washing powder, and it was heavy.

"Nawl you ain't gonna leave me, I'm right behind ya daddy". I said, trying to catch my breath at the same time. I wasn't that far behind, but it was hard keeping up. My father stopped and turned around to wait for me. His face black and shiny in the sun.

"Hurry up boy, dis shit here heavy, you want to trade?" He said in his big deep voice. Every other word was always a curse word out of his mouth. That's really how all the grown-ups talked around here, at least the ones I'd been around. All but the man that owns the Laundromat. I never heard him curse. Maybe it was because he wore a dress. My brother Lil Walt told me that man was a Fag...

"Any man wear a dress is a Fag". He said;

I caught up with my father.

"I'm tied". I said; I put the big box of washing powder down and sat down right there on the curb. My father looked down at me. He still had all the clothes on his back.

"Boy, you better get yo ass up for I drop all dis shit on ya. It's hot out here, I ain't got time to play. I need a drink, shit! You thank I want to do dis shit? Hell nawl, but a man's gotta do what a man's gotta do. Boy dis shit ain't gonna wash itself, now get yo as up and come on now". He said; then he turned and started walking across the park. I knew not to say another word. I got up and headed behind him as fast as my legs would go. It was around 11:00 am on a Monday. School started today, but I didn't go. I had a doctor's appointment for my shots, I was changing schools again. The sun was out, and it was warming up fast, a beautiful day it looked to be. The park was empty, everybody else was in school. By the time I caught up to him, he was crossing the basketball court, about to head up the hill to the Laundromat. He wasn't slowing down at all. I guess the clothes were getting heavy. I know the washing powder was. I started to run and ran right past him.

"Hey boy, don't cross that road," he said. He was out of breath.

"Ok," I answered. I stopped in my tracks right on the curb and waited. My father walked up behind me and said; "Aye Boy, remember what I told ya bout dis Muslim man in there. You don't say shit but yes sir and no sir and always look a man in his eye." He told me the same thing every time we came here, and I never heard my father curse inside the laundromat. He always talked properly and said some words that I couldn't understand when he spoke to the man in the dress. The laundromat was located at the corner of Oak and Atwood, directly across the street from the park. The building was about the size of two houses. It had two sides. One for washing clothes and the other, a small store. The Laundromat had four washers and four dryers. The store was very small, with two isles and one refrigerator. It was a homemade business at its best. The man in the dress was sitting on a bench outside of his store. My father looked both ways, then we crossed the street. We walked right up to the man in the dress. He stood. He was the tallest person I'd seen in my life so far. He was taller than my daddy.

"Assalamualaikum brother Walt! How can I be of service to you and your son?" The tall man in the dress asked; as he extended his hand to my daddy.

"Walaikum Salam brother Rap. We were hoping you had some machines open, needed to do some washing, and let me and my boy get two cold drinks on the books. I got the money for the wash,"? My father asked as he shook the tall man's hand. My father knew everyone in the neighborhood, and they knew him too. He had credit with all the stores.

"All the machines are open for you. What kind of pop would you brothers like? I'll get them while you put your clothes in." He replied; his voice was smooth and proper. I hadn't heard anyone talk that way before. Like every time I asked for a drink, he would say, here's your soda pop.

"Two Cokes, please, Rap," my father answered.

"I'll be right over". He said; then turned and walked inside the store. I opened the door to the laundromat and held it until my father came in. My father started loading the machines up. I sat down on the bench next to the door. The tall man came with the drinks.

"Here you are, nice and cold brother Walt. How is the rest of the family? Hopefully blessed by Allah". The tall man said;

"Everybody, good brother Rap, thanks for asking. The girls are in high school now, they are getting big fast. I gotta watch them. Lil-Walt works at the corner store you know," my father said.

"Don't worry Brother Walt, my people and I watch over all the young ones around here". He replied;

"Believe me Rap, I know you do and thanks again. I'll be by Friday to pay the book off". Father said;

"Ok then I leave you men to your chore,". He turned and walked back out.

After my father finished loading all the clothes, we walked over to the park to drink our cokes. We sat on a bench and I handed my drink to my father. He opened it with his teeth, then gave it back. I took a sip, then asked a question.

"Daddy, why does that man wear dresses?"

"Boy, that ain't no damn dress. It's called a dashiki, Muslims wear them. It's a part of their culture and he ain't no sissy because he wears one." He answered;

"Lil-Walt say he a fag and............" He cut me off.

"Lil-Walt don't know shit that man ain't no fag. He wears that shit because it is part of their religion. Just like our Rev. Stovall gotta drive a Cadillac, that shit part of his religion and a lot more of them crooked motherfuckers that preach." he said; then started laughing. He stopped then said;

"Ok boy don't tell yo momma I said that I was just bullshitting. Imma tell you the truth about Muslims. You just listen well and don't ever forget. That man that Li-Walt say a fag is a very dangerous nigga. He robbed a bank in Philadelphia and shot the police."

"Did he kill them?" I cut in;

"Hell nawl, he didn't kill them. If so, we wouldn't be looking at that nigga today boy, but he fucked him up, fucked up a lot of folks. That nigga a killer, I'm telling you. He used to be in that Black Panther Party shit. They was niggas trying to police other niggas. I heard they used to go around killing drug dealers until half of them got on the dope, went to prison, or got killed. That one over there used to be big time in that shit. That nigga famous, he in books and shit boy. That's why you gotta read, crackers hide shit in books. He wrote some books too, one called "Die Nigger Die" and that nigga made a speech one time and said some shit like "murder is as American as apple pie." I knew then he was fucked up in the head. They say he tried to blow up some people in a courthouse, too. But see Rod, we ain't on this Earth to judge nobody. Maybe he had reason to do the shit they say he did. If he did it, I know it's a lot of bitter niggas on this earth. Crackers did a lot of fucked up shit to us and we did and are still doing a lot of to ourselves. But I can say shit better now boy, I tell you that. That man Luther King made it better for us, not no niggas walking around with guns. Crackers got all the guns anyway, everybody knows that. You can't out kill these crackers. They had to show them Japs. You'll see before these crackers give up power, they'll blow up the planet. Yeah boy, you better believe that. America is the most powerful country on this planet. This country was built on Christianity. You know the stuff you hear in Sunday school. They teach you from the New Testament. They teach you about our Lord and Savior Jesus Christ and how he died for our sins, so as Christians we must forgive. You see, it was another bible before Jesus called the Old Testament. Muslims don't believe in the Bible. They believe in a book called

11

the Quran and the Quran ain't shit but the Old Testament. I ain't saying they ain't all good books. Don't tell nobody I told you this. God didn't write any of that shit, Rod. A man like me and you wrote The Old Testament, The New Testament, and The Quran.

"What? I don't............" I tried to cut in, but he cut me off.

"Boy, shut the hell up and listen. Dis the Truth. Most niggas just believe what they hear. I done read all those books more than once, boy. They all good books if used the right way. The bible kept us in slavery for hundreds of years. The KKK, the biggest Christians in the world. They really read the bible and get an understanding that crackers are better than everybody else. You'll learn about people like that. They call them people false prophets. That man over there in that wash house, he is a false prophet. Any man that uses the Bible to brainwash another man, to believe what he wants them to believe and not what God wants, is a false prophet. The Old Testament had this world at war. Jesus died on the cross to bring forgiveness to earth. The New Testament teaches forgiveness. The Quran is the Old Testament, before Jesus died for us. People believed an eye for an eye, a tooth for a tooth. You kill my dog, I kill your cat, you know what I mean?" I shook my head yes, so he went on.

"If a man can't forgive, he will never have peace and Muslims don't believe in our Lord and savior Jesus Christ. They don't believe he was the son of God. They don't believe he died for our sins. They don't believe in forgiveness and most of all they don't believe in eating hog. I don't trust no nigga that don't eat poke no way. But they believe in having five or six wives. That's why these niggas in the West End joining that shit. Boy, don't you ever be no follower. Follow your heart. The world is going to keep changing. It's changing for the best for us, so why hold on to the past? Why live in the Old Testament? We better get ready for the New New Testament. Like I said, man wrote the bible. As man changes, so will the bible. They're gonna put Luther King in this one. We can't stop change. That man in the wash house should move to Iraq, Baghdad, Afghanistan or some shit like that to live like that. I don't dislike Muslims Rod, I just don't trust him. I don't trust no man that don't forgive. Them mother fuckers have been fighting for a thousand years in the Mid-East and will fight a thousand more. Now they slowly but surely bring that shit over here. Believe me, boy those people are dangerous. They bring a lot of hell wit them," I had only one question on my mind;

"Why don't they eat poke"? I asked;

"I don't know but they are some sick Mother Fuckers, ain't they? All that Assalamualaikum shit! I be wanting to tell that nigga......just sell me some bacon," my father said, then burst out laughing at a joke I didn't understand.

"What does Assalamu alaik mean daddy," I asked.

"Something bout God and peace but don't you worry bout none of that shit you hear these Muslims talk, if it ain't English. God got a plan for them people. I ain't telling you to treat them bad are nothing like that. Cause Jesus and Dr. King didn't die for us to do people the way people did them. You treat everybody the way you wanna be treated. But don't let no nigga fool you twice. Aye, look at me. Don't repeat shit I said, you hear me?".

"Yes sir," I said looking him in his eyes.

"Now come on, let's check on our clothes. If these Muslims steal like they kill, we ain't got a pair of draws left in there." He said and laughed at himself as we headed back over.

"As-Salaam-Alaikum," the Arabic greeting meaning "Peace be unto you," was the standard salutation among members of the Nation of Islam. The greeting was routinely deployed whenever and wherever Muslims gathered and interacted, whether socially or within worship and other contexts. "Wa-Alaikum-Salaam," meaning "And unto you peace," was the standard response. Muslim ministers and audiences regularly exchanged the salutation at the beginning and end of lectures and sermons. Common in the Arab world, the greeting was one of the few linguistic

My father was a funny man, and everybody loved him. He knew a lot more back then than most people know now. Not all of it was factual but most of it close enough, like he used to say.

"If it walks like a duck and quack like a duck, it's a damn duck...............".

Rap was born in Baton Rouge, Louisiana. He became known as H. Rap during the early 1960s. His activism in the civil rights movement included involvement with the Student Nonviolent Coordinating Committee (SNCC), of which he was named chairman in 1967. That same year, he was arrested in Cambridge, Maryland and charged with inciting riot as a result of a speech he gave there.

He appeared on the Federal Bureau of Investigation's Ten Most Wanted List after avoiding trial on charges of inciting a riot and of carrying a gun across state lines. His attorneys in the gun violation case were civil rights advocate Murphy of Baton Rouge and the self-described "radical lawyer" William. Rap was scheduled to be tried in Cambridge, but the trial was moved to Bel Air, Maryland on a change of venue.

On March 9, 1970 two SNCC officials, Ralph and William ("Che"), died on U.S. Route 1 south of Bel Air, Maryland when a bomb on the front floorboard of their car exploded, completely destroying the car and dismembering both occupants. Theories of the origin of the bomb are disputed. Some say it was planted in an assassination attempt, others say it was intentionally carried to be used at the courthouse where Rap was to be tried. The next night the Cambridge court house was bombed. [2]

Rap disappeared for 18 months, and then he was arrested after a reported shootout with officers. The shootout occurred after what was said to be an attempted robbery of a bar in 1971 in New York.

He spent five years (1971-1976) in Attica Prison after a robbery conviction. While in prison, Rap converted to Islam and changed his name to Jamil. After his release, he opened a grocery store in Atlanta, Georgia and became a Muslim spiritual leader and community activist preaching against drugs and gambling in Atlanta's West End neighborhood.

It has since been alleged that Rap's life changed again when he allegedly became affiliated with the "Dar ul-Islam Movement".

LIL WILLY

We made it home and put all the clothes up. The garage house we live in is a 3 bedroom upstairs flat. The only thing that could fit in the rooms are beds. It was around 2:00 pm. Daddy and I were home alone. All the kids were at school and Mama was at work. Daddy made me a bologna sandwich, and I went to my room to look out the window. We only had one TV, and it was in Daddy's room. At night, we all gather on the bed and watch Sanford and Son, but I like looking out of my window. I have a view of the apartments next door. So many people came in and out. Mostly because of Lil-Willy selling that stuff, mother told me. What all stuff he sold, I didn't know, but I did know he had a bootleg house (Liquor house) and he drove a nice long white Caddy, just like Rev. Stovall. He's a nice little short man that gives a whole dollar just to take his trash to the dumpster. I like Mr. Willy and his girlfriend, Ms. Sonya. They're always nice to me. My momma says Willy is old enough to be that girl's granddaddy, but she got a baby. Daddy says Sonya's grown. I spent a lot of my time looking out this window. There was a big dumpster for the apartments right across my window and I would save a little piece of my sandwich and throw it out the window, so I could watch the rats fight. Daddy said this Christmas he's going to get me a BB gun so I can start killing them off. Here comes the roach man Pete, on his bicycle. Now, I get to watch him get in this dumpster and go through the trash looking for roaches. Ever since we moved here, I see him do it almost every day. The first time I saw him doing it, I told daddy and all he said was.

"That nigga nasty ass in that dumpster, looking for roaches,"

I thought he meant real roaches for a long time, and I told everybody. Until Lil Walt told me Pete was a junkie looking for weed roaches, not the real bug. I was watching him go in each bag that came out of Lil-Willy's apartment.

"Rod, I'm bout to go next door to see Lil Willy, don't leave this house boy," daddy said, peeking his head in my door.

"And boy what I told you bout looking out that damn window all the time. Go in my room and watch cartoons. Woody Woodpecker is on," he said.

"Ok," I said. He turned and walked away. Then I heard the front door close and the sound of him going down the steps. I sat right there and watched as daddy came into view as he walked across the lot headed for the apartments. I didn't have a view of Willy's front door, only the steps leading to his walk way. I watched Pete for a little while longer. Then I went to my parent's room to watch cartoons in black and white until I fell asleep.

The familiar tones of Sanford and Son's and my momma's voice awakened me.

"Alright boy, get yo ass up so everybody else can have room," I opened my eyes, and all eyes were on me.

"Yeah lil nigga get up! You didn't even go to school today," Lil Walt said, shoving me so hard I almost hit the floor.

"Boy, don't do him like that. You know he had to get his shots. That's what got him so sleepy". My big sister Kim said; she always took up for me, but I could be so mean to her.

"Alright alright y'all sit ya'll asses down and shut up or get out," daddy said. We all followed suit. Fred was funny as always and like always I didn't understand why TV had to show commercials. When the show went off I was told to go to bed. Tomorrow would be my first day of school this year. I didn't mind, I was ready to look out the window at the women in the short skirts going in and out of Lil-Willy's apartment, no commercials. My brother and I slept in the same bed, but he was still watching TV. I went to sleep wondering what all was going on in Lil Willy's apartment. The next morning everything was routine. Lil Walt and I walked to school together, and we attended J. C. Harris. Lil Walt was in the seventh, I was starting the third grade. Kim and Karen walked together. They attended J. E. Brown High School. I think they were in the tenth and eleventh. Both schools were only about a mile away in opposite directions. This day at school I'll say wasn't my best, and it turned out to be the worst. I met a friend while I was waiting in line at the water fountain. This very short lil boy just walked up to me and said,

"My name, Charles. Will you be my friend," he asked. I said, "Yeah, I'm Rodney, you can jump me,"

"Oooooh Mrs. Shine. Rodney let Charles jump, was Rosanna, the prettiest girl in the world, but she was always telling. Then I heard her again.

"Mrs. Shine, Mrs. Shine hurry Mrs. Shine, Walter having another seizure hurry!" I looked back and near the end of the line Walter, the biggest kid in our class nearly the biggest in the school, was on the floor, on his back shaking around foaming from the mouth. I'd seen him have plenty of seizures last year, but my new friend Charles had not. He burst out laughing.

"Oh, he nasty," Charles said. Everybody in the class laughed. After his fit was over, he gave me the universal sign for a black eye. After school I didn't wait to hear my brother say, fight like a man. I took off running down Lucile Avenue, feet not touching the ground. Walter was right behind me, but I was pulling ahead. When I got to Holderness St., he was just crossing Atwood Street, a block away. I was almost home now, and I was about to turn in the driveway, the one we share with the apartments. I peeked back once more, not a soul insight. I think I broke my record. I turned back, still running full speed.

Bam. It was like I hit a brick wall. I fell back so hard that the back of my head hit the pavement. I was dazed and confused by how Walter got in front of me. Then a familiar face came into focus, or was it familiar?

"Hey young brother slow down, did you hurt yourself?" A very familiar voice said.

"Yeah. Excuse me," I said. I was already up, running. I didn't look back. I ran up the steps, unlocked the door, and ran to my window. The man was gone. I didn't see anybody, no cars, nothing. I sat there and watched. Lil Walt should be walking up soon. It was a rule in our house everybody came directly home from school unless you had something to do at school. I had to use the bathroom because we had that pizza today. When I made it back to the window Lil-Walt was walking up like clockwork.

"Boy, where you think yo scary self-going? That nigga done ran you home already, get yo butt back in the house or Imma tell daddy," Lil Walt said meeting me at the bottom of the stairs.

"I gotta get my money from Willy and take out his trash". I pleaded;

"Nawl boy. You should have done that when you was doing all that running. I gotta go to work. Don't worry bout Willy's trash I'll get that money today, and imma tell daddy you got ran home from school by the same boy again," Walt said while pushing me up the stairs.

"Stop pushing me boy. Imma tell on you too," I yelled. I was getting mad fast.

"Make me stop pushing you, sissy," Walt said and pushed me in the back of the head. I took off running to the kitchen and grabbed a butter knife from the dish drain and headed back. I was ready to see some blood. I heard a door slam and I could hear Walt laughing behind it.

"Imma get you nigga. You gotta come out to go to work. Imma stab you just like momma did daddy. Watch," I screamed at the door. I was crying mad, and Walt knew he better let me cool off.

Walt was much bigger than me, but I was much more dangerous. I banged on the door, but he held it closed. This went on for about ten minutes.

"Ok Rod, I'll give you a dollar and take Willy's trash for you," Walt tried to bargain.

"You gotta give me my dollar from Willy too, when you get off work," I bargained back.

"Yeah yeah I know. I gotta go," He said.

"Slide the dollar under the door," I replied. He slid it under.

"Now go in the kitchen so I can leave out the door," Walt said. He didn't trust me when I got mad. No one did. I went to the kitchen. I was ready for him to leave. I was ready for my window time. I heard two doors close almost at once. That's how fast he ran out. I went into our room and posted up in my window. A police car was parked in the driveway. Walt was walking by. Police cars were common in this area, so I paid them no mind. I went back into the kitchen to get some Kool-Aid, as I poured a cup.....

Bang-bang-bang! "Rod Rod open the door". It sounds like Walt; I wasted my Kool-Aid all over the floor.

"Who is it," I yelled.

"It's me boy. Open the door," Walt demanded. I ran to the door, thinking Walter may have been after him. I opened the door and Walt was out of breath. He came in and locked all the locks. Then I went into our room and looked out my window. His eyes looked wild and confused. He looked at me.

"Lil Willy and Sonya dead," Walt said

"What? Boy, stop playing and give me my other dollar. I know he gave it to you," I said with my hand out.

"Boy look out the window, all them police. Somebody shot Willy and Sonya point blank in the head and they say the blood is still warm," Walt said as I looked out the window. I counted at least 20 police cars in the driveway that fast. My heart dropped to my stomach, and a tear came from my eye. Willy and Ms. Sonya were nice people.

"Why? Who? Who would do that to them? They ain't never did nothing to nobody, they're good people. God don't let that happen to good people. Why? Who did it, Walt? Who killed Willy? I want my daddy. Get my daddy," I said. At this point, I was crying hard, not understanding at all.

"I don't know who killed them but Old Man Coon found them. He heard the shots. Rod, you need to stop crying. I liked Willy too, but he was a drug dealing pimp. Ain't no telling who shot him. Probably got robbed, that's what they're saying. Damn! I hate fine as Sonya had to get it. She ain't did shit to nobody," Walt said. His eyes were glazed.

"I don't believe you, how you know all that," I said to him. I could feel the rage coming on.

"Rod that man drove the cleanest Caddy I ever seen, cleaner than any in a magazine. That nigga ain't have no job. I heard daddy say that nigga sell anything that'll get you high, boy, girl, weed, pills, and most of all pussy. Damn Sonya baby, imma miss seeing that ass! God why," Walt said. I jumped up and ran out the door. I had to see for myself it was just too hard for me to believe. As I ran over our rocky yard I could hear Walt saying, "You gonna get in trouble!"

But I didn't care, I had to see. I ran up the other driveway on the other side of Mr. Coon's house. Before I made it to the street, I stopped and gathered myself. Daddy will be home in about an hour. Momma, Kim, and Karen don't get home until dark. I stepped out onto the sidewalk. Wow! The entire street was jammed with police cars all the way to the corner. Everybody was out watching. I walked across the street so I could get a view of the apartment. I couldn't see the front door. There were too many cops standing around. I found a good spot on the top steps of an empty house. I sat down and watched. I was across the street from the scene, out of the way, but not far awa⌐ ⌐⌐⌐

sky was grey overhead, like it always is when something bad happens to me, but this was worse than anything I had ever experienced in my young life. I didn't know what death was. I'd been to a funeral before. My mother's brother was killed by his wife, momma said. But I was young, and I didn't know him. I see Willy and Sonya every day. He told me I was a cool dude. He even let me crank up the Caddy. I feel some kind of way inside. A way I don't like feeling. The preacher said when you die you go to a better place, but Willy had it all. His heaven was right there where he laid dead. So I guess he's lucky to get two heavens, if that's the way it works. I know I'll miss him and Ms. Sonya. I cried and watched the crowd get larger. Then the moment came.

The front door of Willy's apartment opened, and the cops spread like the Red Sea. A second later, the stretcher came out. Two men were pushing it. One in the front, one in the back and one lying on it. In the middle was unmistakably none other than Lil-Willy. His afro gave him away. It pushed the white sheet up like a big round tent. The crowd erupted in screams. They pushed forward, but the cops formed a wall. The stretcher rode through the sea of cops headed for a van that had the words County Morgue. That's the same van that picks up all the people that get killed on the news. Then came the next stretcher. No doubt it was Sonya. All I saw was a shape under a white sheet. But if that's not her, where is she? Not in the crowd. I'd already prayed to see that. I was feeling a little ill. I scanned the crowd. No Sonya, but I saw Mr. Coon standing off to the side talking to a white man not in uniform but a suit. He had a nice hat on, like the kind Willy might wear when his hair was braided. The white man in the suit had a chain with a gold badge hanging from it. Mr. Coon was talking and pointing. I looked back towards the park and there was the man I ran into earlier. He and three other men all wearing beanie hats and dashikis walked up behind the crowd. For some reason, my heart seemed to beat faster. I was about to leave, when H. Rap, the tallest of the three men turned and looked me directly in the eyes. My hair tingles all over my body, and I had to pee really badly. The tall man smiled a smile that stopped my heart and stole my breath, like I was just hit in the chest. All I could do was jump up and take off running, and I did. I ran home straight to my room and got in the bed and cried myself to sleep.

"Rod Rod wake up, boy. Get yo ass up and wash yo face," my father's voice awakened me. I jumped up still half asleep and stumbled my way to the bathroom. Hurry up boy, we gotta talk," Daddy said. I was washing my face when I remembered Lil-Willy. Had I dreamt it all? I was about to find out. I walked back in the room and sat on the bed.

"What time is it daddy?" I asked.

"Why, where you gotta go? Don't worry about what time it is, Rod. I know you've been in here crying bout what happened to Willy and Sonya, and ain't nothing wrong with that. He was always nice to you and everybody else round here. Imma miss him but Willy chose his life Rod, let this be a lesson learned. You live by the sword, you die by the sword. That nigga was a drug dealing pimp from Memphis, Tennessee. Ain't no telling who killed poor Lil-Willy and we never will. No pimps and drug dealers die in vain. Don't nobody give a shit, that nigga wasn't paying no taxes. They ain't gonna even investigate that shit. I know you liked that nigga but don't you ever think about being like him cause you'll end up like him. If I don't kill you, somebody will end up shooting you in both of your eyes like they did Lil-Willy. But ya see that young girl Sonya, she ain't never did shit to nobody. She's just a casualty of a cold world. A real sick mother fucker did that to that girl. He was real sick," daddy said.

"I know who did it! I think I saw them," I said. I don't know why I said it. It just came out and I wish it hadn't.

"Boy, what the fuck you just say? What are you talking bout," daddy asked me with his eyebrows up in attention. I told him the story about me running into Rap in Li-Willy's driveway around the time everything happened and about how they walked up to the crowd. When I finished, the first thing I heard was my daddy's belt unbuckle.

"Listen real good you dumb motherfucker. Who all you done told that shit to? Tell me now boy," daddy asked in a voice I'd never heard before. I was visibly shaking.

"No-no-nobody but you-you, and Lil-Walt I-I- swear," I stuttered it out. My daddy looked me deep in the eyes.

"Take yo clothes off boy and don't say another word or I'll kill ya. Get on yo stomach". I wanted to beg, but I was too afraid. This wasn't my daddy, I didn't know this man at all. My Daddy had never beat me. My mother was the punisher, and he even kept me from that madness. I didn't know this man, so I obeyed every word. I laid there on my stomach and recited the 23rd Psalm to myself, Granny said that will protect you from all evil in the name of Jesus.

"The Lord is my Shepherd, I shall..............ahhhhhhhhhhhh," I screamed.

The pain was like nothing I ever felt before.

"Why is my daddy beating me like this"? Is all my mind could ask me; as I felt the pain from his belt again? Then I got the answer.

"Boy yo dumb ass don't even know how you will put my family in danger. Didn't I tell you that man is dangerous? Didn't I tell you," daddy asked. I didn't know if I should answer or not, but the next lick told me I should.

"Yes, daddy yes daddy!!! Please daddy I'm sorry I'm sorry!!! I ain't gonna say nothing else. I promise please Jesus," I begged for my life.

"So what man you ran into today," my daddy asked. I was quick to answer.

"Rap Bro...........ahhhhhhhhhh," I screamed as pain went through my body.

"You dumb motherfucker. Who'd'you run into," my daddy yelled like a mad man.

"Nobody daddy nobody I ain't run into nobody I ain't seen nobody ahhhhhhhhhh," I screamed as the belt struck me again. The pain was unbearable, it felt as if my skin was coming off.

"Listen boy! You don't know that man, you ain't never seen that man nowhere. If anybody asks you anything, you don't know shit bout shit! You better not ever speak that man's name again. You hear me, boy? You hear me,"

"Yes- yes sir. I hear you," I said looking at him with tear-filled eyes. He was breathing hard and sweating all over. This wasn't the daddy I loved. This was a big black bear, just like my momma calls him. What had I done so badly? All I did was tell the truth. The Bible says the truth shall set you free. The Bible says the 23rd Psalm will protect me, but it didn't. Or maybe it did.

"You lay your ass right there and don't leave this room for shit, even if you gotta shit. Hold it or shit on yourself. I don't care what you do, just don't leave this room. I gotta go over to the store and talk to your brother before he runs his mouth. Don't leave this room, boy! I don't care if the house catches on fire, you better burn up," daddy said, then turned and headed out. I couldn't leave this room if I wanted to. My backside was on fire, and I was afraid if I moved my skin would burst. I just laid there and processed everything that happened so fast. Life can change in an instance, I'm too young to think about so many things. Plus, I know I must fight Walter tomorrow. I said my prayers the way I'd been taught, then I sent up a special prayer for Willy and Sonya R.I.P. I went to sleep wondering if it hurt when a bullet enters the brain.

394 HOLDERNESS

It's December now, Willy and Sonya have been in the ground for four months. No one had been arrested yet, and daddy said nobody would. We never said a word about the day he beat me. It was like it didn't happen. That man's name was never mentioned again. We even stopped washing our clothes at his wash house. All our things were packed, and we were about to move again. This time right around the corner to a big house with a big backyard. Daddy got mad after the tall man put speakers on the telephone poles around and near the park. About four or five times a day somebody would sing a song in a foreign language, some kind of call to prayer for the Muslims. It was driving daddy crazy, so he found a house at the dead end of Holderness.

"At 394 Holderness, you can't hear all that noise down there by the expressway". Daddy told all of us; at the time the song was playing. I was happy to be moving. All my friends from school lived on Holderness and we were moving into an actual house.

394 Holderness Street was my first and only real home. It was a very nice yellow house next to the last house on the deadend street. The boys and girls still shared rooms, but the rooms were much larger. We have a big basement and an even bigger back yard with grass. The best part about the new house was the dead-end, which was really a fence blocking the expressway to I-20. We used that fence to block our baseballs when we played stickball all summer long. Across from our house were two sets of apartments, and one duplex. I was seeing everything in color now; it was like this street opened my eyes. I remember all the

hot summers and very cold winters. I could sit on the back porch and watch the cars and big trucks go by on I-20. All my friends from Lucile Ave. came down to play on the end, as they call it. I also had friends on Greenwich & Atwood Street. Lil-Walt knew everybody in the neighborhood. Mainly because he worked at the store. In a few years Mr. Author, the owner, told me he would give me a job too, if I stayed out of trouble. I couldn't wait for that day. The store was on the corner of Lucile & Holderness. It shared a building with the notorious motorcycle gang, The Outcast, and an old diner that closed down called Ribs. The members were the nicest guys I knew, but Lil-Walt used to come home every night with a wild story about how they beat, stabbed, or shot somebody. I could see the cops' blue lights up there all the time. The Outcast members always wore black. There were maybe a hundred of them and they all had funny names. Like Cuz, Foots, Superman, Slow Roller, Killer Joe, Bandit, Handgun, and so on. Their names fit their characters, and I knew most of their names. I used to go to the store for my parents and people in the neighborhood. I got to pass by the door of their clubhouse at least four times a day, on a bad day. I always tried to peek inside, but it was always dark inside, the only light was from a drop light over the pool table. Was I crazy to want to go inside that cave or should I say like my momma (death trap). I love walking by all the nice black & chrome Harley-Davidson motorcycles that line the street in front of the store. It reminded me of the cowboy movies I watch with my daddy. Everybody wore black vests and black boots but had bikes instead of horses. Daddy never hung out at the Outcast clubhouse. He told me it was too dangerous inside and too much going on, but he was really cool with most of the guys. Some he knew from the military, most of the Outcast were Vets.

Like my daddy, they'd seen a lot of men die, so I guess that made them brothers. My brothers in death, my daddy called them.

Lucile Groceries was the name of the corner store. The owner's name was Arthur Pope. I don't know how my daddy and Arthur got to be so cool, but they were, and that meant I would soon cut meat for people in the back of the store like Lil-Walt is doing now. I just got to do good in school, learn how to read a scale, and learn to cut using a meat saw. But daddy said I have to get taller for that. The store wasn't small like the one at the park. It was four times that size with four long isles and a fresh meat market in back, and they sold fresh vegetables. The store and the clubhouse are the heartbeat of the West End. People came in and out, day and night.

Just like Mr. Skeeter's house. That's who I make the most of my store runs for. Mr. Skeeter runs the biggest bootleg/gambling house on the westside. My momma says he makes more money on a Sunday than the store makes all week. The store can't sell beer on Sunday, not in Georgia, but Mr. Skeeter does. I've seen the cops there drinking and laughing. They say Mr. Skeeter gets a pass because he marched with Dr. King. I guess Mr. Skeeter had a dream too, because his life ain't bad. He lives better than anybody I know, even better than some white people on T.V. He got the biggest house on the block and he doesn't rent. He owns his house, gets people out of jail with it all the time. Lil-Willy was minor compared to Skeeter. That's what my daddy said, and I believed it. Mr. Skeeter is the nicest man in the world to me, and the oldest. He's at least 60 but looks 80, I think the cane makes him seem older. Daddy told me Mr. Skeeter was an old Gangster from Miami, Florida. He's slicker than slime, but a good honest hustling man. That meant he wasn't a drug dealer, just a bootlegging hustler, gambler and a killer. I never saw him without a pistol hanging out of his pocket, or sitting in his lap. He keeps bankrolls big enough to choke a mule in every pocket. I'm the only kid that is allowed on the front porch, but sometimes I have Lil-Twon, he's only four, so I guess he doesn't matter.

Lil-Twon lives in the apartments across the street from my house. He's so red he looks white, and he has funny eyes like a cat. His real name is Antoine', and he's my little friend. I treat him like my big brother treats me. He follows me everywhere, even to church. He's like the little brother I never had. My daddy had to be a daddy to a lot of the kids in the neighborhood. My friend that lives next door to Mr. Skeeter, Rodney S., has a father, but nobody else around here has a live-in daddy, but me. My daddy promised me he would never leave us, and I believe him. If he was going to leave, he would've left after the first time my momma almost stabbed him to death. Now he's in his third or fourth life. I learned at a young age how dangerous a woman could be. My momma is a deadly woman if provoked, and it doesn't take much to provoke her. When momma and daddy both get drunk together get ready for a bloodbath, and daddy is the blood source. When the cops and ambulance come, daddy tells them it was all his fault so they won't lock momma up. Lil-Walt told me married people fight because they stuck with each other, kids, and they broke. It made me wonder if I ever wanted a family of my own. Love seemed to hurt too bad for me. Lil-Willy used to tell me. "Love em' and leave em.'" But daddy says "A real man doesn't leave what he loves, if he does he'll be lost forever". Maybe that's true, and maybe that's why none of my friend's fathers can find their way home. They are forever lost. All I can do is keep going to church and asking God not to let my daddy leave. That's what my big sister Kim told me to do. If I miss church, daddy might not come home from work, is what she tells me. I believe her because my friend Shane's daddy left them for another woman. Kim says because those people don't go to church at all, not even on Easter. Most of the people living on Holderness St. are Christians one way or the other. I think about God a lot and I know right from wrong, I can feel it inside of me. Like when I steal a dollar out of my brother's pocket, I know it's wrong and I feel bad, but after I buy me some Now & Laters I'm thinking about another dollar, however I can get it. Lil-Walt says I'm a candy junkie. He hopes I don't get on the real junk. I ask myself why bad feels good and good feels bad. Like when I have to share a Now & Later with Twon, even if I don't have but two left. I do it because I know that's what God wants, but that's not what I want. Everybody says my sister Karen spoiled me like this, I am the baby. Life is good for me, so good I have no idea how poor we really are. I think it's a part of life. My daddy and brother have to fight and kill enormous rats in the middle of the night, for momma to wipe the walls down with bleach water when the insurance man comes. This keeps the roaches away for a while. That's what everybody on Holderness does, fight roaches and rats. The rats got so bad the city had to come out and put acid or something in all the holes to kill them. When they put the acid in we could feel the ground tremble. They cemented all the holes they could find. The smell lasted from the 4th of July till Christmas, but no more rats. We took the good with the bad and kept the roaches at bay. Like I said, all was good when things were so bad, no heat in December, daddy said in the winter time real men chopped wood like in the Western. He made it fun. Like he did with the hot plates, that was the quickest way to heat water. The stove is slow. That's what my daddy means to me, never knowing the worst, like Jesus turning water to wine. My daddy turned water to the sweetest Kool-Aid you ever tasted, and he made the best ketchup sandwiches. That's genuine love, built on God's love, only a daddy can love. "Nigga! That's that, you're starving love! I bet that's what Lil-Willy would say, but if I am starving I didn't know it. All I know is love.

The year is 1981, I'm ten years old now, and we've been living on Holderness St for three years. I started the 5th grade this year, and I like school. I really don't have a choice, my daddy will kill you about school. In our house education comes first, even before church. Daddy says it's hard for a nigga, but for a dumb nigga it's impossible, he going to jail or hell. So I try to learn as much as I can, and I watch the news every day after school. Daddy says I know a lot, to be only ten but I still can't throw a curveball. But I know the president's name is Ronald Reagan. I got a Jim Plunkett football for Christmas and the Raiders won the Super Bowl. I know the Braves ain't never won the World Series but daddy says they will, and the Atlanta Falcons I don't think we ever made the playoffs. I know it's a citywide curfew for all the kids in Atlanta. I saw on the news, young black boys are still coming up missing, and then found dead. So, I would say that I'm kinda smart.

ATLANTA MISSING & MURDERED CHILDREN

We used to live next door to Jeffrey. I played with him every day. He came up missing about two years ago; they found his body last year, nothing but bones. He lived not a mile from Holderness, and attended J.C Harris with me, his sister Wanda is my classmate. All the missing and murdered kids made our neighborhood closer. The Muslims are really out to catch whoever is doing it. They started having community meetings at Mrs. Betty's house. Her son Tony and I are friends. He told me the Muslim's asked Betty to let them use him as bait at the park. The Muslim's patrolled the park and always has before the murders. If you are not from around here, you wouldn't know it until it's too late. Now the Muslim's patrol the entire neighborhood, and they teach self-defense classes. They put flyers out to tell people not to be afraid of the cowards who are taking our kids, because if they make the mistake and try to take another kid in the West End, Allah bless their soul.

It's a million dollar reward out, dead or alive, that's what Lil-Walt said. The Muslims and a lot of other people think the Ku-Klux-Klan are behind the missing kids. But daddy didn't think so. He had another theory. I overheard a conversation he was having with some of his friends in our basement/newly renovated bootleg spot. Daddy opened up a bootleg spot in the basement on

New Year's. I'm sitting on the top steps, out of view.

"Let me tell ya'll dumb ass niggas something. Listen to them mother fuckin' Muslims if you want to. Those Muslims just wanna kill some crackers. Cause ain't no Crackers taking them kids. Hell nawl man, I don't believe that shit." Daddy said; to all the men in our small basement. It's a Friday night and the regular crew is over. John, my father's boyhood friend, Foots, Killer Joe, Fast Black, all members of the Outcast, and Charlie Brown, he's the house man at Mr. Skeeter' s spot. Our basement wasn't as nice as some other bootleg spots, just a dim room with a record player, a homemade bar with four stools, a card table with four chairs, and our old refrigerator that used to be upstairs. We didn't serve the top shelf liquor, just the cheap stuff, and daddy put water in some of that, but for some reason people kept coming. Everybody just loved Big Walt because he can talk politics. He taught me how to pour shots, so I served people when daddy wasn't home. Sometimes I get tips.

"Ah-ah-ah-ah Wal-wal-Walt-who-who you thank doing it?" That was Charlie with his deep raspy stuttering voice, like a big bullfrog.

"Yeah, Tatar Brown you used to be a police. Whatcha thank?" John asked in his slow, smooth voice. He knew daddy better than anybody in the room; he always called my daddy by his childhood name, Tatar, and knew how to heat him up. That didn't take much, they were all half drunk and about to be all the way.

"Fuck you Nigga, I wasn't no police, because you know that was some military shit. But Charlie Imma answer yo question, really its common sense but these niggas round here can't see through the hate they got fo crackers man. That's why they ain't solved the case," Walt said.

"Yeah, Walt you right bout that, these niggas blind, this shit been going on fo years now. That nigga Mayor we got. It's like the blind leading the blind. That's Foot's; he and daddy always agreed.

They're Air force buddies.

"Yeah, Foot's you know I'm right. Now imma give yall country niggas the business bout these kid's man. If these kids were coming up missing in Buckhead where rich people live, then it might be the Klan. These kids are coming up missing in the hood. Projects kids, street smart kids. I knew Jeffrey Mathis, we all did. We know everybody in the family. His brother Moe was over here last night. The only way Jeffrey got in the car with a Cracker is they ran him down and put handcuffs on him. That boy was the worst kid in the West End, steal anything he can". Walt said;

"A-a-amen to that Wa-wa- Walt he wa-wa was hell. God Bless the de-de-dead." Charlie put his two cents in. I couldn't see him but I bet he just down his drink and baited daddy to pour another by agreeing.

"But hear this Charlie, then imma pour you a big one. How many cracker's ride round here that ain't the police or the insurance man or some shit like that we know em all. Right or wrong?"

"You right Walt".

"Yeah-yeah-yeah you right Wa-wa-Walt,"

"Preach Tatar Brown." Everybody said at the same time, I guess everybody wanted a free drink. I could hear daddy pouring up.

"Alright niggas this shit ain't free, I'm putting it on yall books. I ain't that drunk, but I'm gettin there. First off, that nigga Mayor we got, he ain't no nigga. He's a white nigga, just look at him, he is as close to white as a nigga can be, hair and all. But what make me not trust that nigga is when he became Mayor.

Why didn't he move out of the West End?" Daddy asked them.

"Cause the man real Tatar! What's wrong with that," John asked.

"John any nigga that will live over here, and aint gotta, they are real. Real motherfucking crazy, that nigga faker than yo shoes nigga. Mayor ackson, man fuck that fag. Me and Foots didn't vote for the nigga, anyway. He's a puppet for crackers. He's on television with a room full of money, no questions asked, cash reward money. How much cash that was Foots," daddy asked.

"At least a half a million, I wish I could find the cracker, nigga, whoever the fuck doing it for them greenbacks. Nigga what," Foots said. He was getting hyped.

"You got damn right nigga, whoever, if my momma was doing this and I found out. To jail her ass is going, and whoever helping her. That kind of money make kin turn on kin, and it'll make the Klan turn on the Klan. That right there would tell a dumb nigga whoever taking them kids doing it by themselves, or else he'll be in jail because niggas tell for free. But for a half a million he'll tell on Jesus, God, and these Muslims round here, they'll even tell on Rap, The Prophet Muhammad, Allah, and eat sum poke wit that bread." Daddy said; and everybody burst out laughing, but I didn't get the joke. The kids missing wasn't a joke at all. It seemed like every day a little boy was coming up missing.

In the summer of 1979, Edward, also known as "Teddy," and Alfred, also known as "Q," both 14, disappeared four days apart. (Terry, who went missing in early 1981, lived in the same apartment as Edward.) Their bodies were both found on July 28 in a wooded area, Edward with a. 22 gunshot to his upper back. They were believed to be the first victims of the "Atlanta Child Killer". The next victim, Milton Harvey, also 14, disappeared on September 4, while going to the bank on an errand for his mother. At the time he was on a yellow 10-speed bike. His body was recovered later.

On October 21, 1979, nine-year-old Yusuf went to a store to buy snuff for a neighbor, Eula. A witness said she saw Yusuf getting into a blue car before he disappeared. His body was found on November 8, 1979, in the abandoned E.P. Johnson elementary school by a school janitor who was looking for a place to urinate. He was still wearing the brown cut-off shorts he was last seen wearing, though they had a piece of masking tape stuck to them. He had been hit over the head twice and the cause of death was strangulation. Police did not immediately link his disappearance to the previous killings.

The next victim, 12-year-old Angel, was the first female victim. She disappeared on March 4, 1980. She had left her house wearing a denim outfit around 4 pm. She was last seen at a friend's house watching Sanford and Son. Angel was found six days later, in a wooded lot possibly 3 blocks away from her apartment. She was found in the clothes she left home in. Someone's white panties were stuffed in her mouth, and an electrical cord bound her hands. The cause of death was strangulation. On March 11, 1980, 11-year-old Jeffrey disappeared while on an errand for his mother. He was wearing gray jogging pants, brown shoes, and a white and green shirt. Months later a girl said she saw him get into a blue car with a light-skinned man and a dark-skinned man. The body of Jeffrey was found in a "briar-covered patch of woodlands."

On June 9, 12-year-old Christopher went missing on his way to a local pool. He was wearing blue shorts, a light blue shirt, and blue tennis shoes. The body of Christopher was found in a wooded area, clothed in unfamiliar swim trunks. The cause of death was undetermined. On June 22 and June 23, seven-year-old Latonya and ten-year-old Aaron went missing. The extended wave of disappearances and murders panicked parents and children in the city, and the government struggled to ensure the safety of children.

The murders of two children, Anthony and Earl, occurred in July 1980.

Between August and November 1980, five more killings took place. There were no known victims during December. All the victims were African-American children between the ages of seven and fourteen, and most were asphyxiated.

The murders continued into 1981. The first known victim in the New Year was Lubie, who disappeared on January 3. Lubie's body was found on February 5. Lubie's friend Terry also went missing in January. An anonymous caller told the police where to find the body.

In February two murders occurred, believed to be linked to the others. In March, four Atlanta linked murders took place, including that of Eddie, the first adult victim.

In April, Larry was murdered, as well as adult ex-convict John and Jimmy Ray.

After William went missing on May 16, 1981, his body was found close to his home. The last victim added to the list was Nathaniel, 27 years old.

Investigator Chet created a map of the victims' locations. Despite the difference in ages, the victims fell with the same geographic parameters. They were connected to Memorial Drive and 11 major streets in the area.

"Yeah Walt, I think you're right. Some freaky ass faggot motherfucker is kidnapping them little boy and fucking them for as long as they like. Then kill em and throw em away like trash. Yall know a lot of fags done move to this city. Go down on MLK and Ashby Street. That shit is despicable, that's who that freak need to be killing. Yall seen em," Charlie Brown said.

"Hell nawl nigga. I aint seen em. The last one I seen, I killed it with this," Foots answered as he pulled a pistol from his boot.

"Nigga put that shit back in your boot and yall stop talking that sissy talk' in here I got boys I don't want them hearin' none of that fag shit. I don't even want them to know shit like that exists. Put that gun up, feet fo you, shoot your other foot off, then what we gonna call you Nubs. I gotta go upstairs and piss, I'll be right back," daddy said. I jumped up fast without making a sound. I've had plenty of practice. These stairs are like the window I had on Lucile, only I can't see. I can only listen and picture all the stories I hear. For my age, I've heard much more than most ten times my age. Some of my stories were make believe. I would take pieces of other people's lives and create fantasies I didn't know then that thoughts become things. In most of my fantasies I would make believe I was Lil-Willy riding around in that white on white L-dog, with a fine woman in the front and back seat. Just like Willy used to ride around, poor Willy R.I.P.

"Rod Rod where yo ass at boy," daddy yelled at the top of his lungs.

"Yeah daddy, I hear you," I answered as I ran up to him as he came out of the bathroom.

"Here boy it's almost 9 o'clock yo brother bout to get off, go up to the store and get me a pack of cigarettes. I snatched the money out of his hand and ran for the door.

"Boy y'all come straight home don't make me come a looking for you". Daddy yelled; at my back I hit the door and jumped all the steps, I was running up the middle of the street. Until I heard,

"Lil-Rod get yo ass on the sidewalk fo you get ran over," Mr. Skeeter screamed. He was in his chair, looking out the door as always.

"Yes, Sir Mr. Skeeter," I yelled and jumped on to the side. I wasn't even breathing hard yet. Skeeter house is halfway up the hill from the dead end. In 2 seconds, I was turning the corner.

THE OUTCAST

"Get in here you faggot motherfucker," Cuz's voice said. He's one of my favorite Outcast members. The other guy I didn't know. Cuz had a gun in his hand and pushed the tall skinny guy inside the club. He smiled at me and closed the door. I ran by and into the store as if I didn't see a thing the way I had been trained. "The Cast business ain't nobody's but the Cast business" that's what I always heard Foots say. I did know when that door closed it meant bad business for somebody. When I busted in the door Lil-Walt was behind the counter running the cash register like a grown man. Lil-Walt was smart and good at math. I was smart enough to know he owed me two quarters because cigarettes cost one dollar and fifty cent.

"Here Lil Walt. Daddy wants a pack of cigarettes and give me the change so I can play pinball. Hurry up. I ain't got much time to play," I said. Walt took the money, hit some button on the register and I heard a ching, and the money was in my hand. The store on the corner is ten times bigger than the Muslim store at the park. It had four long isles with a meat counter in the back. That's where everybody in the neighborhood bought their meat. Lil-Walt used to work the meat counter, but he moved up to the cash register. Mr. Arthur, the store owner, promised me this summer I would be the new meat man, after Lil-Walt trained me on all the different meat saws.

Like my daddy said, by summer I'll be tall enough not to cut my hand off. On one wall of the store is a long row of glass drink coolers, with every drink in them that you could name.

Across from the front counter, the only thing on my mind was "The Triple Tilt" pinball machine. The only problem Shane was playing and Lil-Jorge was waiting, but I had a plan.

"What's going on Shane how many credits you got," I asked.

"Lil-Rod you may as well go on home boy, like I told Lil-Jorge, I ain't sinking fo the store close," Shane said. He was playing the game so hard you could hear the iron ball hitting the glass. I knew he would not sink before the store closed. He's really good.

"Well, I guess I'll go outside and see who the Outcast just closed the door on. Come on Jorge, let's go see," I said.

"Rod, you bet not be lying. If I lose my spot for nothing, you gotta give a quarter," Jorge said.

"That nigga lying. He just trying to trick you, I'm telling you all that nigga do is lie. You go out that door, you lose your spot, and I'm playing again. Shane said; still keeping the ball out the hole.

"Rod, you hold my spot. Imma see if the door is closed," Jorge asked me. Then the store door opened. In came Pissy Coon.

"Lil-Walt, why the club door closed," Pissy Coon asked.

"I don't know, what did you see Rod," Lil-Walt asked me.

"I tried to tell ya'll, Cuz had his big 357 in his hand and told some nigga I ain't seen before to get his faggot ass inside and told me to get on and closed the door," I answered. Everybody got excited and ran for the door.

"Oh, shit! Somebody Anna get fucked wit a pool stick," Pissy Coon said. He was the first out the door. Shane left out with his five credits still left, just like I knew he would. Lil-Walt and I are all that remains. I really came up tonight. I didn't have to spend my money. I got on the game and started playing. Lil-Walt came over the counter and opened the door so he could see. I wanted to see myself, but I had to play this pinball machine first. I dream about this game at night and in class. I'm playing for free today, it must be my birthday. I'm not good at all, at this game, and daddy doesn't like me playing. I tell him it's just like baseball practice makes perfect. I lost three balls back to back. I can't help but think about what's happening to the poor man next door. That's probably why I'm playing so badly. I've heard some stories Foots told as I hid out on the basement steps. Sometimes I'll stay up all night unable to sleep. My mind unable to shut down or block out the stories I heard about what happens to niggas that disrespect THE OUTCAST. The club is full of killers but Bandit, Fast Black, Handgun, and Superman are the worst. Foots said as soon as the door closes Bandit gets a pool stick. Club members would beat them and have no mercy, then strip and torture whoever for whatever they wanted. Foot's always said, The Cast got rules, and the number one rule is no dope selling on not one corner on Lucile and Holderness. If you got caught Bandit had a big black pool stick ready to go up your ass with it. If you got caught again, no talk Fast black would sneak up behind you with that black .44 bulldog, the one with all the red rubber bands on the handle, and blow the back of your head through your nose. Foots said every time Black killed a nigga, he would put one of those bands on his gun handle. You couldn't see any black on the handle, it was all red now. Foots tell lots of stories and I don't know how many are true. When I hear so many gunshots, I have to wonder if they will ever stop. Then blue lights on the corner, I know we will have yellow police tape to play with in the morning. I guess that makes most of his stories true.

"Truth is, it is what it is! They on the corner! You want it? You gonna have to take it," daddy would say after every murder.

"Them niggas don't on that corner and one day them crackers gonna show them niggas. They gotta beat fens ass and make' em buy that step on shit. Fuck the corner, I can stand on the moon with my dope. I got that real Jack and Jill". Lil-Willy would say.

"I wonder did it hurt"? I would ask;

I snapped out of my trance as my last ball sank. Good, now I can get to see some blood. I turned and headed for the door, almost running.

"Boy, you better take daddy his cigarettes. I'mma, call the house," Walt said to the back of my head.

"Call him, he told me to come home with you. Imma be over Shane house," I said without looking back. I was in a full run now. Shane lived one house from the corner on Holderness, his house faced the side of the building that housed the club, diner and store. Shane's driveway is directly across from the alley that ran behind the building where all the back doors are. I ran across the street where a small crowd had gathered, mostly just kids and a couple teenagers. I guess the word had spread fast.

"What done happened," I asked; to anyone that would answer.

"Nothing yet. You know you owe me a quarter for my games, nigga. Give me my money for I do you like The Cast doing that nigga," Shane answered. He's only 12, but he's the biggest, blackest and dumbest in the crowd.

"I don't owe you shit. I didn't get to even play. My brother playing yo game. He say if you don't come get it now ain't nothing you can say," I answered. He says all I do is lie, so I lied.

"I don't even care, my fingers hurt. I been playing too long. I wanna see some blood now. Rod, you better gone down the hill fo Big-Walt come outside. The streetlights been on nigga," Shane said, trying to get some laughs. He did.

"Mind yo own business smut black you need to go in the house we can't see you unless the streetlights on". I cracked back; and got a better laugh.

"Get out my driveway nigga you wanna jone somebody," Shane said. He headed down the drive at me. As he did, the alley lit up with a small bit of light. We all froze and got our eyes focused on what we came to see.

"Get yo punk ass out here nigga find somewhere else to slang that shit. If we ever see you again you dead nigga". A very familiar voice said; a body flew out, and the door slammed closed. We all stood there for a few seconds before we saw a naked body appear from the darkness. The man was a bloody mess, he was crawling as fast as he could, but he was about to run. Like always, Shane and Lil-Jorge had gathered a pile of rock.

"Nigga, you better start running," Lil-Jorge yelled as he cast the first stone. It hit the man right on the side of his ribs, I heard a crack and one loud groan. Then it seemed like the sky started raining rocks all over the poor bloody man. He stumbled to his feet as my first stone struck him on the side of his face. That woke him up I think because somehow he ran not fast, but at least he was moving.

"You better run mother fucker! Did you hear Foots? We'll kill you round here nigga! Run"! Pissy Coon yelled; the man ran, but we ran right behind, casting our stones, punishing this sinner. He was running up Holderness just as he made it to the corner. Charlie Brown turned the corner. The naked man fell in his arms.

"Wah-wah- what the fu-fu- fuck man get yo na-na-naked ass off me," Charlie Brown stuttered. His face was in shock. It had to be shocking to run into a naked man bleeding out the mouth and ass. I was already turning around, headed home the second I saw Charlie Brown. I ran as fast as I could.

"Please, sir. Help me please they trying to kill me," the bloody man cried out.

"Pissy Co-co-coon wha-what the fuck is this shit, ma-ma-man all yall niggas going t-t-to jail wha-wha-what kind of freaky shit is this". Charlie Brown stuttered some more. I heard nothing else, I was too far away. I hope to God Charlie Brown didn't see me and I hope that rat Pissy Coon doesn't tell. If the police come he's telling, because he just got out of jail for stealing. All he does is rob and steal him and Lil-Walt bout the same age, but Pissy Coon doesn't go to school. All he does is hang around the corner, I don't even know where he lives. Pissy Coon is the son of old man Coon, but old man Coon doesn't claim him, he doesn't even talk to him. I have to say Pissy Coon looks just like the old man, light skin, skinny, and tall. We named him Pissy Coon as a joke, because old man Coon is rich, or should I say like daddy (nigga rich).

Thank God my daddy never found out I was involved in that assault of that poor bloody man. Shane told me the ambulance came and got the guy and that was that, like always. The police knew if anybody got beat or killed on that corner; The Outcast did it. Daddy said the club pays the police, that's how they get away with their wrong, and the club got members that are police officers. Most of the members of the club are professional people, and most are Vets.

NO BOOGEYMAN

This school year is going by so slowly, maybe it's because of the curfew. It's still a sicko going around snatching kids. We had to be in the house when the lights came on, but I never saw the police ride down Holderness. I stayed in the window or on the steps, no football in the street this year, no park, no mall, no nothing. But summer came soon enough, and even better news.

It was around the second week of summer, I'd been going to Harlem Boy's Club every summer for as long as I can remember, had to get that free bag lunch, or stay home and eat ketchup sandwiches. We didn't eat but two meals a day at home, and that's summer, Winter, Spring, and Fall. The Boy's Club sits in the middle of Harris Homes. We walked there and back every day. Most of the kids from my block, ranging from teenagers to seven-year-olds, maybe 12-15 of us on any given day. The walk from Holderness to the Club is only about a mile. We ran it most days. The club was cool; I knew almost everybody, and the first place I can ever remember living is on Baldwin Place. Last summer one of my friends at the Club house caught on fire and he was burned severely. Jerome's face looked like melted plastic. He's still my friend, and we would fight anybody that picked on him. This was his first summer back since the fire. We played pool all day, every day. He would always walk with me to the top of the gate trying to get the last tag of the day and today he got it.

"Tag! I gotcha. See you tomorrow," He ran back into the club. I'll get him tomorrow. He caught me snoozing. Too many kids coming up missing for me to let my guard down like that. We left the club everyday around 4pm. When I made it in the house, it was 4:15. Daddy and my sisters Kim and Karen were sitting on the sofa, eyes glued to the small black and white T.V. Daddy looked up and smiled.

"I told you they was gonna get that motherfucker didn't I boy," daddy said.

"Get who," I asked.

"Look at the TV boy, that's that freaky motherfucker right there, been raping and killing all them lil boys," daddy said.

"They ain't charged him with no little boys' daddy. That man that they fished out of the river is grown," my oldest sister Kim added. Kim's 17, my sister Karen is 16, Lil-Walt is 15, and I'm 10 ½ now. Momma said I was a mistake, that's why Walter and I are 5 years apart, but daddy says I'm his blessing.

"Nawl daddy that man way too small to be done killed all those people by himself. I think the Muslims are right, the Klan doing it and they bout to make that li-man the scapegoat," Karen put her two cents in.

"Ya'll shut up. Ya'll don't know how no killer look. It ain't about being big, it's about being smart and that nigga right there thought he was smart. Y'all would be surprised what a little candy, reefer, shit don't have no hot donuts from Krispy Kreme, what kid over here wouldn't get in the car wit that little fella there. Evil has many faces, and that's one. That nigga rode round here selling these kids dreams, tricking them all out of they life. That's why I tell ya'll don't jump for shit that glitters. Anything that sounds too good to be true, it is what the fuck it is. Things too good to be true can cause you more in the long run. It cost them kids they life. I hope they fire that motherfucker," Daddy said, with disgust as I looked into the eyes of the Boogeyman. He was a small guy not much bigger than me, he wore glasses and had a short afro. He didn't look like much of a threat. He looked nothing like the monster in my nightmares. The half man, half wolf I'd been dreaming about for years it seems. He had claws and long teeth and ran me all over the city trying to eat me. No, he wasn't that creature, but he had the same beady eyes. Daddy told me never to trust a man with gold teeth or beady eyes. I wonder if my nightmares stop now. We all sat there and listened to the black news lady Monica Kaufman give details about how they caught this creep.

As the media coverage of the killings intensified, the FBI confidently predicted that the killer might dump the next victim into a body of water to conceal any evidence. Police staked out nearly a dozen area bridges, including crossings of the Chattahoochee River. During a stake-out on May 22, 1981, detectives got their first major break when an officer heard a splash beneath a bridge. Another officer saw a white 1970 Chevrolet station wagon turn around and drive back across the bridge. [3]

Two police cars later stopped the suspect station wagon about a half mile from the bridge. The driver was 23-year-old Wayne B. W., a supposed music promoter and freelance photographer. The Chevrolet wagon belonged to his parents. Dog hair and fibers recovered from the rear of the vehicle were later used as evidence in the case against Williams, as similar fibers were found on some victims. They were found to match his dog and the carpet in his parents' house. During questioning, Wayne said he was on his way to audition one Cheryl J. as a singer. Wayne claimed she lived in the nearby town of Smyrna. Police did not find any record of her or the appointment. Two days later, on May 24, the nude body of Nathaniel, 27, was found floating downriver a few miles from the bridge where police had seen the suspicious station wagon. The body had extensive water damage and may have been in the water for up to two weeks. Based on this evidence, including the police officer's hearing of the splash, police believed that Williams had killed Nathaniel and disposed of his body while the police were nearby.

Much circumstantial evidence led the police to consider

Waynemas the prime suspect. First, he was the only person stopped during the month-long stakeout of twelve bridges, and Wayne had stopped on the bridge immediately after the splash was heard. He denied stopping his car on the bridge, claiming instead that he had turned around in an adjacent lot. Second, police noted that Wayne's appearance resembled a composite sketch of the suspect, including a bushy afro sticking out from the sides of a baseball cap, and a birthmark or scar on the left cheek. Indeed, investigators who stopped Williams on the bridge noticed a 24-inch nylon cord. This cord seemed to match the choke marks on Cater and other victims. Furthermore, Wayne admitted to spending much of his time seeking out and auditioning African-American boys whose ages matched many of the victims. Notably, he failed an FBI-administered polygraph examination—although polygraph results are not admissible as evidence in criminal courts.

Even more evidence seemed to implicate Wayne's fibers from a carpet in his residence were found to match those observed on two of the victims. Additional fibers from the home, autos and pet dog were later matched to fibers discovered on other victims. Furthermore, the witness Robert H. claimed to have seen Wayne holding hands and walking with Nathaniel on the night he is believed to have died. On June 21, 1981, Wayne was arrested. A Grand Jury indicted him for first-degree murder in the deaths of Nathaniel and Jimmy, aged 22. The trial date was set for early 1982.

FBI Agent John E. D., who had previously conducted a widely reported interview with *People* magazine about profiling the killer as a young black man, has admitted that when the news of Williams' arrest was officially released (his status as a suspect had been leaked to the media anyway). He stated that if it was Williams, then he was 'looking good for a good percentage of the killings,'. This was widely reported across media outlets as the FBI effectively declaring Williams guilty, and Douglas was officially censured by the director of the FBI.

I don't know if he killed all those boy's or not, but he did stay in the West End, well Dixie Hill that's close enough about 3 miles from Holderness but 1 mile from South Gordon that where we used to live next door to Jeffrey Mathis and where Jeffrey was last seen. That makes him very guilty to people around here. Plus, no more kids came up missing. The summer flew by and now it's Christmas, but all people seem to talk about this year is that creepy killer's trail. It was all over the TV.

The trial officially began on January 6, 1982, with Judge Cooper presiding. The most important evidence against Williams was the fiber analysis between the victims Williams was indicted for, Jimmy and Nathaniel, and the 12 pattern-murder cases in which circumstantial evidence culminated in many links among the crimes. This included witnesses testifying to seeing Williams with the victims, and some witnesses suggesting that he had solicited sexual favors.

The prosecution's presentation of fiber statistics, particularly in the testimony of FBI special agent Deadman and in the summing up, has been criticized for being based on speculative assumptions and misleading phrasing of probabilities, to an extent that in some jurisdictions might have resulted in a mistrial.

On February 27, 1982 - after eleven hours of deliberation - the jury found Wayne guilty of the two murders. They sentenced him to two consecutive life terms in Georgia's Hancock State Prison at Sparta.

THE DEVIL IS A LIE

My world was normal again, and the boogeyman was in jail forever. I started working at the meat counter at the store. I was making $2.50 an hour 8 hours a day in the summer and 6 hours after school. My daddy would take 50% from everybody that worked. When I added it all up, I decided I liked sports better. My daddy had a baseball in my hand from my first memory. Lil-Walt was better than me but he never got to play in the park leagues, we were too poor to pay the admission fees. Lil-Walt didn't seem to mind, he was too busy working at the store making $5 an hour. My daddy taught any kid that wanted to play baseball, we had big games in the West End Park, and people came to watch. At one of those games we met Coach Jerry, he coached the Reds 12 and under baseball at Adams Park. Adams Park was a park on the other end of Cascade Rd. That's the end where all the uppity nigga's stayed. Well, that's what momma said. I didn't really know, I never leave the West End, and when I do it's going downtown. Momma takes me with her to the Curb Market to get her fresh vegetables and meat. The Market is in the heart of the city, close to where Dr. Luther King grew up. We have to catch the bus #2 Westview to get downtown. I love riding MARTA. I get to see and hear so much. If I had money, I would ride all the time, but not downtown. People downtown are so weird and crazy to me. Like the last time momma and I went to the market, we were on our way back, waiting on the bus right outside of Rich's. This old man was doing some corner preaching, but I wasn't listening. Until he tapped me on my shoulder.

"Son, do you know God," the very short, bearded, faceless, homeless looking man asked me.

"Yes sir! I do," I answered, looking him directly in the eyes. We were the same height.

"Do you believe Jesus died on the cross for our sins," he asked. That's when I noticed his eyes. They were green.

"And on the 3rd day he rose from the dead," I answered. I just played along with this lunatic. When I said it, his green eyes glowed. He reached under his dirty red hat, then held out his hand to me.

"Now you little angel, get to know God's most famous angel Lucifer." the man said. At the same time, he placed a bill in my hand. I looked down at it and it had a 5 and a 0. I worked at a store. I've seen every bill up to one hundred. This was a 50, if it was real.

"Ah thanks mister," I said, but the man was gone. That fast, did he disappear into the air or the crowd of people that was walking by? I didn't waste time trying to find him. My eyes went back to my hand.

"Boy, let me see what that short, nasty lookin', crazy ass man gave you," momma said. She tried to look down into my hand, but I closed it. Lord knows I didn't want momma to see this money.

"It's just a piece of paper momma. That's all," I said, trying not to get excited.

"Boy open yo hand," she said and grabbed me by my arm.

"No stop! I ain't got nothing. Let me go," I said. I snatched away from her. I knew if momma got her hands on my money, I would never see it again.

"Open yo got damn hand nigga fo I break yo fingers. Imma already beat yo skinny ass when we get home for showing out on me down here in front of all these folks, wait til I tell Walt," she said, between clenched teeth. Other people heard her, but I'm the only one that understood her. She was mad and getting madder, and you don't want to make my momma mad. She had my wrist so tight my hand got numb, I opened my hand.

"Holly shit, the devil is a lie. Come on boy fo that crazy nigga come back," she said. She was walking and weaving through the crowd so fast I thought she was tryna to lose me. I had to run to keep up.

"Momma, Momma. Wait, give me my money back," I screamed behind her. She stopped in her tracks.

"Nigga shut the fuck up. I ain't got no money nigga. What you trying to do? Get both of us killed? You damn dummy. I was gonna buy you something now you ain't getting shit. Front me out, like I just robbed you. Nigga wait til I get you home. Now bring yo ass on and don't say another word or I'll push yo ass out in the road," momma said into my ear. Then she looked me in my eyes, and I could really picture her pushing me in front of a bus. So I didn't speak another word until I made it home.

"Daddy, daddy, daddy. Girl where my daddy," I screamed as soon as I hit the door.

"Boy, what's wrong with you? Where's momma," Kim asked as I passed by her headed to the basement. From the steps I could smell the smoke from cigars and cigarettes. My daddy was behind his hand made bar.

"Boy, what you want now? I ain't got no money for that damn game," Daddy said. It was the same old crew and a few other faces that I didn't pay any attention to. They were sitting around telling lies.

"Momma took my $50 that the preacher man gave me at Five Points," I said as fast as I could everybody in the room burst out laughing.

"Rod if a preacher gave you 50 greenbacks and yo momma took it all these niggas in here together ain't gonna get that money back from Artie. What you'll get is a butcher knife in yo neck ask yo daddy he know, look at all them cuts on his ass," one of the others said. It was Jorge, Li-Jorge daddy. He was one of my daddy's homeboys from down south. He was a regular in the basement. Everybody got a good laugh out of that, everybody but me.

"Here boy gone up to the store and play the game I'll ask Artie what happen," Daddy said while handing me a dollar.

"I don't want no damn dollar. I want my money that man gave me," I said before I knew it.

"Boy, who the hell do you think you are talking to? Get yo ass in yo room before I kill you motherfucker. What the fuck wrong wit you nigga? You smelling yo self? You wanna try me, motherfucker? Get out my face and don't say another word, and don't leave that room," daddy said.

I went to my room. I didn't wanna go anywhere without my 50 bucks. I thought about all the things I would have done with my money. I got more and more upset. My anger was turning into hate over 50 bucks. Is that why the man told me to get to know Lucifer? Is money really that evil? I know men are evil. I read about evil in the bible, one Holy war after another. Everybody killed in the name of God, or was it in the name of greed? Rev. Stovall said, "If you love money you will never love anything else, but money and money don't love you back. He preaches money is the root to all evil. Is money the root or route of all evil? That would mean it's the foundation, it starts off evil. If it's the route to evil that means it will lead you to evil. Either way, it will doom you if you love it. I don't know if I love it, but I know I always feel good when it's in my pocket. Now I'm mad and in my heart I want to get even, but instead I do like my preacher said, pray! I prayed to God that he will take away the hate I feel for my momma right now. I prayed that he would stop my heart from beating so fast. I prayed it was all a dream.

FROM THE LITTLE LEAGUE TO THE BIGS

Summer of 1982, I was spending most of my days at Adams Park practicing baseball. Coach Jerry took me around the kids momma would call uppity, and kids that daddy would've called ghetto, but they were all cool with me. I played park ball all over the city, football and baseball. I had a lot of friends in high and low places on my team. The Mayor of our city, Andrew Young's son Bo Young played on our team, and I have to say he wasn't soft, but I wouldn't go as far to say he was hard. Tyrone Pope was hard with him and the rest of the Boat Rock Kimberly Courts project crew. We won the football Turkey Bowl at J.A. White Park the first season I played. We had our banquet at City Hall. We were served on a silver platter! Burger King!!!!!! Gave us all some plastic trophies and put us out in 30 minutes. Coach Jerry didn't like that at all. He said they were cheap, stealing MF's. The next day he took the team and our families to the Smothers Board Buffet on Cleveland Ave. That's where our Baseball team went after we'd won big games. Coach Jerry always paid for everybody, Daddy said, he should because he wins so much money off y'all. Coach Jerry was a big gambler, and he didn't lose much, he made sure of that. We got the best players from the worst places. He gave us hope and put us in real uniforms like the pro teams. I could care less that he gambled on us, it made me play harder because like the coach said when we win he wins, when he eats we eat. We ate a lot because we came from starving to be eating at buffets is wonderful. All the coaches did the same thing, or you didn't stand a chance at winning. I learned a lot from the coach, not about baseball, that daddy taught me. I learned how to be a winner from Coach Jerry, and that winning did mean everything that losing didn't mean shit, but sadness. If you don't feel you're the best at what you do, don't do it. I put it in my mind that I'm the best at everything I do. That's why I don't play basketball, I'm not great at it. Being good at sports is the key out of the ghetto, at least that's what I heard. That's what everybody is trying to do. It's one big hustle, so I met so many young hungry kids like myself all over the city. Little did I know then that another hustle would present itself years later?

NEW NEIGHBORS

Winter of 1983 was a big turning point in my life. I was in the 7th grade at J. C. Harris. This would be my last year. Next year, I will be going to Brown High. Kim and Karen are in College at Morris Brown, and Walter is in the 11th grade. I'll have one year at Brown High with him. Everybody does well in school but me. I think I could do better, but my mind wonders a lot. It's like my teacher Mrs. Polite said, I don't apply myself. I like Reading and P.E. My daddy is a firm believer in education and he's very hard on us. Everybody gets A's but me. I'm happy to get a C in anything but Reading. That's a B+. I overheard momma telling daddy that I was slow, and they could get a check for me. Daddy wasn't hearing that and cursed my momma out bad for saying it. Truth is, I'm not slow. I just think a lot, and most of the time it's not what the teacher is teaching about. I know I'm smart because I pass all my tests, that's when I concentrate the most. I really hate school. All I want to do is play baseball and football, but I know without school nothing will be possible. All daddy talked about besides baseball is education. He always said education is something nobody can take from you, but it seems so hard to get. I have so many distractions in my life, and to make matters worse, I get butterflies in my stomach around girls now. The same way I do when I'm playing baseball before it's my bat. Lil-Walt told me;

"It's because girls are like baseball, if I keep swinging, one day you'll hit a Homerun".

"I don't get it". I said; looking at him puzzled.

"One day believe me you will get it, just don't get nothing with it". Lil-Walt said; and started laughing. I had no idea what was so funny and really didn't care that day because I was sitting on the front stoop being nosey watching the new neighbors move in next door. We have a new edition to the dead end, and they were moving on the very end, the last house on the dead end.

"Oh my God, I know that girl. That Muslim girl!!!!!!! Daddy Daddy Daddy!!!!!!!!" I screamed; as I ran in the house. Daddy was sitting in his chair watching the Nfl playoffs. Another year our beloved Falcons are watching with us.

"Boy, what the hell you want, don't come in here wit no bullshit, I'm watching the game," he said, not moving his eyes off our new Renter Center 25 inch color TV.

"Some Muslims moving in next door". I said; I couldn't wait to see his reaction. My daddy has always been anti-Muslim, he believe Muslims are very violent people, that are living in the past.

"Boy, get outta here wit that shit I told you I was watching the game. Don't come back in here, if you do you takin yo ass to bed". He warned me; still not taking his eyes off the TV.

"Daddy! I'm for real. I know them Muslim kids from school. I ain't lying, come see, if I'm lying, I'll go to sleep for a week," I replied and laughed a little at the end. That got his attention. His eyes snapped to mine like magnets.

"Boy, don't be playing wit me, if you are imma put yo ass to sleep," he said as he put his cigarette out and stood up. It was the beginning of January, football playoffs were on, but it wasn't that cold outside. My daddy walked right past me, bare feet no shirt onto the front stoop. I stood inside the door and watched. They were moving their things in an old gray beat up pickup truck. There were three women, all their faces covered like robbers. One of the women looked very white, she was very light-skinned, and all I could see was the bridge of her nose and their eye sockets. There was one man with them. He was tall, slim and very light-skinned, but I could tell he was black by his nappy beard. There were more kids than I could count. Their ages looked to range from newborn to maybe 4, plus the two I went to school with were the Muslim girl Bosha and her brother Jamil. He's a year younger than us. I like Bosha and Jamil. We walked home from school every day. I never knew where they lived. They are from Philadelphia wherever that is. All I know is the Eagles and Phillies play ball there. Bosha talks real funny just like a white girl, she's the one that's been giving me butterflies every time she talks. Her voice is unlike any I've heard. It's like she's singing a song when she's talking, it's enchanting. She and I have a lot in common, we both like sports, Pac-man, Good times, Sanford and Son, and most of all music. We both loved Michael and Prince. New Edition had just come out with Candy Girl and took everybody's girl, I'm glad I didn't have a girl. I wasn't into love music, but I did take a liking to rape music. Everybody was walking around with big boom boxes blasting. All the Rappers are from New York City, and I can't understand a word they are saying, but I love the beats. Bosha is very smart, 10 times smarter than all the kids at J. C. Harris, and smarter than some teachers. She knows all the words to all the latest songs and sings them every day on the way home from school. Bosha's tall, slim, with smooth pecan brown skin. I hadn't seen her hair, she always keeps it covered. Her face is never covered, and it's very easy on the eyes. All the Muslim women around here keep their faces covered, but not the girls. Lil-Walt says it's because they ain't got their period yet.

"As soon as they come on the rag, the men cover their face wit a rag," he said. I didn't know what all that meant, but I knew what a period was, I have two sisters. At school some kids used to pick on the Muslim kids until they found out that they would fight and they all stood together. Before Bosha I was always neutral, but Bosha used to fight every day when she first moved here. I found myself in a few fights on her side that meant "the Muslim side" to the kids at school. Really, I don't know why people feel like Muslims are so different from us. We like the same things we just don't believe in the same bible.

"The Quran is older than the bible Rakil, the bible was written using the Quran. But they are only books. People are the religion, not the books, we all read the same books, but for each of us it may have different meanings. If you truly believe in God and pray for the true meaning, you will receive it Rakil," Bosha said to me one day. She called me Rakil. She said because I reminded her of a friend in Philly.

"That ain't what my preacher says," I replied. I wasn't not being serious.

"I bet yo so call preacher drives a caddy fool". She said; Bosha loved to talk about religion. I'm learning a lot from her, and now she's moving next door.

"Hey how y'all folks doing? I'm Big-Walt looks like we gonna be neighbors. Y'all must be some of the good brothers' people? Any friends of the Iman is a friend of mine. You need any help, I got two strong boys over here," Daddy said. He sounded very fake. Sometimes you have to fake it to make it. These people will never know how much he didn't trust Muslims, but my daddy had a way with everyone. He's a people person.

"Assalamualaikum brother. Thank you for your kindness, but there's no need. Iman and some brothers are pulling up now. I look forward to being a good neighbor to you and your family brother Walt," the light-skinned, nappy bearded man said. I could see a dark green station wagon out of the corner of my eye, as it pulled to the curb behind the truck. The station wagon was packed full of all kinds of household things, and two mattresses on the top of the car. I could also see three heads on the inside of the wagon, two I didn't know but one I did. Iman Jamil (H. Rap) and the head of the snake, as Foots would say, I knew well.

"Oh ok, I didn't see the car coming. Nice to meet you, man. I hope to be a good neighbor to y'all too. Imma head back in and finish watching this game," my daddy said.

"Assalamualaikum Big Walt, how have you been brother, how's the family? I see Lil-Rod peeping out the door. How are you doing, Rodney," Rap asked.

"I'm doing fine Jamil," I answered. I knew he didn't like kids calling him Rap and never sir or mister. I remember one time he gave me a soda at his store, I said;

"Thank ya, sir," I said.

"Slavery is over, Lil-Rod. Thank you and calling me Jamil will do," he said. From that day on, I called him Jamil.

"Yeah, he fine as long as I don't have a dime. How you been doing Rap? Ain't seen you since they caught that monster Wayne Williams," daddy said.

"It's been about a year, I'm doing well thanks to Allah! Big Walt, our kids still aren't safe. There's a monster coming for us. White people are always planning a way to kill us or put us back in slavery. A lot of our people still have a need to be enslaved. Crackers got them brainwashed, if not on drugs, that's the new slavery," Rap said. He was about to get deep.

"Well, I see ya got more than enough help. Imma gone back in here and watch the game. Ya'll need anything give me a holler," daddy said.

"Come on, boy. We gotta talk," He said to me. I followed. Daddy and I were the only ones home. We walked into the living room and we both sat down. Daddy turned the TV off.

"Boy, I know you got the eye for that lil skinny Muslim girl, but you better take it off her. You see them people over there, they don't think like us. Now that don't make 'em wrong, it make 'em different. To them we different too. I ain't telling you not like a person cause they're different, but first you gotta understand why they're different. You don't understand that shit now but I do, and I'm yo daddy and I'm telling you to stay the fuck away from them people. You better not bring no trouble to my peep hole". Daddy said.

"Why I"? I spoke.

"Why my ass nigga! I don't wanna hear shit bout that cause you just don't know, you don't know shit. But I will tell you this, that man you call Jamil is a killer, and he ain't gonna stop killing, like a thief ain't gonna stop stealing. Look at me, boy! Those people are dangerous! I been all over the world when I was in the service. I been places that still stone people to death, boy. The shit the Muslims believe won't move this world forward, it will only keep us at war. Cross the water them motherfuckers been at war for over a thousand years and ain't gonna stop no time soon. Look around you Rod, the more of them mothersfuckers you see the more danger this world will see. They got more faith in death than life, like in that war movie when the Japs flew their planes into our battleship. Kamikaze is what they call it, but that shit ain't nothing but suicide. They killed themselves because their religion said it's cool. It's a better world waiting on you with plenty of money and hoes, cause you killing people and yourself in the name of Buddha, Allah, Jesus or God. What kind of God would want some shit like that? Not the one in my heart. My God is a merciful God, he believes in forgiveness, not pain. Jesus suffered enough for us. Those people over there, if you cross one of them once, you better kill 'em all twice, they don't forgive or forget. Remember that shit, boy. Now go get me a pack of cigarettes and tell Author to put it on my book. I ain't got no money." daddy said. This was one of his serious conversations. He didn't talk about God much, only when he was drunk or very serious. He hadn't had a drink, but the day wasn't over yet. My momma and sisters were at that church. Lil-Walt was at the store like always, and that's where I was headed. I still worked at the store, just about every other day. I got my own book account, but I can only credit $5 thanks to my daddy. Walt can credit whatever and I'd get him to credit me $5 for $6 back, he calls it juice, I call it being a Jew.

"Hey Rod-Rod," my shadow Twon said. He's the little red, green-eyed boy and the little brother momma never had.

"What you want nigga? I'm busy," I said in my tough guy voice.

"You don't work today nigga, stop lying Rod. Buy me a drank. Imma pay you back. Why you ain't watching the game," Twon asked.

"Nigga all you do is beg and ask questions". I was saying; but before I could continue.

"Dem some Muslims moving next door to ya'll my grand momma said, yo daddy gonna have to stop all that hell raising. His bootleg business bout to go to shit, and ain't nobody gonna wanna hang in that basement no more," Twon said in a voice like his granny, Mrs. Sweet Mabel.

"Nigga shut up! Yo grandma old as hell. She don't know what she be saying, she just be saying shit. Look at all the bootlegging she doing plus the police stay going up there, she needs to mind her own business. This a dead end nigga, one way in and that's the same way out," I told him. To say we see all the cars that come back and forth all day, people know what's going on even if they don't see it.

"My grandmamma ain't old nigga she blessed. Now come on man and buy me a drink. I'll steal you two back when Mable come home. Tag boy," Twon said. Then he took off running past Skeeter's house, and I was right behind him. I really love Twon like a brother, I'm close with all the kids in my hood. Derek D., Rodney S., Rodney T., Shane, Reggie H., Demil P., and Tony. That's just naming a few. I was cool with everybody from Harris Homes to Dixie Hill. But Twon is my little brother. His grandmamma was a bootlegger, my daddy was a bootlegger, and we knew all the same people. But we didn't know how our lives would change. I caught up with him right before he made the corner.

"Gotcha lil red nigga! You thank you fast, don't ya," I said.

"Ah, Rod," Shane yelled from inside of his screen on the porch. Shane lived in a nice brick house across from the store.

"What's going on Shane," I yelled back.

"Say it ain't so man," he asked me.

"What ain't so nigga," I yelled.

"Big Walt done let Rap move right next door," he yelled back. That got people on the corner to look around.

"No, he ain't," I said and headed into the store.

"Yes, he is nigga! I saw them riding down the street loaded up. Maybe they moving in wit y'all then". Shane said; I could hear him laughing. I didn't want everybody asking me who was moving where, and like Mable said, Muslims are bad for business. As we walked past the clubhouse, I could hear pool balls breaking and somebody cursing. Across the street Black John, Pissy Coon, and one of them Eggleston boy's. I don't know which one of them it was because they all look alike with their California curls. Daddy says all them boy's bad news and they are all going to jail or hell. I hope not because I like them, and they all give me money. They were congregated in their usual spot, shooting dice around the steps that lead to the apartment building. It wasn't cold, but even if it was freezing a group of people always stood there. They had to because it was against club laws to stand on this side of the street and deal. If you got caught, that pool stick wouldn't be busting balls, it would be busting your ass. Twon and I walked into the store. Walt was behind the counter, and Lil-Jorge was playing Pac-Man. Times had changed no more Pin-ball, it's Pac-Man and Atari these days.

"What up Jorge? How many credits you got left," I asked.

"I'm gonna let you play cause when Big-Walt finds out you moved yo lil Muslim girlfriend next door he gonna kill you nigga," Jorge said. Everybody got a laugh.

"That ain't my girlfriend nigga and my daddy already know, I told him. You nosey ass nigga," I snapped back.

"I ain't nosey nigga! Those niggas on the dead end nosey, they tied of Big-Walt raising all that hell down there. Rap gonna put an end to that shit. You better gone and fuck that lil bitch. They

fuck real young. I done fucked them all but Bosha but she next,"
Jorge said. He loves to talk shit, and he's good at it. He wasn't
gonna get his laugh off me.

"Fuck you Jorge! Let's go Twon," I said. We headed out the door.

"Wait Rod! I was just playing man, but have you smelted that
pussy yet? Muslim pussy smells different ask yo brother," Jorge
told me. We walked out of the store not knowing which way to
go.

"Rod you like that skinny, ugly Muslim girl for real man? Nigga
I'm thirsty, I'm going back in the store. You can go play with yo
ugly girlfriend," Twon teased.

"Say it again nigga imma black yo eye," I said.

"Say what she ugly or she yo girlfriend," He asked like he really
didn't know.

"She ain't ugly and she ain't my girlfriend nigga, don't say that
shit no more! You dig," I said. I was getting more mad by the
minute.

"Alight man. I won't, let's just go back in and get us a drank,"
Twon asked. He knew when I was getting mad so he did like any
other little brother, backed down. I don't know if I was getting
mad at him calling her my girlfriend or at him calling her ugly.
Both made me feel some kind of way.

"Alight man, but you go in because I don't wanna hear that shit
from Lil-Jorge. Get two Cokes on my book and a pack of cigarettes
on my daddy's book. Walt knows how to write it up, just hurry
up," I said as I shoved him to the door. He went in. I stood and
watched across the street the crowd had grown, but all the same
faces from the days before. I know them all, if not by name, by
face. As I'm watching the green station wagon pass by I could see
Jamil driving and the two other heads still inside, but the wagon
was unloaded. I waved, Jamil nodded, and his eyes scanned in
the direction that mine had just left the apartment steps. But
now the steps were empty. Only Pissy Coon remained. He stood

6 foot 2 inches as skinny as a rail, skin red and pale. He was waving and smiling like he was watching a parade. Daddy says Pissy Coon will never be shit but a thief and a junky and a rat or one day them Muslims will catch up to him soon. I watched the taillights of the wagon as it turned right on Dragon Place. and headed down by the park where they belong. I looked back across the street and like magic, everybody was back.

"Let's go Rod, Lil-Jorge finna to come out here," Twon said. He was already running. He had a brown paper bag under his arm like a football. I took off behind him. I could hear my name being called from all directions as I ran down Holderness.

Everybody was trying to be noisy. Word flies fast around here. There were only a few house phones on Holderness and we got one 755-1802 everybody got the number. They should just call my daddy and ask him who moved next door, but they know that will be a quick way to get cursed out. So they kept calling me.

"Rod,"

"Lil-Rod,"

"Rodney". They just kept on calling; and then before I made it to Greenwich Street.

"Rod Brown bring yo ass here boy, don't you run by me boy," the old raspy voice of old man Skeeter said. I had to stop for him at least. I get paid for what I say. Skeeter and daddy are good friends, and he is like a grandpa to me. A rich one at that.

"Yes, sir," I answered as I put my breaks on.

"Twon hold on," I yelled to him. He stopped and turned around.

"Imma wait right here, I'm thirsty," Twon said, then took a seat on the curb, opened the bag and popped his Coke. I turned and headed up to Skeeter's front steps, and there he stood. Old and handsome, tall and lean used to be every woman's dream. He still is let him tell it.

"Boy, why you keep running by here all fast not speaking to

nobody? They say yo girlfriend done moved next door to ya down there. Is that true boy? Dem Muslims done snuck their way all the way to the dead end," Skeeter asked. He already knew, because he's shaking his head.

"Yes, sir. It's true," I answered, looking him right in the eyes.

"Well I be damn, but I don't give a damn. Imma keep making it do what it do, you do? Dis my street, fuck the Muslims and the pigs. Here you go as he held his hand out. I took his hand and felt paper inside that had to be money like always.

"Now go tell yo daddy to call me". Skeeter said; Mr. Skeeter is the nicest man I know. He ain't nice to everybody, he shows me much favor. He makes more money than anybody in the West End bootlegging, running numbers, cards, and loan sharking, no drugs, no girl, no boy, not even reefer. But daddy says Skeeter's nephew Rufus, he just moved here from Miami. Word is late at night when Skeeter is asleep Rufus turns the house to a dope house. I don't know how true it is, but Charlie Brown told my daddy and Charlie lives there. If I knew soon Skeeter would know. I could hear people on the inside now, cursing over the game.

"Who winning the game," I asked.

"The Cowboys playing like some cowgirls! You know that Rod! Who you took," Skeeter asked; he already knew who I liked this year. He asked me almost every day. I pick teams better than anybody my age, Mr. Skeeter said. I pick winners like none other in baseball and football. The reason is that in my house, we watch all the games like its homework. Daddy says watching the best can only make you better and teach you the history of the game. I love watching football, but sometimes baseball gets boring watching. I'd rather play.

"You know I told you not to take yo cowgirls yesterday. I to ok the Rams, but next week the skins will kill them. The Rams not big enough," I answered. Skeeter scratched his head.

"You know what Rod? You damn sho right". Skeeter said; a little under his breath.

"Well, I better be going. Thank you, sir. See you later," I said, and I was off.

"Let's go boy," I said to Twon as I blew by on the curb. He was up and running in less than a second. I was feeling how many bills were in my hand, 3 bucks for a little news ain't bad. I could feel the cool air blowing by my ears as I headed to my front yard.

"Got you nigga! I caught you that time," Twon said, pulling the back of my shirt.

"Nigga you ain't caught nothing. I was stopping. Look nigga I'm home, so why should I keep on running I ain't no slave. Take yo nasty ass hand off me nigga," I said slapping his hand.

"Rakil! Do you not know that boy's name," Bosha asked. I couldn't see her because of the screen on the porch, but I knew her voice from anywhere, I wonder who else is on that porch.

"Yeah! I know his name. You must wanna know it," I replied.

"No, I don't wanna know his name. I just want both of you to use each other's name instead of that bad word y'all keep using. Rakil, you know how I hate to hear you talk that way. I told you we not niggas we are kings and queens that were kidnapped by these crackers, and taught to think the way you thinking and..."

"Rod--Rod get in here, boy" daddy cut in. He cut Bosha off with her black power shit. She really does hate the word nigga, but I don't know why. My momma says no matter how much money or power a black man gets, he will still be a nigga to a real cracker. A nigga will always be a nigga.

"I gotta go. See y'all later. Here I come," I said; I stepped inside the living room, but I didn't see my daddy.

"Daddy where you at"? I screamed out;

"I'm in the basement boy, come on down," he answered. The old wooden stairs made cracking sounds under my weight. The basement was cold, very dimly lit, and smelled of stale smoke.

Our old black-and-white TV was behind the bar and the game was on.

"Why you come down here? It's cold," I asked with my arms wrapped around my body.

"Sit down, boy. We gotta talk about a lot of shit," he said. He had a glass in one hand and a fifth of Seagram's Gin in the other. This wasn't going to be good.

"Rod, I know ya like that lil nappy head girl next door, and ain't nothing wrong wit liking girls. As a matter of fact, everything is right wit that shit and don't let nobody tell you no different. But boy, that Muslim girl will be trouble for you and our family," he said at the same time, pouring himself a shot. "Why daddy," I asked as he downed his shot.

"Why? Why? Ain't got shit to do wit it Rod, it's about, we. We are Christian's they are Muslim's just like white and black boy, you get it? We live by different rules. You see how that lil girl talks to you? I heard all that shit, they don't think they nigga's, they living in yester years. All that king and queen shit been gone for us. Dem niggas over there stone age men, and if you mess wit that lil girl you gotta be one of them. That means no more pork, you think you can live wit out pork chops, and pork ribs nigga please? Shit nigga you can't even eat bacon no mo'. Can't no nigga live wit me that don't eat pork, so you gotta get the fuck outta here and move next door". Daddy said; then burst out laughing. I didn't see anything funny about nothing he was saying, or was this a joke, so I laughed with him.

"That was real funny daddy, you know you can tell good jokes," I said. My laugh wasn't genuine.

"Mother fucker I ain't joking, you hang around them Muslim's you gotta get the fuck outta here fast nigga no joke," daddy said and took another shot.

"You for real," I asked. "Dead for real! Like how dead you'll be fucking wit them people. Let me finish telling you what I gotta say. Like I be telling you bout saying nigga all the time, some people don't like that word, and I can understand that. I say nigga all the time in my own house around my own people. Dem people next door, not our people. You seen that white woman, didn't you," he asked me.

"She ain't white, she just light-skinned. I ain't never seen no white Muslim," I answered and laughed for real this time.

"Boy, you need to read more, you dumb ass hell. Muslims come in all colors, just like Christian's. That woman over there is a cracker if I ever seen one, and she got the blue eyes to prove it. That lil girl got way more sense than you boy, so stay away from her. She'll trick the shit out of a dumb ass nigga like you, and what's wit that name she called you (Rakil) some shit like that? You let that lil smart bitch know yo name Rod or Rodney ain't nobody gonna be calling you that shit boy. If I didn't know better, I believe you wanna be a Muslim," he said. Then I took a drink right out of the gin bottle this time.

"Nawl I don't wanna be known Muslim. I love pork daddy," I answered.

"Yeah, I know you love pork, but pussy better than pork. If that little girl gives you some pussy it will change yo religion I'm telling ya. You see, in that religion you can have more than one wife. That red nigga over there got three wives. Shit all that pussy that nigga ain't thinking bout eaten no pork all he do is poke". Daddy said; and he got a real good laugh out of it too. My mind started to race.

"For real daddy? I don't believe you, swear it to God". I asked; I didn't believe it, I thought stuff like that was against the law.

"Boy, I'm telling you to read a book this shit is only a secret to a dummy. I ain't gotta swear on that shit it's a known fact Jack. Stay away from them people. They'll reel yo dumb ass in so fast. That shit ain't nothing but bait don't get caught fool. The church don't accept that kind of sin. If any church I go to and pay my tithes accept that kind of shit or that homo shit they will lose this member. Some shit just ain't right for kids to see. Things

69

might change one day. God knows I hope not, but I guess crackers felt the same way when the slaves were freed. They believed they were doing God's will. It took over five hundred years for them to realize we are humans like them. When I was stationed in Germany nothing but a white woman over there, and boy let me tell you them bitches thought niggas had tails like monkeys. I told one of them whores, yeah I got a tail but it don't come out my ass it hangs between my nuts. That's why I look at these nigga politicians on TV and I laugh. They don't thank they nigga's no more, like them fools next doe, they thank they gonna change these crackers world. To the crackers that count, you will always be a nigga. That's why I don't see nothing wrong with a nigga calling a nigga a nigga. It's slowly taking the power from the word. When slaves came over that's the only name we knew to call each other. We didn't know English, and crackers would cut our tongues out if they heard us speaking in our own language. Crackers don't like to hear that word now. It makes them feel guilty. I think we should never forget that word or stop using it and remember a lot of niggas died just for being a nigga, and they were happy just being a nigga. Now niggas wanna be all they can be, and I'm wit that, but you still gonna be a nigga in this white man world". Daddy preached; my mind was wondering faster than his mouth was talking. Is it right for a man to have more than one wife? Is it right for a man to sleep with a man or a woman to sleep with a woman? When it comes down to sissy's. Rev. Stovall always says if it doesn't happen in nature and it shouldn't happen with man. It means that if two boy dogs won't have sex, two men shouldn't. I wonder what he would say about a man with more than one wife. I know one thing: he can't compare that to a dog, because my dog Bear stays locked up with a stray bitch. Dogs don't care as long as it's a bitch dog he is going in. Did God make man the same way? Who was first on earth, man or animals? That's the question that I needed answered. I think animals were first, because God had to have something here for us to eat. If that's a fact, it would make Rev. Stovall right. We had to learn from nature to become what we have become.

"Boy, you better be listening to me one day dis shit might save yo life," daddy said. He snapped me out of my trance.

"Why is it wrong for a man to have more than one wife in the bible? Solomon had seven wives," I asked;

"What? What you say? Nigga all that shit is Old Testament if you would read the bible instead of just listen to that nigga Stovall recite shit out of it. Read Rod men created some shit called civilization. People next door living in the Stone Age. In civilization shit is always changing, we just gotta keep up, what's right today may be wrong tomorrow, just like a friend today can be an enemy tomorrow. But shit just can't stay the same enemy's turn to friends, shit that was right, is now wrong. Muslims don't change. They have been killing for the same shit for over a thousand years, some shit bout some holy land. I know you slow but get what I'm saying. People who don't change end up living on a Reservation, you can ask the Indians about that. All they wanted to do was follow the buffalo, but these crackers came and wanted to fly like the Crow, so the Indians had to go. This shit is called progress. I'm living a dream compared to my daddy. Boy, just stay the fuck away from them Muslims, and whatever you do, don't put yo lil wee-wee in that Muslim girl. If you do, you gonna have to marry her and all her momma's too," daddy said then laughed his ass off. I wasn't even smiling. Why did this man like to talk in riddles, it's hard to know how for real he is. I headed up the stairs, daddy was still laughing. I didn't want to hear any more talk about Muslim's or Christian's, but I did get it. One religion changes with the times the other is trying to stay the same in a constantly changing world. I like how the world is changing. God knows I couldn't have been a slave. I don't even like taking the trash to the curb. I would've gotten beaten everyday back then, it took change for that. After slavery niggas still wasn't free here in the South, my daddy told me. After Slavery the Klan got worse than ever, and niggas still didn't have rights. Niggas in Texas didn't find out they were free until two years later on June 19th, 1865. Daddy always says niggas celebrate Christmas like its Juneteenth. He lived in the times when the Klan ruled, but his great granddaddy was a slave. The Klan had to be stopped, things had to change, and they did. Thanks to The Rev Dr. Luther King and a lot of great Christians.

Christians are the power core in the civil rights movement. Christians believe in Jesus and Jesus believes in forgiveness and forgiveness changes the heart. When people's hearts change, the world changes. All you gotta do is look around you, I still see racist faces, but for the most part we are blessed. I'm not a Muslim and never will be, but I don't have anything against them. We are all God's children, we all just don't know it yet. I'm not gonna stop feeling the way I feel. I don't think I could if I tried. Bosha is my friend and her friends are my friends. We're from the dead end that makes us dead end friends. From Shane to Bosha, they are all my dead end friends.

IS THIS THE END

It was the last day of school, the last day of elementary school, I was feeling sad. Even though I knew this was just another step to manhood. I had already got the speech from daddy. This school year went by so fast, I think Bosha had a lot to do with it. We were what they call going together now, whatever that meant. I just know she makes me feel some kind of way. She's my motivation to get out of bed and go to school every morning. I know when I open my door rain, sleet or snow her and her family will be waiting at the light pole in front of my house. Then we headed up Holderness for the rest of the crew. At the corner of Lucile and Holderness we met up with the kids from Lil-Jorge apartments and more Muslims from the park. On most days it would be around 20 of us, then we would head to J.C Harris, all ages, all sizes. It was a three block trip and more kids would tag along the way. Most days we walked to school slowly like we all really didn't want to go, we all talked shit and told jokes. At the corner of Oglethorpe and Lucille one of my best friends Lil-Jamie would be waiting, he's a year younger than me, and I'll miss him next year. I'll miss all of this like Bosha says we're family, but like I say time for shit to change. After school we all waited for each other then raced home as fast as possible, but Bosha and I had been walking slowly lately. Trying to make this time slow down.

"Rakil," she called. She still called me that, just not in front of daddy. Like everybody else, she had grown to love and respect my father. We were on our way home from school for the last time. Everyone else was home or almost home by now, we were just crossing Hopkins St.

"Yeah, B. What up." I answered. She was walking a little ahead of me. She stopped in her tracks.

"I found out last night after the summer I'm moving back to Philly for high school". She said; but did she really say what I thought she said? My heart skipped three beats.

"What? You told me you going to Brown wit me, stop playing B," I replied. My voice was a little shaky, maybe because I knew when she was joking and she wasn't.

"I know, I know. But my Pops wants me back home, man. Just me man and that shit ain't fair. My little brothers and sisters can stay," she said, looking me in my eyes. I could see she was about to cry. It was the first week of June and a big black cloud just rolled over the sun, blocking it completely. I was feeling as gray as the sky and praying to myself not to cry.

"But why, Bosha why," I pleaded.

"He said someone told him I was falling in love with a kafir, the schools down here are too far behind, and he said this city is cultureless," she answered; but I had no idea what she was talking about.

"Who the fuck is kafir? What is that, you got a boyfriend or something I don't know bout? Speak in English Bosha, I don't understand that Muslim shit and you know it"? I asked; really confused, a lot of Muslim's speak Arabic, Bosha speaks it well, I can barely speak English. Maybe our schools are behind, and everybody from up north laughs at how we talk. They call us country niggas because we don't talk proper like them, but I have to say they are smarter. I can barely read out loud, but Jamal Bosha's brother reads better than anybody in the school besides Bosha, and he's two years younger.

"Calm down Rakil and stop cursing at me. You know I don't have a boyfriend silly. You are the Kafir they speak of, but like I told sister, you are not a kafir. You believe in Allah or do you not? Do you submit to the will of Allah or do you not?" She asked; as if she knew the answer. Sister was the white Muslim head of household.

"I believe in God! I submit to his will, and I don't care. Sister can call me all the names she wants. I'm going to heaven," I said. I hate when people talk about me behind my back.

"God is Allah and Allah is God they are one in the same Rakil how many times I gotta tell you that. I call you Rakil and your family calls you Rod, but your name is Rodney. Our God has many names. So many not even I can name them all, but he is the creator of all heaven and earth. If you believe in the creator and submit to his will, that makes you Islam. Islam is the oldest religion back in time if you believe in God that made you Islamic. This is back before Jesus and your bible. Back then if you didn't believe in the creator and submit to his will you were considered a Kafir, non-believer. That's all that word means, but Sister is wrong. She said it's a sin to marry a Kafir and I agree. You're not a Kafir, you love and fear Allah, he's in your heart and he surrounds your soul. I told her that, and that bitch still crossed me. I could hate her and wish her ill, but I'm not. Imma just leave it to Allah. Let him do his will. You know what I do wish Rakil? I wish everyone was the same color and religion. I think that would make this world so much simpler, and we could be together without judgment. Only Allah could judge us then, we would be living in much less sin. Now close your eyes, I have a surprise. I have been saving it for you for a very long time," Bosha said. She sure had a way with words; She has a power gift sometimes her words can be poetic, and in a way hypnotizing or should I say motivational. This little girl is way before her time, she's 13 going on 33.

"Why I gotta close my eyes, just give it to me". I asked;

"Just close em or I'm not giving it to you". She snapped back; so I closed my eyes, and what happened next I will never forget.

I felt something warm and wet on my lips, then something poking and prying trying to separate them, and it did. Bosha's tongue was in my mouth, rolling around. The kiss only lasted maybe 5 seconds, but to me it felt like five hours. I took it all in every smell, every taste, every sound, and definitely the feeling. I'd never been this close to any girls except my sisters and they always smelled like soap or a sweet cheap perfume. Bosha smelled like an onion, her tongue tasted like a pickle. The sound of it splashing in my mouth made me feel like calling earl.

"Tag Rakil," she said in what I guess was her sexy voice. I'd never heard of it before. I opened my eyes to make sure it was Bosha that had kissed me. All I saw was her back and the black scarf she wore on her head blowing in the wind. She wasn't running fast. I took off behind her, but I wasn't trying to catch her. I felt embarrassed for some reason. I didn't want to see her. I let her run up ahead of me, knowing she would be in her house before I got there. As I ran, I felt the first of many drops of rain that were about to fall upon my head, so I ran faster. The rain felt so good all over my face, I hope it washes away the smell of Bosha. We made it to our houses at the same time. I didn't even look her way, I just went inside. Before I could open the door to my room that Lil-Walt and I shared, I could smell his feet. Walt's feet smelt so bad his shoes weren't allowed in the house.

"Walt yo feet smell like shit and the rain is making them smell worse," I said as soon as I opened the door. Walt was lying on his bed reading a book.

"Nigga shut up you just graduated and I bet you can't spell smell dummy," Walt shot back at me. I was used to all the spelling jokes. The truth is, I'm a very poor speller and not a good reader. I guess they both go hand in hand, I really can read but only to myself. When I read out loud, it just sounds like I'm just calling out words. When Bosha reads she sounds like a reporter, like that black lady on TV Monica Kauffman. I sound like a S.P.E.D. Everybody tells me I don't read enough. Only Bosha said something that made me feel like I wasn't a sped. She told me the reason I don't read well out loud, but read just fine in silence is because I'm a thinker.

"Rakil you are much too smart not to be able to read. It's your shyness, in time you will overcome it, don't shy away from reading. You are a thinker, your mind is always grinding, you want answers. All the answers are in the books. Read in silence or read only to yourself until you feel better about how you sound, but you gotta read Rodney Brown! I wouldn't want you to become a clown," she told me.

"Nigga I can spell, I just like spelling to myself, like I like thinking to myself," I told him. Walt got a good laugh out of that.

"Alright whatever man I'm just glad you graduated. You finna to be in the 8th grade and it's time for you to get some pussy. I ain't gonna be at Brown but one year wit you, don't embrace me. You gotta get a girlfriend in the 8th grade or niggas gonna call you a sissy". He said; Walt was a smooth operator. He didn't need a girlfriend, he used his job at the store to have his way with grown women, I've been a witness to it.

"Man, I already got a girlfriend. You late on that," I said. I knew I shouldn't have.

"Boy, you ain't got no girlfriend. Who you talking about? Oh, I know that little skinny Muslim girl next doe. Nigga that ain't yo girlfriend. If she yo girlfriend, she'll let you fuck it or at least touch it. Which one she let you do," Walt asked as he sat up on the bed like he was about to hear something good. I thought about lying, but I told the truth.

"Nawl we ain't did all that yet, but she let me kiss her," I answered. Walt's eyes got big, and he stood up.

"Nigga you lying put yo hand on the bible and say it," he asked and got our bible off the dresser. I put my hand on it.

"God, you saw me kiss Bosha," I began. It was all I could get out. Walt ran out the room.

"Daddy, daddy, daddy. Rod been kissing that little nasty Muslim girl," Walt ran out screaming. What a dirty rat. I lied once and told Walt I kissed a girl that goes to our church. He never ran and told that. He was too busy telling me all these nasty sinful things to try next to an innocent young girl inside the church. Walt has never really hung around any of the Muslims, because he works all the time, but he did know most of them. Walt listened to daddy and stayed away from them, but I was hard-headed. I had to know why people felt how they felt about Muslims. If I was smart, I would've just read a few books on it, and I wouldn't be in this trouble.

"Rod get yo ass down here boy". My daddy screamed loud enough to shake the house and knew they heard him next door. We are the TV, their TV they never got to watch, and the houses are only 5 feet apart. I headed out the door and downstairs to the basement, or should I say the lion's den. Lil-Walt was sitting in a chair right in front of the stairs. Daddy was standing behind the bar as soon as my feet hit pavement.

"Boy, you just won't get outta yo own way, so as a father, I gotta get you outta yo way for you. Guess what, Rod? We moving I ain't paying no more rent. I been giving this shit some thought since them barbarians moved over there. See you, my dumbest child. You don't believe shit stank, yo dumb ass got to try to smell it every time. One day you gonna smell the wrong shit nigga, and I pray to God, it don't kill you, so you just keep on sniffing, you got bout 90 days nigga. Congratulations for getting promoted. Now it's time for a fresh start all the way around, by the time school rolls back around we will be gone. You can go play or go kiss that nasty girl some more". Daddy said; then dismissed me.

"Dem folk don't even brush they teeth. Rod nasty ain't he daddy"? Walt chimed in.

"Shut up, boy and get yo ass outta here too, I need to think," daddy snapped dismissing Walt as well.

Move? Move where? Move how? Was he serious? Daddy has been depressed lately, not just because of our new neighbors, it's the old one on the other side. Old Slather was here when we moved in and daddy knew him before then. He passed away last month. Sad part is he wasn't even sick, he died in his sleep, and they say that's how the good ones go. Some say after the Muslims moved on the dead end he was never the same anymore. Momma says he was 85 years old. It was time for him to go. Now his house has a for rent sign in the yard, and daddy has been saying more Muslims on the way. Things around me are changing so fast all this bad news in one day.

I think I need to go to church like my grand momma Bell says, when things seem bad the lord will take away all your sadness. So I just prayed and started being a good boy going to church every Sunday. I even read the bible to myself and this Sunday I had some questions.

CALVARY

Calvary United Methodist Church, 1471 Ralph David Abernathy Blvd it was located in the heart of the West End. This church is my family's home away from home. My sisters and momma spend at least 3 days a week here in God's house. Lil-Walt and I only came on Sundays, daddy came maybe once a month give or take, and that's giving a lot. But he was here today, his big black forehead shining like a black bowling ball. Everyone in our family was here on this 3rd Sunday. I was in my Sunday school class, all of us were. It's a 30 minute class before church service. We talked about Jesus and read from the bible, so we'll know what the preacher is preaching about. My Sunday school teacher's name is Mrs. Webb, and she's a teacher in real life. Mrs. Webb is an angel, that's the only way I can describe her. She is the nicest woman I've ever met. She has two kids of her own Keisha and Shawn and we are all around the same age. Shawn being the oldest. Older than me by a year, but I'm older than Keisha by two years. Mrs. Webb treats me as if I was one of her own. I'm a very shy kid, most people think, but really I just got to get to know you. I know all these people at this church. We are a family. I'm comfortable here. We were inside one of the small classrooms in the back of the church. There were only 10 members in the young adolescent Sunday school class. We always started our class with the Lord's Prayer, after the prayer we got to talk about our week, and ask questions. Bosha had me thinking a lot about religion. There were so many questions I had that I never had before and now was the time to ask them.

"Mrs. Webb, was Jesus a prophet? I asked; already knowing the answer.

"Oh yes Rod, Jesus was the profit of all prophets". Mrs. Webb answered quickly; with a big smile on her face, like she was proud of me.

"What about Luther King, was he a prophet too? Just like Jesus, he came with a message from God. Just like Jesus, he had hater's and non-believers that wanted him dead. Just like Jesus, they killed him because of his message. I wanna know the difference between the two"? I asked; I'd been practicing what I was going to say and how I was going to say it all week, with help from Bosha. She read to me out of the Quran what a prophet was. A prophet is a spokesman for God, one who relates the message of God to the people. They were usually unpopular among their people.

"Well Rod, that's a good question, and I hope my answer will help you out. Dr. King was a great man that did a lot to help a lot of people white, black, red, and yellow. His message was from God. I believe he was a God sent man. Do you hear me, Rodney? Dr. King was a man. Jesus is the son of God. He was never a man," Mrs. Webb answered, still smiling. Her faith is always unfazed now and forevermore.

"But Mrs. Webb Jesus was born from a woman a lot of people say that makes him a man". I said; like I was really saying something.

"Rod people say a lot of things, that's why you chose well the people you discuss your faith with. Be strong Rod, it's all a test the same way Moses was tested. God has his own ways of making us strong and keeping us strong, we don't question how. I don't know who you've been talking to, but you let them know that Jesus loves them too, and they are welcome to come serve him with us anytime. Now we must move on to the lesson for this Sunday". Mrs. Webb said; she never took her eyes off me. It was like she was looking for me. Was I lost? I don't think so, I'm just wondering around in my own head. I'm not confused. My daddy told me the truth about religion long ago, and it was simple.

"Rod religion is man made. God made us. When man can make man, that's when we will know the truth about our God, but all it takes is a good writer to write a good book, and our bible is The Good Book". That was all he said; but it made me understand a lot. No, I wasn't lost. I was just wondering who might be close to right about what our true purpose is on Earth. Deep inside of me I know only death will tell me that, because I know one purpose we have is to die. Daddy says any and everything that has life will one day die, if man doesn't kill everything first.

After Sunday school I joined my mother, father and brother on the 3rd row on the middle aisle side to the left of the preacher. Kim and Karen were singing in the choir, so they weren't seated with us. We've been sitting in the same seat since I could remember. Everything inside of our Church is white with nice brown wood trim that matches the color of the pews and pulpit. The pulpit has three big chairs behind the preacher's podium, the biggest in the middle, with two smaller chairs off to each side of the main pulpit. Those chairs are for the acolytes. I'm an acolyte, but it's not my Sunday. It's Cedric Thomas, Gloria's Son, and one of Lil-Walt's best friends. Cedric's family lives on Lucile right next to the store, Gloria, her husband Robert, Jerry Gloria's sister and Jerry's baby daughter Ramika, they don't live together just in the same building. I'm happy because it's so hard not to go to sleep sitting up there. There are nice big gold crosses surrounding the pulpit, but the biggest cross in the church is up on the wall behind the pulpit and the choir. It's made of lights, and it gives off a glow. This is a nice place. Momma said white people used to really take care of the church. Now that's it's mostly nigga's here now it will go down.

I looked around just to count how many whites were still left. I could only count six. Three very old married couples, Mrs. and Mr. Johnson, Mrs. and Mr. Taylor, and my favorite, Mrs. and Mr. Hughes. Mrs. Hues used to keep me at her daycare when I was small. She really treats me like I'm her kid, and she always has something for me. As I looked her way she smiled and showed me a Snicker bar, my favorite. It's a few more whites that are still active members, but they are not in church today, and the rest are too old and sick to come, but they send money and we send our prayers. They were sprinkled throughout the congregation like old ghosts, like daddy said everything gotta change.

"Rod turn around the preacher is coming in," momma said. I turned around to see a fat black bald man in a black robe. It was the one and only Rev. Stovall. Automatically, the church came to order.

"Let the Church say amen," Stovall said in his giant, deep voice.

"Amen," we all said back in cadence. Even daddy said amen. His forehead was shining like a black light bulb, and his cheap cotton dress shirt was already wet with sweat, and I could smell a hint of Gin coming for his skin. I was sitting in between momma and daddy. Lil-Walt was on the other side of momma, and daddy sat on the end of the aisle. We started service with the Lord's prayer. After that Rev. Stovall told us to turn our bibles to Luke 1:3-9. I pretended to do as everyone else. But my mind was far from Luke, John, or Mark, I was thinking about Bosha and Rod. She would leave soon, and I was feeling some kind away. After the kiss, I stayed away from her for a while, but not for long. Last time we were alone she asked me if I wanted to touch her down there, and I asked her what for. Because I belong to you, Rakil. So this belongs to you, she said. She took my hand and put it between her legs. I could feel the heat like her pants were on fire. I snatched my hand back and ran as fast as I could. My heart was racing so fast I had to stop, and when I stopped, I could feel the inside of my pants was beating faster than my heart. It scared me, but it felt so good. Ever since that day, I have been trying to get that feeling back, and only Bosha can do it. I got to move fast before she's gone.

"The doors of the church are now open," Rev. Stovall's powerful voice said. It shook me out of my trance. The door opened and the light from the outside illuminated the sanctuary, and made the gold crosses shine like the sun. I still had my bible open. Lil-Walt looked over at me and just shook his head. Church was almost over, and I couldn't tell you anything about his sermon. So I prayed to myself. God, please forgive me for letting my mind drift away again.

"If there is anyone here today that wishes to be born again in Christ, please come forward. Come to the altar. I don't bite and neither does Jesus, we are in the business of healing the body and saving the soul". Rev. Stovall continued; this is the part of the service when people come up to the altar to be saved by Baptism. After this it will be time to go, if don't nobody comes up to the altar. I already scanned the Church. Everybody today is a member, we're already saved. Just like I said, no one stepped up today, so like always Rev. Stovall had the ushers pass his gold money trays around. As the trays went up and down the aisles and the choir hummed a nice sweet hymn, Rev. Stovall stood there watching each hand slide in and out of his money. As the tray reached me I had second thoughts about putting my only two in the tray, but one look at the good Rev. and I did the right thing. Like they say when you give money to God you get it back double, but the only person who I hear say it is Rev. Stovall. I really don't think God needs money as much as I need it, but my daddy has begged for so much money out of this place, it's only right I give back. I just wish I had enough to give and not worry about how I'm going to get it back. I get tired of being broke, and I ain't even grown yet. When I get older, money ain't gonna be my problem, because Imma be a baseball player or a football player. I already know I'm gonna ball. Imma be a baller. I gotta get me some money.

"Boy, get out yo head and get up. You always daydreaming. Let's go," daddy said. Just like that, church was over. Now I had to wait for all the kisses and handshakes. I walked around and spoke to most of my good brothers and sisters, and collected my goodies from all the sweet old women that paid me to squeeze my jaws.

Then I was on my way to the car.

"Lil-Rod, don't you sneak out this church without giving me my hug," a soft voice said. It's Mrs. Webb, the sweetest lady I've ever known. I turned around and went back to embrace her. At my age I was still taller than her, we hugged.

"Rod never forget your roots. A tree can grow 200 ft high, but not an inch without a root. Always take care of your roots, I love you, boy," she said. She then kissed me on the forehead, held both of my hands in hers, and closed her eyes for maybe five seconds.

"I love you too, Mrs. Webb," I said.

"I know baby, I know and Jesus loves us all ". And she moved on to bless someone else. When I opened my hand a neatly folded five-dollar bill was there, God is good. I was the first to arrive at our car. A 1975 Gremlin daddy bought this bug looking car from his nephew Don. It's the ugliest car I've ever seen, but at least we don't ride MARTA everywhere anymore. I stood there outside the Church on Gordon St. watching the cars roll pass, trying to guess the make before it made it to me. I was feeling good the church will do that to you. Plus, I just got five bucks. Soon everybody filed out of the church and piled into this super small bug car. It was so small I had to ride on Kim's lap. We were squeezed in like sardines in a can, but we only had a brief trip. It was a hip and a hop, only four blocks and one stop. The Ice Cream Parlor, it's one and a half blocks from the church. Straight down the street headed to Dixie Hills, right across from Westview cemetery. We stopped by there when we left church in the summer. They sell the soft ice cream out of the machine. God forgive me, but that's why I don't miss church in the summer. Momma loves the ice cream more than me, so I know it's always a sure go. We went through the small drive thru, and all ordered double cones, and mine was gone before we got half way home. Just like always, daddy gave me the rest of his. I love my daddy. When he turned the green Gremlin on to Holderness, BBQ grills were smoking. Everybody was out. Skeeter's house had cars parked everywhere.

Mr. Skeeter barbecued almost every day. He said the smell of pork ribs keeps the Muslims away. I think niggas around here believed that shit because we kept grills going on Holderness. We made it out of that small coffin and into the house.

ONE SHOT

It was 1:15pm, so I had time to hang out before dinner. It would be ready at 4:00. Daddy did most of the cooking and he was very good at it. I went to my room and started to change clothes. My door opened.

"Rod don't go out there and get lost. Don't be late for dinner, I got some shit I gotta talk to y 'all about. Boy stay away from Skeeter's house too much shit going on up there," daddy said. I laced up my Chucks, and I was gone. It was almost the end of summer and it was hotter than hot. I could smell the aroma of barbecue and marijuana in the air, I could hear kids playing and music jamming. This is Holderness and this is my hood.

"What up Rod where you headed"? That's Derek Duffy; he lives across the street. He's one year older than me, and we have been friends for as long as I have been on the dead end. I stopped and waited for him to come down the hill from his apartment.

"Nowhere just tryna see what's going out here," I said as we gave each other some dap.

"I just saw Twon, he says Lil-Gorge got the fire hydrant on at the Deadman's Curve. That's where he went," Derek said. That's like Six Flags for us.

"For real Dee? Just yesterday the police came and ran us all off and cut the water off. Lil-Gorge trying to go back to juvie," I told Dee. He's making a career of it.

"Man, you know that nigga don't care. It's like he left something in there," Dee said.

"What a boyfriend," I cracked. Dee started laughing and couldn't stop, I did too until I turned and looked at the difference in old dead man Slaughter's house, it's right next door to ours. The grass had been cut, and the for rent sign was gone.

"Ah man who stole the for rent sign out Slaughter's old yard," I asked; he looked in the direction I was looking.

"Ain't nobody stole it. I think somebody bout to move in, and it ain't nobody good cause that nigga Winnie Head was with them. He's the one who cut the grass and took the sign with them. He was wit a skinny light skinned lady wit white hair in a brown Caddy," Dee said.

"Man, I don't even care. It ain't our house, fuck it. Let's go watch Gorge go to jail, and dis the last day for the festival and I got five dollars nigga I'm gone". I said and took off running, but I couldn't outrun Dee. He was passing me real fast. I hope he just keeps running if he ain't got no money, cause mine spent. The West End Festival is an annual event held at the West End Park. People come out and sell all kinds of goodies, and knick knack's, it's like the Fair without the rides, and there's a stage that sits right in the middle of the park for concerts. I was here all day yesterday listening to music. It was like a big talent show. I got a good laugh outta all these country niggas trying to rap. Some of it was cool, but everything ain't for everybody. I tried to rap like Kurtis Blow, but the shit didn't sound right. Bosha said niggas from the south can never be rappers because we talk funny. I don't know, but all I know is things change. Paul McCartney left the Beatles that changed music. We already got one nigga from our city to change the world Luther King, so it's possible one of these country niggas will figure that rap shit out sooner or later.

We made it around Deadman's Curve, and it was a real block party going. Everybody was out. Lil-Gorge was sitting on top of the fire hydrant with a board pressing the water, making it spray a hundred feet in the air. The water was shooting all the way across Lucile Ave. into the park, and the park was packed again today. It had to be the hottest day of the year by far. Everybody was playing in the water, even some drunk grownups. The first person I spotted was Bosha hair covered with pants rolled up in the water. God knows I will miss her. There were a lot of Muslims playing with the Kalfas today, but I guess it was because we were playing close to the park, their park. All my friends were already wet. Shane and his black ass sister Sari, she's blacker than him, JD, Twon, Rodney Smith and his two sisters, Monta and his brother Quan, Sean Tiger and all the rest of the Eggleston's. It's about twenty of them alone, Bennie, Stacy, and a lot more of them bums from the top end of Holderness, my project crew Jeron, BB, Lil-Jesse, Dennis Butler, Black Corey, and my man Carlos.

"Rakil you not going to get wet," Bosha screamed. Wow, why did she do that? I'm a shy guy, but then I thought, don't nobody know me by that name but the Muslims and.......

"Yeah, Rod get in the water with us," Twon's big ass mouth said. Now people were looking my way, they knew Twon was talking to me, but who was that Muslim girl talking to? That's what I was thinking. Then the echoes began.

"Rakil, Rakil. Who the hell is Rakil," Lil-Gorge was first to chime in. He made himself sound like a little girl. Then he started a stupid song.

"Rakil and Bosha sitting in a tree K-I-S-S-I-N-G.........BOOM! The sound was as loud as thunder, but there wasn't a cloud in the sky, and that sound could I identify. That's the sound you hear right before somebody dies. Next came the screams, and the crowd running out of the park. I didn't run. I just stood there, wondering who got shot or worse killed. People were running in all directions with their heads down, but all I heard was one shot, one shot in the park. Then I saw Pam Landy, Lil-George's oldest sister. She was crying. George grabbed her.

"Pam what's wrong? Why are you crying? Where's daddy? Who got shot, what happened girl," George pleaded. We all stood there. We had to know. She stopped crying.

"It's Youngblood. Big Al shot him in the chest and he fell dead off the big wall. He was dead before he hit the ground. You got a cigarette, Koon"? she asked; All her tears were gone. Big Al was one of my daddy's closest friends. He was one of the nicest old men I ever met, but daddy told me he was a dangerous old hustler. He came by our house 3-4 times a week, he was like family, and I never saw him without his Smith & Wesson 44 bulldog. It's a short, fat pistol with a short barrel and it really sounds like thunder. I should've known that was the sound I just heard. He shoots it on New Year's, and it's just as loud as Rap AK47s. What about Youngblood, the thug that's Weenie head's brother? That nigga ain't nothing but trouble. We barred him from the store, but really I liked him. Well, I did like him cause but if that 44 hit him in the chest, he's being laid to rest for sure, I gotta go see.

"Come on, Twon. Let's go see," I said. Then, I headed across the street. I looked back and everyone was following. I could hear the screams from his mother now.

"Lord my baby ain't never hurt nobody". Miss Frances was screaming; anybody that knew that nigga knew that's a lie, and she did too, but it's sad. I think he's about 21 or 22. I made it across the street. Fat Al was pacing around, the bulldog still in hand. Old man George was trying to talk to him, but I couldn't hear what he was saying. Just a lot of head shaking and hand waving, so I kept walking to the edge of the 10 feet wall that went around the back of the baseball field. Just like a back stop it rose on each side at the highest point it was at least 10 feet. That's where a few people were looking over. I walked to the edge and took my look. His eyes were still open, but life had left his body. The only sign of death was a white tee shirt that was bloody red now. One of his friends Snag was pressing it to his chest, right over his heart. Snag was crying, cussing, sweating, and screaming.

"Help help somebody! Please help! Blood don't die on me! Nigga, please don't die on me! If you do imma, kick yo ass for real nigga," Snag was so drunk, he didn't have any idea what he was saying to a man that was already dead. I thought to myself, this is how death looked. Not like a casket dead, like I've seen at church. This is murder dead, blood and everything, momma crying, brothers crying, Fat Al still holding that Bulldog, and now I hear sirens.

"Is he dead," Bosha asked.

"Hell yeah he dead. That bulldog blew his ass all the way to home plate. Damn Youngblood. Imma miss you, man. Here comes the police. I'm gone before Big Al goes to shooting again," Lil George said. That made everyone move, even me. Before I left, I took one more look at death. H. Rap and a few other good brothers stood at home plate. As they turned their backs, I turned mine.

"Rakil, let's go. The cops are coming from everywhere. It's time to go," Bosha said, pulling me by my arm. All I heard was one shot, one shot from the West, one shot in the chest, one shot laid Youngblood to rest. All it took was one "bang" and I'll never see Youngblood again. I thought about the first time I held a gun. Lil Willy let me hold a beautiful silver pearl handle snub nose 38 revolver.

"Don't she feel good Lil-Rod? Don't be scared of that bitch, hold that bitch like she yours. Because she is yours as longs as she in your hand. You see that pretty bitch there spits fire, and you ain't gotta ask her shit. Just put yo finger in the pussy, squeeze the clit, that bitch will go bang, and nut all in who every face you want her to. Now gimme my shit foe you kill the both of us," Lil-Willy told me. Back then I didn't get it. Now I do. We were walking back around to Deadman's Curve, just the Holderness crew and everyone else had headed their own way.

"Youngblood dead for real? Or was he just sleep because if he was dead that means he's gone forever," Twon said.

"Yes Lil-Twon he's gone forever from this life, but the brother is in a better place. He's in a place that you may or not see him again, depending on what you chose for your life," Bosha told him.

"A better place? What? That nigga there is going to hell, he ain't get his life right. It doesn't matter to me. Heaven or hell, I aint trying to die to see which way I go, I like it here, better place my ass". I said; in a better place! I think she really believes that shit. The only fact I know is, that man is down there lying dead in that red Georgia clay. That's not a better place than I saw him yesterday, drinking beer, smoking weed, smiling and talking shit. He seems happier than he is now. Every Muslim I know always says the same thing when someone dies. "They're in a better place" that's some bullshit, people that really want to die just commit suicide. Well, I guess some people live like they want to die, and Youngblood was living hard.

"Rakil, we will all get a chance to meet the maker. Wherever Allah calls me, I'll be ready," Bosha said. She was getting loud.

"Ready for what," I asked. We were all still walking together, almost home. She thought for a minute.

"Ready to die or kill in the name of Allah. That's what I was born to do. Not to fall in love with this unholy world. It is a better place where we all get all looked kindly upon by Allah," she answered.

"Sounds nice, but I don't wanna see that place any time soon. I gotta go eat. I might come back out later," I said.

"Rod, can I come eat with you," Twon asked.

"Nawl nigga not today daddy say no company". I lied; just didn't want to be bothered.

"Ok Rakil. I'll see you later if you come back, hit my window," Bosha said. Her long legs were in the wind, trying to catch her brothers. Twon, Derick, and I walked home in silence. When we made it to the corner of Greenwich and Holderness everybody was still out like nothing had happened.

"I'm bout to go up Skeeter's house. I'll see ya'll later," Twon said.

"Later," Derick and I said at the same time. No one was out on the dead end. It was supper time.

"Later Dee," I said as I cut across the little grass we had left in the front yard.

"Aight Rod," Dee said and headed up the hill to his apartment. I jumped on the porch and headed into the house. The family was at the table, everyone but Lil-Walt.

"Boy, where the hell you been? I just sent ya brother looking for you. Did you see him," daddy asked.

"I been at the park. I came back Deadman's Curve way, that's why he didn't see me. You know......." I was about to say more.

"I already heard Big Al blew that nigga heart out of his back. My friend is gone forever for a nothing ass nigga like that. Al let that nigga play him off the streets. That's why I don't hang out wit none of them niggas. Now go wash yo hands, I don't wanna hear shit else bout that dead nigga. It's time to eat". Daddy said; I did as I was told, and when I return Lil-Walt was in his spot at the table. I went and sat beside him, Kim and Karen sat across from us, and momma and daddy sat at the head of the table. Everyone's plate was already prepared, like always. This Sunday dinner was turkey wings, wild rice, collard greens, cornbread, and some of daddy's sweet ice tea, I was ready to eat.

"Bow yo heads," daddy said, and we did.

"Father God, thank you for the food we are about to receive for the nourishment of our bodies. By his hands we are fed, thank you Lord for our daily bread. And Lord, please watch over Big Al. He's a good man. Lord, they had to do a bad thang to a bad man. Forgive him. Amen," daddy prayed. He went on to say more. "A good man had to do a bad thang to a bad man. I'd like to think that maybe God will write it out like that and forgive them both. God forgive Youngblood. I know he has sinned, but if you can find it in your heart, please let him in," he continued.

"Amen," we all said at once.

"That's sad Blood got killed like that. I know he was a fool and all, but he always respected me and Karen. When he was at Brown High, he fought for everybody from our side," Kim said.

"Yeah, Blood was cool. So was Al," Lil-Walt said.

"Al still alive," I said.

"Alive? Boy, that nigga is dead. He murdered a man in front of a 150 witnesses. He'll be lucky if those crackers don't give him life. Only thang in his favor is who he killed. But still he'll do 20 or better. That shit was worth it at all. That's what this neighborhood has turn into a death trap, and soon to be a dope trap. That's why we moving in two weeks. Walt start bring boxes home from the store, and y'all start packing up all this shit," daddy said without a smile.

"What? Moving where? Moving for what," Lil-Walt asked. He sounded upset. I know it devastated me.

"We moving cross the tracks right off Stewart Avenue. It's a street called Erin Avenue, and it's one street over from Dill Avenue. And as to why we moving, it's time. A storm is coming. It's a dark cloud headed this way, and we gonna be gone before it gets here," daddy said like he was praying. I didn't know what he meant, but it made me feel like I was in church, you know, serious.

"Yeah! Walt, the storm is here. Margo and her 24 kids bout to move next door, selling liquor, dope, and who knows what else. Her other son just got out of jail, walking round here like he's a Prince. They say that boy is the dangerous one," momma added. She was talking about the Eggleston's. Margo is the mother she had at least 8 kids, but I don't think 24.

"Momma, who you talkin' bout Shawn? Y'all scared of Shawn? Shawn is cool, ask Rod. He don't mess with nobody. He got a job and everything," Lil-Walt added. Shawn was cool, but people say he had been in jail for a long time for some very bad things.

"Boy, I ain't gotta ask nobody bout that nigga. I tell you what, you and Rod can stay wit that nigga. We moving. Nigga you talkin' to me bout some scared shit. Let me tell you something sometimes scared can keep you from dead. Like Youngblood, I seen it in him. That nigga wasn't scared of nothing. When you ain't scared of nothing you'll die over anything," momma said.

PART.2

The year is 1986. I'm 15 years old, in the 9th grade, but we are not living on Erin Ave. anymore that didn't last long. Once we moved off Holderness, daddy started drinking real bad again, lights off, gas off, it wasn't long before we had to move again. The best thing about Erin Ave is that's where I met my first real girlfriend, Shanetha Nee-Nee Barnes. She was my heart, and she was still a virgin. I had been getting around a bit. Well, I'll say I've had sex one and a half times. All with the same girl, Shalinda McDowell. I met her at school. She lives in some apartment's right next to Harris Holmes, so she's from the projects. We didn't move far from Erin Ave. We moved right off Dill Ave on Athens. 1469 Athens Ave, a big yellow house on the corner of Athens and Deckner. It was the nicest house we ever lived in. It had three bedrooms, hardwood floors, and a big backyard for the dogs. Things are better now. I was the last child left in the house, Kim and Karen had their own place. Kim was working for the IRS and Karen worked for Atlanta Public Schools. She taught at Dean Rusk elementary, it's in Harris Holmes. Lil-Walt wasn't little anymore, he had joined the Army. He wanted to go into law enforcement. Momma was working at Emory as an assistant nurse, daddy was a head cook at Fat Tuesday's in Buckhead.

He was stealing anything he could steal. I got to work there as a dishwasher/bar back/night cook during the summer and I loved it. I was still very much into sports. I played varsity baseball and

B Team football, but next year I'll play for varsity, that's what coach Hodges promised me. He's the varsity coach. Now I feel like an only child. When we first moved from Holderness, I was sick for months until I met Nee-Nee. She was the only friend I had on this side of town until we moved on Athens Ave. Now I know everybody, just like in my old hood. We all hang out at Perkerson Park. The first friend I made on this side of town was Encre Styles. We both lived on Athens Ave, it's a dead-end street like Holderness. Encre lives on the dead end. I live in the middle.

PERKERSON PARK

We met one day walking to the park, Encre is a fat but fly kid. He is an only child, and it shows he has everything a teenager would want. We hung out a lot. He was born in this neighborhood, so he knows everyone. He turned me on to all the cool niggas in the hood. We all hung out at the park. This park was much bigger than the West End Park, and there were no Muslims to control this park. There's just one big red nigga that everyone seems to fear. His name is Big Slick. He's a monster of a human being. He couldn't have been a year older than 18, but he looked 30. This nigga had to eat a pig for breakfast and cow for dinner. He was all muscle, but not tall at all, maybe 5'10" and his skin is so light. I remember the first day I met him, Encre and I were at the park watching cats play basketball. A light blue Cadillac Seville pulled up maybe a 76-77, I couldn't see the back lights.

"Oh, shit Slick done got him a Lac," Encre yelled out. That caused the ballers to stop balling. Everyone crowded around. It was a nice ride, but where I'm from, all the hustlers ride well, and it's a lot of hustlers in the West End. Like Shawn, he just bought a 72 El-Dog the same year as the Mack. It was gold with a dark brown rag, big gold grill. I saw it with my own eyes, I was riding with daddy. He sells meat to the Outcast every Friday, so I still get to go to the hood. Shawn is a rich nigga now, they say he is bigger than Lil-Willy ever was, but I don't believe that. On the scale of 1-10 this caddy was a 6 in my book, but that's good, it could have been a 1. That would be good, it's a caddy. But these niggas were acting like this nigga was in a Benz. They were high fiving and chanting this nigga's name, but he seemed unfazed like me. He leaned against the front of his car and pulled out a big fat cigar.

"Man, ya'll nigga's go play some ball. I wanna bet some of this money," Slick said and pulled a bank roll big enough to choke a mule. The ball started back bouncing fast, then everybody hit the court but me and Encre.

"Fat Boy you ain't ballin' today," Slick asked, clutching the cigar between his teeth. This nigga moved and spoke like a real mobster, if there was a such thing as a black mobster, but this nigga so red maybe he's not even black.

"Nawl not today, I just got these," Encre replied looking down at his feet. On them, he wore a new pair of Air Jordan's. Big boy always stayed fresh in the best of the best. Really all the niggas on this side dressed good, well better than me. Encre was a fat guy. He's not tall at all, maybe 5 '8 but he ran well and he is very limber. He could ball if he wanted to. I didn't play basketball, was never great at it, and at the West End Park we got the Thunderdome. It's a basketball court with a dome over it. You have to be a real baller to ball there, and a fighter. I saw too much blood on that court, and I love my teeth.

"Oh yeah, I like them! What size you wear," Slick asked. My heart jumped because in my hood, that's a robbery move, and my homeboy Keybo's favorite move. .

"These are an 11 but I should've got an 11 and a half. They a little tight," Encre answered. I looked in Slick's eyes, they were dark and unreadable. We made eye contact, and I remember not to blink. It was hard, but Slick winked. I felt better fast.

"Take them off nigga let me see how they feel on me," Slick asked nicely. Big Boy put one foot on the bumper of the car and bent over to untie. I smiled, maybe Big Boy saw it, because then he stopped and stood back up.

"I ain't bout to get my new socks dirty. Slick, that big bank roll you got, lets ride to the West End Mall. Imma show you where I got 'em," Encre said with a smile.

"Ha, ha. I already got my Jordan's but if you would've taken those off, I would've had yours too nigga. Don't be no lame for nigga's out here. Fat Boy never take yo shit off for no nigga," Slick said. His laugh sounded like Santa Claus.

"You know I ain't know lame, Slick. You had me for a second cause I trust you nigga. How your momma been man," Encre asked.

"She good Fat Boy, but I see you still got yo hand in yo momma pocket book. I done told you nigga. When you ready to get a real bank roll, get at me. Who is this nigga right here? You go to Sylvan," Slick asked me.

"My name Rodney. I go to Brown," I answered fast, looking him in the eyes.

"Where you live," Slick asked back.

"Up on Athens," I answered. I get these questions all the time.

"How you go to Brown if you stay on this side," he asked.

"I was going there before we moved over here," I answered.

"Where you move from," Slick continued to ask.

"The West End," I answered.

"Where bout in the West End nigga? Or you just claiming shit," He asked.

"Baldwin Place is where I'm from. That's on the back side of Harris Holmes. I have lived all over the West End, but I grew up on Lucile and Holderness. What you know bout that," I popped back.

"Ha, ha, ha," Slick laughed.

"What I know bout that nigga? I know all about that. I'm from Mechanicsville and Pittsburgh. Imma westside nigga for real. Who you know in Harris Holmes? Do you know Cowpack," Slick asked. Everybody on the westside had heard of Cowpack. He's the biggest drug dealer in Harris Holmes, but I knew him and his family before all that.

"Yeah I know Cow, his people Lip and Bok too. Do you know Shawn from Holderness St? I used to work at that corner store next to the Outcast. I know all the hustlers on that side," I answered. He seemed impressed.

"Hell yeah I know Pimp Shawn. He just jumped him a clean as El-Dog, that shit is as gold as that nigga's teeth. That's a cool motherfucker for real Fat Boy you ever seen that nigga. That nigga fucking everybody hoe. You gotta a hoe, you better hide her that nigga game loaded. What about those Outcast niggas? I hear they getting money over there too. That's a money getting hood the only thing they gotta worry about is them damn Muslims. They everywhere over there. We used to shoot ball at that park, but a nigga can't even curse around them damn Muslims. They always got something to say. I stop going over there, this one nigga name Rico run that shit we cool but I don't trust that nigga he's a psycho. What about Terry White? You ever heard of a nigga by that name"? Slick replied; this talk got him hyped. I'd heard of Terry White. I also heard he was the biggest drug dealer in the city, but that's all I heard. I never saw him before, just know he's from John Hope Projects.

"Nawl Big Boy, I know Shawn. The Outcast hands are in a lot of shit in the West End, and that nigga they call Terry White, he might be a ghost cause I ain't never seen only heard how rich the nigga is. I got a partner named Pudding, out of John Hope. That's that's how I heard about that nigga Terry White," I answered.

"Ha, ha, ha! That nigga ain't no ghost. That nigga is for real, for real. I done seen him before inside of Joe's Pawn Shop. That nigga was talking shit to them crackers like he owned the place. He was jeweled up and draped down. That nigga had a mink on so fresh it was still dripping blood. You know how I know it was him? That nigga kept saying "Bitch I'm Terry White, call Joe now!" That's a crazy ass nigga ya'll no Joe down wit the Mob and he's a Jew. Joe owns this city. He's the biggest loan shark around here. That cracker is in everybody pockets you dig. Terry White talked to them crackers like they owed him. That nigga a gangster real talk. Last question, you know a lot of people and shit, so why you broke," he asked, then looked down at my worn out Nike Flights. I could hustle, that's a fact. I know lots of dealers, my best friend Junebug works for the Miami Boy's in Craver Holmes. The only reason I didn't sell dope is because I have been hearing not to sell it all my life. My daddy didn't play about drugs. He didn't want it anywhere around him. He always said money is the root to evil, and dope is the quickest way to death. At a young age, I'd already seen what dope could do to good people. I worked on the corner on Lucile and Holderness. Heroin was like a monster eating people alive. One day they had a soul, the next day it was gone. It hurts me to watch black people turn into zombies. No, I will never sell dope, and if I did my daddy would kill me before I got to spend the money.

"That nigga got a daddy, he ain't bout to do no real hustling," Encre answered for me.

"I work and play football man. Everything ain't for everybody," I answered.

"Yeah you right, everybody can't be rich, and then we wouldn't have nobody to break. Ain't that right? Slick, we gotta have broke niggas. If not, it won't be no rich niggas," Encre said. I thought to myself, damn this nigga trying to make me look bad.

"Yeah, you right Fat Boy. But if a nigga wanna ball let him ball. It's money in that shit too. Everybody can't be the next Al Capone. You any good at it? You better be great. What position you play," he asked.

"I play free safety, corner, and some linebacker. Imma head hunter," I said. I'm a very hard hitter, and I can cover.

"Oh yeah! But if you for real bout that shit you better start hitting the weight room hard. You need to pick up some pounds. Y'all know Sylvan gotta go to Brown next year. Y'all should have a good team. Fat Boy you gonna play for Brown cause you didn't do shit for Sylvan," Slick said.

"Yeah man, imma play for Brown. Last year I was getting in

trouble, so momma wouldn't let me play. This my year right here. Imma play ball so I can fuck 'em all," Encre said, smiling from ear to ear. Slick wasn't.

"Nigga don't go over there on no trick shit at a nigga bitch. You know them Oakland City nigga don't like dis side of the tracks. You better get yo fight game up, I wish I was still in school, them niggas wouldn't dare," Slick said, then got off the car and squeezed one of his fists like he was ready to fight.

"What? Big Boy my dawg, he ain't gotta worry bout shit. I been going to Brown, I know everybody. Oakland City niggas, Cascade niggas, Harris Holmes niggas, and man I know all the real niggas. Big Boy my main man you fuck wit him you fuck wit me. That's here, there and everywhere. I got his back". I said; looking slick in his beady eyes.

"I like you nigga, give me some". Slick said; we locked hands. He pulled me close to his chest and said.

"I fuck wit you nigga,"

"Capone, what the fuck you got going on," Corey Watson yelled. Corey is the thug of the hood and one of the best running backs in the city. He was short built like a runner. He was only 18, but he looked 38 in the face. He had an afro, full beard and mustache. He was walking up the hill with Junebug, and my get high buddy Black.

"Rod that's you? Bring yo ass on man we been looking everywhere for you," Black said. He's ready to smoke some reefer, me too.

"What up y'all? Here I come. Aightt Big Slick be easy. Encre you coming," I asked.

"Yeah, give me a second. I'll catch up," Encre replied, as he walked over to Slick. I headed down the hill, as Corey and I passed each other we dapped up and kept it moving, we were on two different missions today. When I made it to Junebug and Black, there wasn't any dapping.

"Put 'em up nigga. You done had me walking all over the hood looking for you. You thank you the shit now nigga let's do it". That's Black crazy ass; he pushed me on my forehead and went bouncing around like Sugar Ray. Black is as thin as a pin, but he stands over six feet tall, smooth and blacker than blue. He's the cool young nigga, but I could never tell him that.

"Yeah slap the shit out that nigga Black, he always telling lies. I ain't gonna let that nigga smoke now anyway," Junebug said. We were around the same size. He's light with so many teeth in his mouth, not even a dentist can count. This nigga looks like a light-skinned shark.

"Come on niggas imma knock both of you motherfuckers out. Swing nigga stop all that dancing shit," I yelled out, then got into my fighting stance. Junebug put his bag down and started circling me.

"Man fuck dis shit, I'm tired and ready to smoke. Let's go under the hut and roll up," Black said. We always slap boxing, but usually after we smoke. The hut is a big pavilion in the middle of the bottom part of this lovely park. It has a lot of tables under it, and it's the size of a basketball court. Perkerson Park has two levels, the top level has a basketball court and three baseball fields. On the bottom a small court with a low rim for the smaller kids, a nice big recreation center, and two tennis courts. It's a nice place. This is a nice neighborhood, all the lawns are cut, and I guess that's why all the white people ain't moved yet. Unlike the West End, the white people that lived over there are Muslims.

"Nigga you always wanna smoke but you ain't never got shit on shit," Junebug said to Black. It was true, we were broke. Junebug is the man, he keeps a bank roll as big as Slick, but it ain't all his money, he's a worker, but he's been working well.

"Who you talkin' to nigga? Boy, I done told ya'll niggas just because ya'll go to Brown that shit don't mean shit to Black nigga. I'll take yo shit nigga and pull some of them teeth out yo mouth," Black came back. Black talked more shit than anybody, but I ain't never seen him fight.

"You fak-fak- fake ass Big Daddy Kane looking nigga. Wai- wait to I get yo ass over to Brown we-we gonna jump yo skinny ass wa-wa-watch nigga," Junebug stuttered. He loves to play the dozen, and he's good at it. Junebug will talk about you so bad he will make you fight, and unlike Black. I've witnessed Junebug fight more than once, but there won't be any fighting today, just smoking and talking shit, we're all friends.

"Fuck all that shit Bug let's smoke man, ya'll niggas play too much," I said; trying to stop the bullshit.

"Let's smoke let's smoke that's all ya'll niggas say, I should make ya beg, but imma a real nigga. Let's go, fags," Junebug said. He picked up his bag and headed to the hut. We followed like soldiers in the army. I've been smoking weed now since the 8th grade, I remember the first joint I smoked. It was me, Mario Turner, and Rico McCray we were at school on the Catwalk. That's where everybody went to smoke at Brown. Mario just pulled it out and lit one. At first I thought it was a cigarette until I smelt the aroma. He passed it to Rico. He pulled on it hard and passed it to me. I pulled on it like I'd been smoking all my life and ended up coughing so hard I missed two passes, but I caught the last one and smoked easily. I was so high, I had to take a test for the next period. I sat there at my desk just staring at the test paper, then I looked at it and just bubbled in anything. I didn't care if I passed or failed. I just wanted to get high some more, I can do this class work anytime. That's how weed makes me feel, and it was getting worse. Junebug pulled out two 40's of Colt 45 out of his bag. I wasn't a drinker at all, but reefer made me want to do more, so we're drinking, talking shit and telling a few lies, and here comes Encre wobbling down the hill looking like the Kool-Aid man. He had on an all red Nike suit with a white Kango and the new white and red Jordan's, Big Boy was fresh to death.

"Hey Kool-Aid," I screamed out like the kids on the Kool-Aid TV commercial.

"Oh yeah, oh yeah," Black and Junebug chimed in. We made it sound just like the commercial. Encre really hated it when we called him Kool-Aid, but when we got high, we didn't care about anyone's feelings. Big Boy heard us and headed our way, running fast. For a fat boy, Encre moved real light and smoothly on his feet, and he's fast.

"Keep talking shit niggas. Imma smash all y'all," he yelled, as he ran across the grass right at us. All we could do was laugh, I guess it was the reefer because Big Boy was on me before I knew it.

"Say that shit now lil bitty ass nigg. I'll power slam yo ass," Encre said. He had me in his signature bear hug and my feet were off the grown.

"Put me down nigga before I throw up on you," I said. Big Boy didn't stop, he slammed me on one of the picnic tables and I didn't like it. My entire life I've had to try to keep my temper under control, but it's been a serious challenge. Encre doesn't know me well enough, because if he did he would let me go now. Junebug knows me, we are both from the West End. Junebug is Troy Lee's nephew. We blood in, hood blood.

"Ah-ah Fat-Fatboy get the fuck off my nigga," fuck all that wrestling shit. You blowing my high nigga. Let 'em up," Junebug said; I knew he was serious, he was talking like them Miami Boys, all that my nigga my nigga shit. I was mad as hell now, I was so mad. I had that feeling of ants crawling all over my body.

"Get me off em nigga! You thank you bad now cause you working for them Miami Boyz," Encre said. Damn! It's about to get ugly.

Click! It was the sound of a gun hammer going back.

"Oh, hell nawl. Bug put that shit up, we don't need that! Them niggas just playing. They do this shit all the time, you don't be around. Rod tell 'em to put the gun up, man," Black said in a panic. Junebug kept him as a problem solver, a little black deuce revolver, and he's quick to pull it out. Bug and I were a different breed. Over the last year, my life has really changed, hanging with Bug. I was doing grown men things. That little 22 he was holding was our money maker every weekend before Bug started selling dope. We used to hit a lot of small time licks like snatching pocketbooks. We would do anything but be broke.

"Get the fuck off me nigga! You wanna get shot? Don't shoot Bug, I got this man," I pleaded. Encre jumped off me fast.

"Oh nigga you gotta gun? Nigga I'll take that lil bitty shit from you," Encre said, then started walking up on Junebug. Encre ain't no coward, and Junebug ain't no killer, but don't push him.

"Ah big boy dis shit ain't no game nigga. I don't wanna bust you," Junebug said as his gun hand rose. I moved fast and jumped in between the two.

"Put the pistol up nigga shit cool. Big Boy we cool, ain't we," I asked them at the same time. Big boy looked me in the eyes and sucked his teeth.

"Yeah, we cool Rodney man, but what's up wit dis nigga and that lil bitty ass gun. That's all them Miami Boyz let you hold nigga. I got my own shit nigga a big 357. I call that bitch Heaven, but the bitch spit fire like she hell nigga," Encre said. I knew he was mad, but now wasn't a good time to show it. Junebug still had the gun in his hand.

"Where that bitch at nigga, I don't see her, but I do see that gold nugget watch you flexing," Junebug said, without a smile. Black burst out laughing.

"God damn Fatboy! You ain't never got a bitch when you need one, huh? Junebug yo ugly ass need to put that piece up. It ain't that type of party man. We all family, we can still fight shit out like players, and then get high some more and laugh about the shit you dig. Cause nigga you shoot Fatboy you gotta shoot all of us," Black preached, trying to bring peace so we could continue to get high.

"Alright you black motherfucker, I'll shoot you first then,"

Junebug said. He used his thumb to pull the hammer on the 22 back again. Then came an awkward silence. The sound of a man laughing broke it like a seal. Junebug had a laugh like no other, it really didn't sound human at all, and he loved to laugh at himself. He is the Joker, and he looks the part.

"Man, I smell pussy ya'll niggas hoes. Just think about it 3 against one. I won't be able to get off maybe one or two shots, but yall better move fast before I blast," Junebug said.

"Nigga imma show you pussy if you don't put that shit up, you play too much monkey ass nigga. Imma count to three nigga, then imma charge yo ass you ain't gonna shoot me. If you do and I don't die, imma kill you. If I do die, my spirit will hunt you down and skull you two times and put you somewhere you will never be found nigga, that's on Allah. So you better not kill me. One nigga, get ready yall, yall know I can't count," I said. We all looked at each other, and the laughter began again, but this time everybody was laughing. Junebug put the gun back in his back pocket. He was laughing harder than anyone.

"Man, that shit ain't funny roll another J. Ya'll niggas done blew my high for real now. This nigga go to talking all that gangster shit. Then this nigga go to talking all that Muslim shit, nigga please let's get high," Black said. He was always ready to smoke.

"Man, that nigga ain't no Muslim. Black don't believe that bullshit," Junebug said.

"Nigga I ain't never claim to be no Muslim. I believe in Jesus, but you no imma from AK Ave. Motherfucker Lucile and Holderness. Imma dead end nigga. Ask yo Uncle Troy Lee what that means. He from the West End. I really don't know where you from, you might be a country nigga," I popped back. I was high, feeling good, and when I'm high, I talk shit like my daddy, but when I'm drunk, I'll cut you like my momma.

"Nigga please! Broke ass nigga you can front in front of these suckers but I done begged you to get some money. Yeah, yo hood a gold mine, but you ain't shit, but a hub cap stealing, pocket book snatching, two bit stick up kid. I told you them crackers giving out 60 months to the door for armed robbery, nigga better change yo game," Junebug came back at me.

"Nigga what you talkin' bout? You better than me now? You were doing the same shit last summer. Now you done sold yo soul to them niggas wit mouths full of golds. Nigga I done told you, I know niggas that hunt Miami Boys for a living. Word on the street, Terry White paying a grand for every gold teeth a nigga you can bring him from out of them niggas mouths. Be Careful bug you gotta lot of teeth in yo mouth and they yellow enough to go for gold. I hate to see them motherfuckers in Joe's Pawn Shop". I cracked right back; that got everybody laughing. I was going in hard on Junebug, and he didn't like it, so he tried to shoot me a low blow, literally.

"You sound like you wanna jones ole one nut ass nigga. That bitch Peaches stab you in yo right nut nigga. She fucked you up, now you ain't got but one kind of seed left. You will never have a son. The damage has been done. Y'all know, right nut boy, left nut girl," Junebug said. He would say anything to get a laugh, and that really got everyone to laugh. It was true Peaches stabbed me, but not in the balls.

"You ugly lying motherfucker. I got both of my balls. You wanna see em nigga," I said, then started unzipping my pants.

"Show me nigga, so I can shoot that other little BB off," Junebug said. That got the biggest laugh of all, and once again June Bug won the joning match. I wasn't mad we kicked like this all the time. Like Skeeter told me if you live in the West End you better have tough skin. After all the laughs and a few more jabs. Junebug rolled a few more joints, and the conversation changed to making money.

"Yeah but for real Rodney man it's time for you to get some of this real money, before them Miami niggas get it all or you catch a murder case. You remember what happened last summer," Encre kicked it off. I don't remember last summer. Last summer never happened.

"I don't know what the fuck you talking bout nigga a lot of shit happened last summer, and a lot of shit didn't. So don't knock my hustle because you changed yours. Get money nigga all that shit green, it don't matter if it's off the muscle or the hustle. The way I see it, ya'll niggas gotta sell dope everyday all day. That's too many chances to go to jail. I can hit a lick a week and come up, fuck a re-up nigga". I snapped back; but was that really why I didn't want to sell?

"Man, fuck all that shit! Ya'll niggas better get some jobs or ya'll all going to jail or hell. Rod man you know better you gotta good daddy just like me. These niggas here, they what you call inglorious bastards, there daddy don't live with them. Junebug don't even know who his daddy is. They live wit they momma. A woman can't raise a man like a man can. Me and you Rod can't sell no dope and live in the same house wit our daddy. They can do that shit living wit they momma, come in and out the house whenever they want, ain't no real man gonna let no boy do that and that's a fact Jack". That was Black; he loved to get high and preach. But what he said this time was the truth. Ain't no way on Earth my daddy would let me sell dope and live anywhere at all, he would kill me.

"Black boy you better watch yo mouth you don't know shit bout me nigga, my daddy dead," Junebug said. He always told that lie.

"Well, I'm sorry Bug, but I bet a nigga killed him, and you headed to rest wit 'em," Black said.

"Oh yeah ole black ass nigga. That might be true, but you won't live to see it if you keep running yo mouth at me," Junebug said, and put his hand in his back pocket.

"Man, fuck you! God got me. Kill me nigga! I'll haunt yo ass while you in prison doing that life sentence, cause my people gonna come to court every hearing nigga. Believe that! They love them some Black," Black said.

"Man, I'm bout to go for ya'll blow my high, hold on Bug for you shoot that nigga. You don't need no witnesses," Encre said.

"I'm wit you Cre," I said as we headed up the hill we could still hear Black and Junebug.

"Come on Bug. We gonna leave you," I yelled. Encre and I lived on the same street which was Athens Avenue. Junebug one street over on Belmont.

"I know my way home nigga. Get the fuck on me and my nigga Black bout to get fucked up some more". Junebug yelled back; that Miami shit was coming out of him more and more.

"Yeah son that's right! Bye lames," Black said sounding like them New York niggas, Atlanta is turning to a melting pot. We started out good old fried chicken and biscuits, now it's like we are turning into a buffet. People come here from everywhere and don't leave, l guess our chicken is that good.

"Rodney man that nigga Junebug don't know who he fucking wit if it wasn't for you. I'll go get my bitch and fire that pussy ass nigga up," Encre said. He was getting excited. I stop walking and look at him.

"Listen nigga that's my homeboy, plus he's Troy Lee nephew, please don't do nothing crazy. Cre all that shit will fall on me, man. That nigga Bug he cool just silly as hell, he play too much and them Miami Boyz got em talking all kinds of crazy shit, but the nigga love me so you cool man I'm telling you," I pleaded. Encre is a psycho, but he really doesn't know it. He's not like the Ahki's in the West End that kill just to kill, but Encre will kill you for disrespecting him or somebody he cool with, he's a cowboy.

"I'm cool as a fan," Encre said with a crooked smile.

"Yeah like a white bitch taking a tan. Nigga you ain't cool wit that shit at all. I know you Cre, get it out of your mind, let that shit go, you getting money now, don't play yo self-off the streets or worst end up in a hearse". I said; looking him in his eyes, trying to let him know how serious I was. It wasn't like I had more love for Junebug than Encre. It's like if Encre was in the West End and

Junebug or anybody else over there robbed him or tried him in any way it's on me. I'll have to get his shit back or blow a nigga wig back, because that's my hood and he's my company. You got beef with my company, you got beef with me. Why do I have to choose a side? When somebody already crosses my line. Anyway, I didn't make the rules, I'm just trying to be a good student. Who knows, one day I may write my own rules in the invisible hood rule book. Shawn and Rico are the authors now in the West End.

"On everything Rodney man I ain't gonna fuck that nigga up, but I wanna fuck his sister bad. You know she works for Tony Tripp, that nigga ten hoe's down, the best pimp in town. Have you heard of him," Encre asked.

"Yeah nigga dis Tripp City right now. That nigga got that shit painted on the back of his Blazer in big letters "Tripp City" and a picture of Atlanta is behind it". I said;

"Nigga you lying,"

"That Blazer be round Junebug house," I said matter of factly

"I ain't seen know Blazer just a white Benz," Encre said.

"Yeah, he be in that too, he's a fly ass nigga man. He be in a lot of shit. He got a lot of hoes. If you wanna fuck Niece just skin down nigga, you big ole Trick," I said, then took off running. We were almost at my house, and Encre had about a block left to walk.

"Hold on Rodney man stop playing. I gotta ask you something for real," He pleaded. I stopped and waited.

"What Big Boy? I'm bout to go in the house, don't come up here playing," I said.

"How that pussy smell Rodney? I know you done fucked her," he asked, with a big smile.

"She at home. Go see for yourself trick. I'm gone," I said, and took off running to my house.

"Ole broke ass nigga," Encre screamed at my back. Those were his favorite words since he started selling coke. That's just how it is either you sold dope or you broke. I am broke, but I ain't gonna sell no dope everything ain't for everybody. I got every reason not to do it, but just one reason to do it. Money! But money is everything and more.

EVERYBODY GETTING MONEY

I walked up the steps of our house and into our home. Our house was just another house on the block; they all looked about the same. But inside it was home we still had all our same things from Holderness give or take, and we had all the love that a family should have. It was just momma daddy and myself now, everyone else was gone on their own. Kim and Karen had their own place out on Buford Highway. Both in their last years at Morris Brown, Lil-Walt is in the Army now, momma still working at Emory NA, daddy is the head cook at Fat Tuesday's where I worked during the summer. Thinking of the summer, a lot of things happened to me last summer. Brown High is just one big high for me, and I'm accepted, respected, and protected there. I have lots of friends from all the hoods that attend Brown. In Oakland City I roll with Corey Allen, Bobby Clayton, Dexter Gates, but I know everybody like Otis Lowe and Sweet Pete, they are just a little older than me. They are already calling shots. I was in the car with Joe-Joe when Sweet Pete hit Bert Pope in the back of the head with a baseball bat. He swung that bat like he was trying to hit a home run. The bib of Bert's hat got stuck in between the top of the car door. Joe-Joe had to open the door to get it out. I watched it fly away in the wind, and I watched Bert run twenty feet and drop like a bowling ball pin. Otis Lowe is the youngest pimp I know, and he's dealing a lot of blow. The two niggas like six and eight, their running mates. I hang out with

Bobby Clayton, Corey Allen, and Dexter Gates. Corey and I used to play eighth grade, and B-team Football at Brown, Dexter is Mr. Football and he's varsity QB. Bobby doesn't play sports, he just gets high. I started hanging with Bobby when I met Dex, we all get high, so I guess that's how we got so cool. Corey was my nigga for real, but he can't stay out of jail to save his life. Corey was the first nigga I hung out with that was a real slanger. He used to sell coke for Otis Lowe for $25 off $100 but he got tired of being a worker, so he got down with Oily. He's from Carver Holmes, I knew him from park league football. Now Corey is getting fronted an ounce of coke for $1200 but he bags up $2500, after going to see Woody for the cook up. Woody is a junky in Oakland City, he knows how to turn powder cocaine into hard cocaine; we call it ready rock. A lot of people are getting hooked on it fast, Woody says when you cook it up it turns into pure cocaine. After you cook it, you can't snort it anymore. You have to put it on a can or in a pipe and smoke it; they call it beaming up to Scotty, like on Star Trek. Cocaine is a helluva drug! It makes people do things they wouldn't think of doing, if they weren't high. Ready rock gets you a hundred times higher, but a $20 ready rock only lasts you 20 minutes. Twenty dollars of powder cocaine can last two hours or more if it's good. Woody is a shooter and a smoker, he stands around 5'5" but his afro makes him six feet tall, and maybe 87 pounds of a man. I've seen him plenty of times with a needle in his arm, and a pipe in his mouth. The last time I saw him he was on a stretcher under a cocaine white sheet. Well, I didn't really see him, but it was him. Who else could it be? All we could really see was the front of the sheet standing up like a beach ball was under it. No doubt that was Woody's afro. That's a fact Corey, and I were about to walk up his steps. Word was Otis and Sweet had some coke so strong and it was too strong to main line. Woody tied up and stuck it in and tried to count to ten, but he didn't make it to five, nigga died so fast he didn't get to close his eyes. Shooting dope kills you faster than ever now, because of this new disease called AIDS. At first they said it was a fag disease, now if you share needles you can die. So a lot of shooters are turning into smokers. Only makes sense if you are a junky. Ready Rock is some real dangerous shit, it kills you slow. That junky ass nigga Bobby Clayton put a rock in a joint of weed and past it to me, not knowing I hit it, and almost died. My heart felt like it was about to burst, and my mouth wouldn't stop moving. When he told me what it was I took off running, I ran all the way from Oakland City to my house on Athens Ave. about eight miles. When I got home, I sat on the front steps, and that shit started calling me. It was like a voice in my head saying.

"You need some more of me now. Get up and run your ass back over there". That was the devil speaking to me, I remember his kind voice. It was the same voice from years ago, that little man who gave me the $50 bill that momma took. Since then I never looked at money the same, I'm not saying I don't want it, because I do, but I don't want the things I see come with it. I don't want to be a target, I don't want to go to jail, or get murdered. The little man that gave me that money, he wanted evil to come out of me, he wanted me to hurt my momma over that money, and I felt a feeling I never felt before.

"The devil is a lie, money ain't everything it comes and goes. God is forever. Amen," Rev. Stovall's voice repeated in my head. That's all I could hear over and over. The little man's voice was gone or drowned out, and I hoped I would never hear it again. That ready rock is a monster like no other, I think it's going to change the world. Black people are already starting to live better, you can see that by all the new cars on the westside.

"How many niggas got to die and go to jail for one drug dealer to get rich," my daddy asked me.

"I don't know how many," I asked back.

"More than a slave ship could hold. Don't be no slave boy, these Crackers are known for setting traps. Dis new shit ain't to be fucked wit at all, they say that shit sound like the pipe cracking when they smoke it. Boy, you know bout it, stay the fuck away from it. If you wanna stay living, it's about to get bad," That was all daddy had to say; but like he said, I already knew how bad it was. It's like a perfect storm, everything is lined up for disaster.

CLOSE CALL

I hadn't spoken to Bobby since that day and wasn't planning on it anytime soon. Dexter and I were still kicking it on a daily basis, he's the QB and the captain of the football team. Dexter saved my life when that bitch Peaches stabbed me at school last year. She didn't get my balls or my bat, but she nicked a main artery in my upper thigh. I almost bleed to death waiting in the hallway downstairs at Grady. When my momma made it to me she looked down and she was standing in a puddle of my blood. I was still bleeding badly, but I didn't know it. I just felt really cold and light-headed. Next thing I know momma was screaming and cursing everybody out that was wearing white. Two minutes later, I was in an all-white room with a mask on my face, people walking all around me dressed in white. One of them held the mask on my face and told me to count backwards from 20. I don't know how many hours had passed, but when I opened my eyes, I was in another room, with other beds, long curtains going around them, and I had a tube in my dick. My memory rushed back to me. I'd been stabbed by my own girlfriend. Wow! Like father like son, I guess this is how my daddy feels when momma put one of her blades in him. I reached down to feel my leg bandaged up. I couldn't feel where I'd been stabbed, it was all numb. I was feeling numb and dumb. How did I let this happen to me? It was all over some he says she say shit. Well! Not really, because I did give that project hoe Special-K a picture of me that my sweet girlfriend Peaches had just gotten developed the day before. I didn't think that hood rat would go to her next class with Peaches and show the picture off just for Peaches to see her with it. That's what jumped everything off. I had managed to avoid her all day, but at the last bell she cornered me in the stairwell. I was with my crew, walking down to wait on the buses. She walked up on me pushing me with her finger all in my face, cursing, and talking all kinds of shit. She wouldn't stop so I mushed her in her face, and ran down the steps to catch my bus, but it hadn't pulled up yet.

"Rodney O," Lee said. He lives on Holderness st, he just transferred from Mays. He was standing up on the hill that overlooks the buses. I ran up the hill to give him and the rest of my Holderness Street crew some dap. I looked back and there she was across the way, her eyes beaming hate at me, as she stood with Shon and Lorraine. I smiled. She rolled her eyes and walked away in the crowd. I will call her tonight and smooth this over, I don't like people all in my business. I told her that. I love Peaches and she loves me.

"There goes yo bus Rodney," Big Wil said.

"See ya'll niggas," I said. We dapped up again and headed down the hill. I was crossing the driveway headed to my bus. It was very crowded, students were passing me on all sides, everybody was saying something to somebody at the same time. I spotted Dexter up ahead.

"Ah Dex.....Oooh shit," I screamed. Somebody just punched me in the leg, and it felt like I got a charlie horse in it. I was bent over my hand holding my leg.

"Whatcha doing Rodney," Dexter's voice said. I stood up and moved my hand.

"Somebody just punched the shit out of me," I said just before our eyes glanced down to the hole in my leg that was spraying blood all over his brand new white Nike Flights.

"Mother fuck! That bitch stabbed you dog, don't worry I got you," Dexter screamed. He picked me up like I was a baby and ran with me up a hill and two flights of steps into the nurse's office.

"Nurse Harris, get yo ass off the phone. This shit is bad," Dexter yelled at her. She looked up at me and all the blood, and just froze. The door opened behind us and there was my main man, my ROTC teacher, and a war vet. He was Mexican looking, but his voice was all black, he's a real cool cat.

"Downtown Brown, I hear your girlfriend scratch you. Put him over on the table for me Dexter, so I can see what we got," he said. He always called me downtown Brown. I never asked why. Dexter laid me down. Sergeant pulled out his knife and cut my pants open. I looked down and I could see blood pumping out of a hole in my upper right thigh.

"That's a lot of blood, Serg. He's bleeding bad," Dexter tried to whisper.

"Boy, what you know bout bleeding? This ain't nothin' but a scratch. Thank you for your help sir, now go outside and tell everybody Downtown is ok. Sarg got this. Nurse Harris, have you made the call? If not, please do so and get me the trauma kit ASAP," Serg said.

"Yes, Sir!" Nurse Harris answered. Serg was calm as a clam just like the first aid, and trauma he taught, and I passed with flying colors. That scared me.

"Sarg how bad is it man, cause you know I know it ain't no scratch," I asked. He snatched a towel from the desk, folded it up, and pressed it hard on my wound.

"Downtown I've seen a lot worse. Look at me. I promise you will live, but I gotta stop this bleeding, so just be calm. This might hurt, but it will save your life. You know the routine," Serg said. I believed him. He applied pressure on my wound.

As they rolled me down the driveway on a stretcher. The same kind of stretcher I'd seen so many dead bodies on. I thought to myself, Damn that bitch got me good.

"Rakil, you alright? Who did that to you? Just say their name, Aki," Jamil yelled. Bosha's brother was up on the hill with some more Muslims. A lot of my homeboys had stuck around, maybe to see if I was dead. Lee and Will were still on the hill calling out my name. I couldn't yell back. I had an oxygen mask on my face, so I put an L in the air, that's my hood Lucile Ave. I had to let them know I wasn't dead yet. The last face I saw before the ambulance door closed was Dexter Gates.

That day Dexter became my friend for life. I almost died that day. A fingernail file nearly killed me. The surgery left me with a scar, an ugly reminder that love can kill. I bounced back just fine. Peaches went to jail, but I didn't want her charged, but she did get kicked out of school, I didn't, but I should've, but I'm good at football.

THE FIRST FAMILIES

My Cascade Rd.-. Cascade place crew Pillhead, Rodney (Boo) Henry, Willy (Killer) James, Lil-Bob, Baby-Flop, now this is my money tree. Everybody I named is family, and I'm in the family. Niecy is the Auntie to all the guys I named, and she is the Cocaine Queen on the westside, and she's my Mother-in-law. Her daughter Keisha is my high school sweetheart, she's two years younger, but what happened to me with Peaches could you blame me for going younger. Keisha was a good girl, and crazy about me as far as she could see, but I could see further now. Her mother Niecy treated me like an actual son, a good friend, and a man all at the same time. She had kids by Walter Lee Freeman. Some say he is a bigger drug dealer than Terry White, but less flashy I really don't know, but if you ask me. They are both way pass nigga rich. Niecy put Pillhead on and Pillhead put all his cousins on and on and on. Niecy is a very nice person, and she's nice to look at, short, dark, and fine as hell just like Keisha. They could really go for sisters like two Twix bars. I'm very attracted to Niecy, but so is the entire westside. She is the queen. I remember the first time we met Keisha was waiting for me after football practice; we were sitting on the steps in front of the gym. A dark blue new Benz slid to the curb right in front of us, rimmed up, and ragged down.

"Who the fuck is dis". I thought to myself; I was busy trying to see through the tint.

"Shhh boy, that's momma," Keisha said. As the window rolled down Keisha stood up and I did too. This is a queen or should I say Queen Pin but where we are from it's the same thing.

"Hey Rodney". That's Nee-Nee; Keisha's little sister, they all look alike. Just a smaller version of Niecy.

"What's going on, lil lady?" I answered. The driver's door of the Benz opened, and out came the queen, all four feet ten inches of her. I couldn't see her until she came around the front of the car, but I heard her.

"What's going on? You tell me, Mr. Brown, how everybody in my family knows you, but I don't," the Queen asked. She walked right up to my chest. I looked down at her as we talked.

"How you doing, Ms. Niecy? I been begging to meet you, but Keisha kept putting it off. I guess she ain't sure bout us". I lied; the truth is Keisha has been trying to get me to meet her momma for months. I was just shy I guess, but I'd seen her plenty of times, her nephew Lil-Boo and I hung out all the time she just didn't know who I was.

"Boy, you better stop lying on me, and lying to my momma," Keisha said. Then slapped me across the back of my head and was trying to hit me again.

"Girl stop! Don't you see I'm talking? Well Rodney, now that we have met don't be no stranger, you can come over anytime. I don't want all that sneaky shit going on in my house, you almost grown and she thinks she grown. Y'all be careful and protect ya'll selves and Rodney, take care of my child. I know yo people. I know Shawn down on Holderness Street. I know everybody. Let's go, girl," Niecy said. I heard most of what she said but I was so distracted by something inside her mouth, every time she opened her mouth a light beamed out. It looked like she had a disco ball inside her mouth, and the lights danced to the rhythm of her voice. It was hypnotizing.

"Rodney, what's wrong with you? Don't you hear what my momma is asking you? Do you want a ride, fool," Keisha snapped. I felt like I was in a trance, but I snapped out of it.

"Thank you Ms. Niecy, but I'll walk, don't wanna take you out the way," I lied. I've never ridden a ride this nice. The closest I've come would be the Caddie limousines we rode in for my aunt Rowena's funeral. It was sweet but not like this and ain't nobody died today. It's sad to say, but it takes a sad day for most black people to ride this way.

"Lame get in the car," Keisha snapped again. She meant nothing by it, and she knew I wasn't a lame for real. That's just how my K talks.

"Keisha, don't you ever talk to a man like that in front of me! Cause you just fronting. I seen this nigga on the football field number 45. I know he can knock the shit out of you. I'm always in the stands sitting right next to Vershon Eggerson, Mr. Lucile and Holderness. That little crew is crazy bout you. Keisha knows Shon wit the pimped out Vet that's yo Aunt Shell's man". Niecy said;

"Yeah, I know him momma. That's what I'm saying, I'm not being mean. This nigga just being shy. He knows Shell, he's just been dodging you. Everybody been telling him you cool like that but he still acting scary," Keshia said.

"I'm telling you it ain't got nothing to do with being scary, it's about respect, but like I been telling you, if you ain't scared of nothing, you will die over anything," I said. I was trying to impress her.

"I like you, Rodney Brown. Get in the car. Imma take you home," Niecy said with a big smile. Keisha already had the door open.

"Get in Dum-Dum," she said. I hopped in and slid over on the soft brown leather seats. The leather and wood grain smelled like reefer and expensive perfume. Niecy got in and pulled away from the curb. The big V-12 engine purred like a cat. It was like riding on an airplane, once it leveled off, or maybe a spaceship. I flew once on a plane. It was a free field trip when I was in elementary school, that's my only time. I have never been on a spaceship, but I imagine it would feel this way. Keisha and I were riding in the back. It was like floating on air. My mind went back to Niecy's mouth. Was she a fire breathing, hypnotizing witch or was it just my imagination? Eric B. and Rakim were jamming out the speakers, thinking of a master plan.

"Keisha, I'm I crazy or does yo momma have lights in her mouth," I whispered in her ear.

"No silly! Those are diamonds," she answered, laughing loudly. I felt like a dumb, but I felt good, like the song was saying. Thinking of a master plan ain't nothing but sweat inside my hand. I was wondering to myself, is this real? I'm riding in a Benz with a Queen pin, diamonds in her mouth, and a ring on her hand that looks something like a peacock.

"Momma, he don't live this way," Keisha said. That brought me out of my daydream. One day I will have a nice car like this.

"I thought you lived on Holderness," Niecy asked, after she turned the music down.

"Yes ma'am I did, but we moved over off Dill Avenue on Athens Ave. My daddy said it's gonna get bad on Holderness, but that's still my hood though," I answered.

"Yo daddy's a smart man. Holderness is a real dead end. I'm glad you don't live over there, but fuck that ma'am shit, you can call me momma or Niecy," she said as she busted a U-turn in the middle of Lucile Avenue. I felt high, like a coke rush. Is this it? The feeling they say you can never let go, like a shot of good dope, once you feel it, you got to get it. That's how I was feeling, and it felt really good.

"Ok momma," I said with a smile. Keisha grabbed my hand with a squeeze.

"Ok baby," she answered. I felt like a made man, and in a way I was. Keisha and I had a good relationship. All she wanted to do was fuck, but I didn't mind. Word was she was fucking everybody, and I still didn't mind. Riding in the back of that Benz, I came up with a master plan. I had to play my hand. Keisha was my ace, and I had to keep her safe. Fuck what a nigga said. Now everything is good!

Niecy told me not to even think about selling dope. She pays for everything. Every concert that comes to town we were there 30 deep. Everybody had on new outfits, real MOB shit, everybody in the family that was tall enough to drive had a rimmed up car, even Lil-Flop and he was 12. Pillhead is the boss under Niecy. We have been down since day one. He knows my family. If I wanted to sell dope, he would be my man, and all the niggas I run with knew it. That's why they begged for me to get in the game, but I wouldn't.

CARLOS

From Beecher St., Rogers, S. Gordon, and all in between was another crew I ran with. The leader of this crew is my ace Carlos Evans, Voodoo Bob's son. We've been cool since park ball, and Carlos was the most popular person at Brown High. Everybody loved Carlos, or hated him. He's handsome, hood rich, and doesn't give a shit. He attracted friends like moths to a flame, or more like fire fighters to a fire. Carlos had everything but a car, but this Christmas he'll get one. He just had to stay out of trouble, but that's easier said than done with Carlos. This nigga is trouble with a big fat T, he's a menace. The crew that ran with him ain't at all better. Cateye Tony, his brother Twon, Tic, his brother Taco, Michael Allen, Maurice Brown, Willie James, and all the Cascade crew. Me and everybody else from Holderness knew Carlos was the man. I don't care if people told me that he and his family believed in Voodoo. My daddy believes in it and he thinks anybody that can kill chickens, and goats just to sacrifice for the devil and not eat them, are sick people. Seriously, my daddy thinks Mr. Bob is a crock, but a good one just like them niggas in Yahweh. Daddy said, 'if you get enough niggas to believe in anything it can happen.' Thoughts become things bad or good. To me, Bob is a good man that's doing well for his family. To my daddy, Bob is a man that's playing with people's minds and money. What's worse he's playing with God's power just like Donnie and Dallas Moe down in Tifton Georgia, it's a price to pay for the roots you dig? I don't believe in root workers, I only believe in God. Carlos could be the Devil himself for all I care, it wouldn't change how I feel about him. He's the realist nigga I know. We go to Summer School together every summer and have to fight our way home every day. During the summer, we may hang 25 deep Carlos in the middle with his shirt off screaming.

"Who wants some beef"? Cateye Tony standing right behind him with his hands in his pants like he is from New York or something, he's not holding his joint, he was holding a real joint, the kind that only needs a finger curl. But really, we would fight fair. The only niggas we busting on sight are the niggas out of Summer Hill. They caught us slipping at a football game at Cheney Stadium. There were a hundred of them, twenty-five of us, and we were joint less. We fought as much as we could. We took off running in and out between cars. These niggas was coming from everywhere like on one of them Tarzan movies. I ran past Carlos and he was flying, we were running for our lives. Carlos came back and passed me on the hood of a car.

"Run Rodney jump on nigga Bang-bang-bang-bang-bang"! Carlos was screaming; until somebody else started shooting. I ran over to a park car to take cover like everybody else. That's when I saw where the shots were coming from a brown Iroz. I knew that car from the 5th ward, Herndon Holmes. That's Sunb car, and that's Sunb shooting a big 357. That calmed everything all the way down, and we could live to fight another day. That's just one of the many adventures we survived. Carlos said it protects everybody that surrounds him from all evils they may fear, and I believed him. I do feel a kind of power when I'm with Carlos, maybe it's because he's full of energy. Explosive energy like a walking, living missile. He's dangerously fun. Fearless he is. Like my daddy always said, 'if you ain't scared of nothing, you will die over anything.' But not Carlos, he just got out of Juvenile for some small shit now he's on probation, so he's been cooling it. He just got his first set of beads. I saw him with them on, with my own eyes, if you believe in what they believe in he's double blessed now. Plus, he gets all my prayers. My God loves all his kids good and bad, that's what Mrs. Webb always said. That's the last crew I really hung with, but really everybody I know hung together at some point.

THE NEW

HOLDERNESS

My hood home is Holderness St. I hang out over there every chance I get, and that's really not much. My daddy got eyes everywhere on Holderness, and everybody knows I shouldn't be over there. Holderness has really changed. It's not a place where kids run and play up and down the streets. It's a place where niggas run back a forward to cars so they can eat. It's like the biggest drive-thru in the world. Car after car pulling up and somebody runs to it, puts a hand in the window and it comes out with cash. We call this rolling, because everything stays rolling. All you need is a couple of lookouts to yell 12 when they see the police. I don't know why the number 12; I think it's some Miami shit. I'm not sure, but I know if it's said on Holderness, niggas scramble like a dozen of eggs. This is the new Holderness, and it's a gold mine. All the same people live there with only a few fresh faces. I think we are the only family that moved, and the way it looked now it wasn't at all a bad idea. Most of my old friends from Holderness are selling dope or being look out guys. Shane, Lil-George, Rico, JD, Pokey and Stacy let me stop, it's too hard for me to name all the niggas I grew up with that are selling dope on Holderness, so I'll name the ones that are not. Derrick Duffy, Rodney Smith, Rodney Tabb, and me Rodney Brown, Antwon wasn't selling yet, but soon he will be, he's a look out now. Twon is only 12 years old, standing on a corner yelling 12, but he got more money than me. I don't knock any of my homies for what they do, because most of them wouldn't dare do the shit I have done, let God be our judge. What has happened to my hood is ungodly. It's like the gates of Hell are slowly opening up upon us. People are changing before my eyes, everybody walking around looking at the ground, when blessings come from the sky. Maybe they've already seen theirs fall and shatter. Now they walk around looking for the pieces or a piece of dope a dealer may have dropped. I got two new homies living in the hood now, William (Big-Wil) Poon, and Samuel (Lee) Sawyer. We were stuck together like glue at school. When they come they both sell coke for William's brother Clarence (CP) Poon. The Poon's are a big family, Joan (Papa Poon) he's the same. Joan Poon and my daddy grew up in Albany Ga., and they all lived on Holderness now. I don't know them all by name, but they all look alike, light skin and curly hair like Mexicans. Clarence, I knew him before he went to prison. He used to hang with big one leg Reno, Shorty, Ball, Pissy Coon, and Youngblood robbing and stealing. He got lucky and went to prison. Poor Youngblood went wherever gangsters go, I wonder if there is a heaven for a gangster? If there is, I hope Lil-Willy is there. He was a good gangster, to me anyway, but somebody else wanted him dead. He told me if a nigga gettin' money a lot of people gonna want you dead. Clarence just got out of prison after doing five or six years. Now he's rich from selling coke in six months. I can remember when he was a junky, now he is almost as big as Shawn. He and his people roll on Holderness. Shawn and his crew work Lucille Avenue, but they all cool, they get high and gamble against each other, and everything is cool. Ain't nobody got killed yet? So much money around now you don't have to kill for it, just deal for it. I'm proud of Clarence with all this dope in the hood and he's not using, robbing, or stealing for it. He just provides people with something that if they don't get from him, they're gonna get it from somebody else. That's what Lil-Willy used to say. I guess it is some truth because if you're the dealer, you cannot have a conscience while dealing death and destruction. Now Clarence is a boss trying to put a crew together. I got that info from Lee. Clarence told him he was too young to wait until next year. Right now Shane, Monique, and a country nigga name Lucky is all that makes up his crew. Lee asked me to get in because I was already a year older. I laughed at him, but I shouldn't have because he didn't know my daddy. Clarence knew my entire family. He would never let me in, even if I wanted in. Lee and I had gotten very close over just a couple of summers. He's really from Adamsville. He's been living on Holderness St. for almost two years. That is why he was going to Mays High School. I met him through Shane, when he first moved to the hood. We got a bond like actual blood brothers, and everybody thought we looked a lot alike. Lee is brown skin but not too light, maybe a shade lighter than me, but we both stood the same height 5 '11, with the same athletic build. We both have sandy brown hair, but it is sandier than mine. At school people get confused all the time, but looks are as far as it goes. Lee and I are like night and day. I am the night and he is the day, my nigga shining for real. Big money, jewelry, all the new brand name shoes and clothes. But what he has that nobody else has that I know for sure is Monique! The neighborhood queen pin. She ain't no Niecy, but believe me she'll do. She got a brand new Caddy, Canary yellow Fleetwood, white leather seats, trues and vogue hoes. Word is she buying a quarter key, and CP front nine more. That's a half a brick, and she sells it all herself out of the blue house, Clarence house. That nigga Lee is all the way on, but all he talked about is me getting on. On what? Death row! Seriously, Lee has big dreams, and he wants me to be a part of them. That's the difference between Lee and all the other friends I have. He doesn't want to give me anything, but he wants to see me with everything. For example, we walked to the McDonalds just Lee and I. Lee had at least a grand in his pocket; I had seventy-five cents for MARTA.

"Let me get ah, Let me get a Big Mac, large fry, ah coke, and ah apple pie," Lee asked the young lady behind the counter.

"Ah nigga get me something," I asked. I was so hungry and the smell inside of McDonald's was making it worse.

"Will that be all sir," the young lady asked. Lee ignored me.

"Yeah that'll do along wit them seven digits you dig," Lee added. He wasn't shy at all. He pulled that dope boy bank roll out and peeled her off a dub.

"Yeah, I'm digging you. Have a seat baby and imma bring it out to ya," she said smiling like she had just hit the number. Lee and I walked over and took a seat at the table.

"Damn nigga you can't get a nigga a meal dis shit done got real". I said; just to see where it would lead, hopefully to the counter for a burger.

"Listen player. I been trying to talk wit you bout some big money shit, but you ain't even wit it. But every time I pull out my bank roll you try to get in it. Dis dope money nigga, dis shit from the devil. Dis the shit Big Walt will kill and bury you bout, but you wanna eat off it. You can't have it both ways you can't eat with the devil and sleep wit God. I gotta plan for real nigga, its called never to see broke again. Imma buy that Fleetwood this weekend I told you bout. That cracker wants five grand. Imma try him wit forty-five hundred, hope he bites. If he do, boy we gonna ride over to Pittsburgh, see pop and get a hundred sacks of that Sess, and we gonna smoke and ride dis city nigga. Maybe that will give you the motivation to get you some money," Lee said. He's got a way with words, everything he says sounds so good. We are kids 15 and 16, I'm the oldest. Lee doesn't even have a driver's license, but he believes everything he's saying, and I do too.

"Man, why me? Why you keep trying to get me to sell dope? I told you the deal on that shit," I asked.

"Cause I fuck wit you nigga and I got a lotta love for ya. I feel you going out bad hanging around junky ass Bob hit them petty ass licks. You know they giving out five years for arm robbery now, and think about what happened last summer, all y'all could be doing life. And for what? What's the most you ever hit for in one night"? Lee asked; he was getting too hyped.

"Nigga listen. Dig dis! Never speak on last summer again! Cause

I don't no what the fuck you talkin' bout," I whispered. I looked around to make sure no one was within earshot.

"You no what the fuck I'm talkin' bout. That bad lick y'all went on. Play dumb if you want to, but it's a body buried somewhere, and you one rat from prison. Nigga you act like I'm wired up," Lee said.

"Fuck what you heard nigga. I ain't did shit! I don't even know what the fuck you talkin' bout. Are you wired up nigga? I'm gone," I said. I got out of my seat fast. Lee grabbed me by the arm with that big baby smile on his face.

"Nigga I'm high! I'm just bull shitin' man. Fuck it, what I say don't matter. Y'all get bang, everybody gets life. You see ain't nobody know fool but you. You doing the same shit and still broke, but I love you nigga! I don't wanna see you go out bad. Fuck wit yo hood nigga, fuck all that life sentence shit". Lee said; with that smile still on his face. I couldn't believe this nigga honestly said I love you. My brother Walt ain't never said that to me. Hell, not even my momma or daddy. I know we all love each other, but those three words are not used. I love you. Wow!

"Hey baby, here is your food, it's good and hot like me. My number in the bag I get off at five, call me, gotta get back," The girl who took the order said. I was truly relieved.

"Thanks' baby! Please believe me, imma ring you up." Lee answered. She walked away twisting her ass like she was working at Montre's. Lee opened the bag and pulled out two Big Mac's, two large fries, and two apple pies. He gave me half.

"That's that dope boy magic nigga I'm loving it," Lee said then took a large bite out of Mac. Out of all the friends I have, Lee is my best and my worst.

THE TOOTH FAIRIES

I went into the house, went straight to my room, laid back on my bed. I was still high as a bird. I went to sleep thinking about my life, or was I really even living.

Boom-boom-boom!

"Who da fuck beating on my door like that," daddy yelled with a lot of bass in his voice.

"Police we got a murder warrant! Open up now," I heard the cops yell back. My heart raced, I jumped up, nothing but Fruit of the Loom on. I headed to my window. Cops were everywhere. My life is over, and it never even began.

"What? You got is the wrong house who the fuck you looking for," daddy yelled back. I could hear my heart beating like a bass drum. Sweat streamed down my face.

"Rodney Brown," the cops yelled. I was up and running. I ran out of the back door.

"Freeze motherfucker, get down," a big white cop screamed at me. I kept running.

Bang! All I heard was one shot. Then I felt the pain in my back and fire through my chest. I could still see as I watched my blood appear. Then I saw darkness, peace, no bright lights, golden streets, or gates. I was so cold, but my body wouldn't shake.

"Rod, Rod wake yo ass up. Boy Junebug at the door you gonna miss the school bus. Get yo ass up," daddy's voice woke me. It was all a dream, but each time the dreams got more and more vivid. It's like my destiny is getting closer and closer. I opened my eyes.

"I'm up! I been up," I said. Daddy was looking me in the eyes.

"Nigga you lying. I been watching you toss and turn in this bed like you fighting for your life. Boy, I don't know what's wrong with ya or what kind of monkey you done let jump on yo back, but you going to church Sunday. Now get yo ass up and get dressed, don't miss that bus". Daddy said; he was serious. I was still shaking, laying in a cold sweat. Maybe church will help me with my dreams, Mrs. Webb can pray them all away. Carlos gave Willy James a beaded necklace blessed to protect him and his thoughts. I want one, but you have to ask to receive it, or you don't believe it. I think I'll try church and get Ms. Gloria to make me one of those nice cross necklaces that she passes out every third Sunday. I jumped up, brushed my teeth, washed my face, got dressed, and hit the door. The bus stop was a half a block away, Junebug was already there with all the other kids from the hood, all from the old Sylvan High.

"What up Bugman," I asked as we gave each other west side dap. I gave everybody else a few what ups, and that was it. Bug pulled out a fat J like every morning.

"Big Walt had to put that belt on yo ass to get up dis morning sleeping beauty. Fire up nigga before the bus roll up," Bug said. That got a laugh out of Arthur (Big Worm) Pitts and a few more giggles. I fired up, hit it two times and passed it to Bug.

"Damn dis shit strong Bug," I said. He hit it two times and passed it back.

"Let me hit Junebug," Big Worm asked. We were all cool like that, so Bug passed it. That nigga didn't hit it twice, but four times on the way to the fifth. It's Bug weed but he ain't saying shit, because he don't know this nigga. I do.

"Nigga two times and pass. Where the fuck you from," I snapped. This nigga was out of order. He hit it again, then passed it back to Bug.

"I'm from Dill Avene nigga where the fuck you from? You talking like you wrote the rules on getting high," Big Worm popped back quickly. He got himself a few giggles from the bystanders, he even laughed at himself.

"I'm finna be from off yo ass nigga. Puff, puff, pass. Nigga. I didn't write the rule nigga, but I see why it was written. For free loaders like you," I said. I had my hand in my back pocket holding my box cutter my momma gave me after that bitch stabbed me.

"Freeloader? Broke ass nigga you the freeloader. I got a bank nigga! Put down big bank, take lil bank nigga," Big Worm said. He pulled out a set of dice. I pulled out my box cutter.

"You fat motherfucker, you trying to front on me nigga? Front on dis," I growled before I started slicing him. I missed his face, but landed a few across his chest before he even saw the blood. When he saw it he stopped trying to fight and took flight. I never saw a person run that fast, but really everything happened so fast no one even knew what happened, not even Junebug.

"Damn that nigga running like his ass on fire. I was bout to jump in foe that nigga cut out," Junebug said, smiling showing all of his teeth.

"Nawl man, I ain't gotta jump no nigga. I believe in one on one. Cause I got something to even any fight up, you dig? I hate disrespectful niggas'" I said. I was trying to be cool, but inside my heart was pounding. I felt hot, like I was about to sweat. I was losing control of myself, living like I have nothing to lose. Like a football game this year, it was a blowout, and we were the ones getting blown. We lost control, the coach said because we felt like we had nothing to lose, game over. Is the game over for me. All I've been thinking about is will I stay free or will I see the penitentiary. Every knock at my front door makes my heart jump. Every time I see a police car pull up at school, I get a hall pass and haul ass. Now this shit with Big Worm may surely put me behind bars. The bus came, we all loaded up and went to school like nothing happened. At lunch time it was a big crowd of kids on the catwalk, and they were all from Harris Holmes and the West End. They were all crying. I walked up behind Dennis

Butler.

"What's going on D," I asked. He turned around, I saw tears of anger running down his face, he hugged me.

"Dem Miami Boy's done killed Cowpac. Shot in the back of his head, he was getting off his motorcycle on Norcross, and they just murdered him," he whispered. My shoulder was wet from his tears. We broke our embrace, and I looked at him.

"What? Why they do that foe? God, no! Not Cow," I screamed in disbelief. I knew Cowpac. I know his entire family. This is tragic. Cowpac comes from a family of drug dealers and hustlers, but he was the biggest. He was the richest dealer in Harris Holmes, that's for sure. They say he beats Shawn out in the most gold contest at Charles Disco every year. Cowpac got gold ropes that drag the ground, and to beat Shawn, that's what it took. I looked around and Dennis was hugging another homie. I walked off looking for my crew; they were nowhere to be found. That meant they were somewhere rolling, so I cut school for the rest of the day. I couldn't focus on anything but murder, it's haunting my thoughts and my dreams. I walked out the front door of Brown High and ran all the way up Peoples St. It's a mild September day, cloudy, surely to rain soon. It seems like it rains every time I'm feeling blue. Today I feel like it's going to rain all over the world. The Cow is dead, murdered in his own hood by niggas not even from this city. I made it to the corner of Peoples St. and Gordon St. that's when the first big tear fell from heaven upon my forehead. That's God crying for Cowpac and drug dealing pimp, I hope so. Maybe God has a heaven for gangsters, the good ones anyway. Just that thought made the sky open up and all God's tears poured down on me at once. Willie Watkins funeral home was directly across from me, and next door to them is a rooming house owned by Black James. James owns a lot of houses and apartments in the West End. All his kids go to Brown and his wife Mrs. Farrell is the special Ed teacher, SPED kids. On the down low, Black James is one of the biggest drug dealers in the city. I heard that years ago sitting on the steps down in my daddy's basement. He was just real low key and slick with everything he did. My daddy really likes Black James, and so do most the girls I go to school with. James was turning the hood into a rooming house village. Like that cracker up north turning house to duplexes, Donald Trump. Well, that's what my daddy said. Shane got a room right here next to Watkins, I just hope he's home. I ran across the street and up the steep steps on the side of the old house. I was out of breath and dripping wet. I didn't even knock on the door. I just turned the knob, and it was open. Even if Shane is not here at least, I'm out of the rain. Shane is the only tenant I know of living here. It was dark, and it felt damp like a basement, but I was on the second floor and Shane lived on the first. I could hear and feel Shane's music blasting so loud it shook the entire house that's why we nicknamed him DJ Shanny Boo. My DJ was playing "Love and Happiness" as I creeped down the steps. Sneaking has become a habit for me.

'Love and happiness. Something makes you do wrong, something to make you do right,' Al Green was screaming from the speaker at the bottom of the steps. I went left and I could see Shane's door cracked open.

I took silent steps, thinking I was going to catch Shane getting head from a smoker, and maybe he would buy me some. Before my hand could touch the knob, something cold and hard touched the back of my head.

"Go ahead, open the door real slow nigga," a voice said from behind my head. I knew this familiar voice, and that scared me even more. This is a gun behind my head for sure. All I could do was pray. I opened the door real slow. It was like stepping into Heaven. Was I dead already? The room was covered with white sheets nailed to each wall, under my feet and over the bed was plastic from wall to wall it was over everything on the floor. The reason for all this interior decorating was sitting in Shane's barber's chair in the middle of the floor. It was a man with a bloody pillowcase over his head. The chair was leaning all the way back like he was about to get a shave. Standing around the chair were Shane, Jamil, and this smiling little light skin dude. I knew his face, but I could never remember his name. But his wicked smile was unforgettable.

"Rod! How the fuck you get in here," Shane asked in anger. I couldn't hear him, but I could see his face and read lips.

"Get yo lil nosy ass in nigga so I can close the door," the voice behind me said as the cold steel pushed the back of my head all the way into the room.

"Yo Aki. Who the fuck dis dude man? Where the fuck did he come from," the light-skinned, no face, but a lot of teeth, wearing a red Kufi said. He he pulled out a big black Taurus 9 mm. My heart skipped three beats. What the fuck did I just stumble upon death or has death stumble upon me? Shane turned the music down fast.

"Chill niggas. Chill. Dis my homie he," Shane said.

"Hold up, Aki. That's Rakil. Him," Jamil said. This nigga still had his gun out.

"Shy be easy. Dis lil Rod. He from the dead end of Holderness, he used to work at the corner store. Nigga what you doing creeping around here? Turn yo ass around," Rico said. I turned and faced all 6'6" of him. He had a smirk on his face, and a pair of lock pliers in his hand, holding them like a gun.

"Damn Rico what you trying to do, scare me to death, man? I just stopped by to get out rain, and to tell Shane the Miami boy's done kilt Cowpac," I said. I didn't stutter a word. I wasn't sure I was safe yet. I looked around the room for a reaction. The ghost face killer put his gun away. That made me feel like I would get to see another day. Rico called the nigga Shy, short for Shaheed. I know this nigga, but this the first time we were in the same room together. All I really know about Shaheed came from Shane, and he kept it simple. We were on the block one day, and Rico pulled up with this same red nigga. He had on a blue Kufi last time. Shane went to the car, chopped it up with them, dapped up, and they rode out.

"That nigga wit Rico! That's the Diablo! The ghost face killer, take a good picture niggas," Shane said, then he walked away. Then Will took over. Wil was a king capper, so you really don't know what to believe.

"Shane ain't lied that nigga is the devil in disguise. That nigga done turned Rico into a psycho. Him and another, up top nigga from Brooklyn. Nigga is a fake Muslim, rapper, and killer. I been did my homework on that cat," Will said.

"How you know all that shit, Will," I asked. Will is known to blow things up.

"Nigga men ain't lied! That nigga will kill anything living and anything that'll die. Nigga who you thank doing all the killing round here and in Harris Homes. Young nigga got gunned down the other day on Sells Avenue. He was an innocent bystander. The actual target was Cutie B, bout a bitch. Ain't that some shit? Nigga who you thank started that robbing and putting babies in the microwave. Dem niggas put dis city on a new carve. Purging season, so you better go home Lil-Rod, it's getting dark". Will said; most of the time I only believe half of what I hear coming from his mouth, but I heard the worst shit about this new cat. It didn't all come from the hustler, a lot of the shit I heard came from the Akis and Bosha. I just never put the face with the name. Now I do, and I will never forget it.

"Nigga stop lying. Say Cowpac ain't dead," Shane pleaded. His face had a confused look, like this was an April fool's joke. Shane is like me, the hood is his heart, and everybody in it.

"Yeah, Shane that nigga dead He took one in back of his head. Miami nigga knocked his brains out of his eyes. I just heard when I went to get the pliers, that's some bad shit. But like I told Lip and Boc weeks ago, I'll kill all them niggas; even the cool one, Convertible Bert. We'll blow that nigga top back for the right sack. See them Miami Boys ain't gonna let no scary niggas get money round dem. That shit was just a gut check and they bout to take over Norcross. Murder nigga's, ain't nobody seen it, but everybody heard it. Well, fuck that shit! The brother is in a much better place. Now let's get this done, I got the pliers, who gonna do the pulling,"? Rico said, as he snatched the pillowcase off the guy duct taped in the barber's chair. Wow! This nigga face looks like a black ass elephant man with duct tape on his mouth. He had knots on top of knots on his head. Jamil pulled the tape from his mouth, even with all the blood in his mouth I could still see all the gold and diamond, a Miami boy for sure. They are about to pull all this niggas teeth.

"Ah imma bout to dip, gotta make it back to class. I see y'all cats busy," I said, as I turned around for the door.

"Boy, you ain't going nowhere! You just stepped in sum gorilla shit. Too early to whip yo shoes. How we know you won't run and tell," Rico asked.

"Man,' you know I ain't no rat," I blurted.

"I know you ain't. A rat needs a tail, but now you got one. Just don't let it grow, we really hate to kill rats, because that means he grew a tail. After we kill the motherfucker, it still leaves a tail and we can still go to jail. So I rather kill you before you become a rat and grow a tail, you dig? Now close the doe and lock it nigga," Rico said. Was this all a joke? If it was, somebody forgot to tell this guy taped to the chair. I locked the door, turned back around, and didn't move.

"Please. My nigga, please! Y'all done got all I got! You ain't gotta do a nigga! You see, I got my eyes closed! I don't know none of y'all! My nigga," the elephant man pleaded with his eyes closed tight. Rico laughed so loud, it made Shane turn the music back up some. He laughed like the Pigeon on Batman. It was chilling how Rico could change his voice up, it sounded so real, so sick.

"Sit that nigga straight up in the chair, Shane. Open yo eyes nigga. Don't waste the rest of yo life in the dark. Face yo final light like a man, cause you gotta die. That lame done came in here now, you know names. You think I want Big Trav hunting for me wit dem choppers. Nigga, please! See ya'll niggas done went too far now. First you come up here paying all the bitches, fucking the price of pussy up. Then you come wit the cheap coke, fucking the price of dope up. Now y'all killing my homeboys, skipping back to the bottom. One ya'll niggas done shot Pete over in John Hope, gave my man wheels for legs, and killed that old lady. That shit really hurt T. W. Now he wants all ya'll niggas dead from here to Bankhead. So my only dilemma is whether to pull your teeth while you dead or alive," Rico said. He sounded like Al in Scarface. If this guy wasn't scared, I was scared enough for the both of us. He opened his eyes.

"You pussy ass fuck nigga. You ain't gonna kill shit or let shit die bitch. Yeah nigga, we fucking ya'll bitches, they mommas, and all ya'll niggas mommas. Ya'll niggas ain't killers. Y'all cowards because y'all allow this shit," the elephant man said. He smiled and blood leaked from his teeth. Is this a joke or what? Can a man really be this brave? Maybe he knew like I really knew. He's already dead!

"My nigga! You a gangster! I dig that shit! That's why I ain't gonna kill you. Kill this nigga Shy," Rico said. He's westside serious now. A pillow appeared over the top of the elephant man's head and then, BANG! The sound was death defying in this small dim place. My ears rang like an alarm clock was going off inside my head. When my eyes came back in focus, a few feathers flew in the air, and one Miami boy sat dead slumped in the chair. Gun smoke filled my nose like a one on one of some good coke. Oh, what a rush. Wow! Look how quick a nigga can get killed. All it took was one word.

"God bless the dead, dis nigga here was a gangster for real. Look at him now. He is dead wit that same smile on his face, but the nigga in a better place. Dem Miami boy's hustle hard, but imma make em die harder," Rico said. I thought to myself. A better place? I think South Beach would be his choice at this point.

"I smell shit. One of ya'll niggas done shitted on yo self, or dis dead motherfucker done shitted in my chair? Help me get him out of my chair before he fucks it up," Shane demanded. Nobody moved, so Shane pushed him out onto the plastic-covered floor. He hit the floor hard, like a big sack of potatoes. That got a good laugh out of Rico.

"Shane, you need to bust a cap in his dead ass for that. Look! Yo chair wet as hell player. Kill that nigga while he dead for that shit Shane," Rico said and laughed some more. I was getting nauseated, I felt like I was about to lose my stomach. It's just something about the smell, gun smoke, blood, shit, and fear. It's the smell of death, up close death. Not shooting in the crowd, then praying nobody dies. These niggas doing shit like you see in the movies. It wouldn't surprise me if they sawed the body up and dumped it in the Chattahoochee River. This isn't these niggas' first rodeo. They have done all of this before.

"Ah son, hold on! I gotta get dis nigga grill. Hand me the pliers, Rico. I don't need no help, I bet this nigga mouth stays open now," Shane said. He laughed at his own joke and went right to work. He turned the body over and sat down on his chest. He opened his mouth up. The pliers went in and gold came out. When he pulled it, I could swear his dead hand moved.

"Hurry up, Ak so we can rap dis nigga up. He stinks," Rico said while holding his nose.

"Yeah! we gotta get this nigga up out of here fast. Want me to see if the DJ is next doe," Shane asked.

"Nawl, we don't need the DJ for dis one. We ain't gonna burn dis nigga. They want dis nigga dumped on Greensferry right there where Miami Trav's crew rolls. Think about the news. A body was found on Greensferry wit their fuckin' teeth pulled out. That's what the headlines will read. That sounds like some Mob shit," Rico said. I had seen and heard enough. I had to go.

"I gotta go, I can't be late for practice," I said, taking a fake glance at my Sir watch. I grabbed the lock and the knob and out I went. I didn't look back, but I heard from behind.

"Keep your mouth closed, or you will lose your teeth," Rico said.

There was a lot of laughter. It faded as I ran up the steps to get out of this madhouse. The windy rain slapped me in my face, but I didn't mind. I was too busy thanking God I wasn't dead, or was I?

THE BRIDGE

It's the winter of 1987, the Friday before Christmas break. It was about to be another year and I'm still here. It's a drug war going on in the Atlanta Streets. Da Miami Boyz against Atlanta, and by my count they were winning. My hood wasn't infected yet, thanks to Rico and the Tooth Fairy's. I've been trying my best to stay clear of that crew, all but Shane. We haven't spoken on anything, that never happened since that day. You dig? It was like it never happened, and that was cool. I had my own demons chasing me.

Carlos finally got out of juvenile, and everybody at school was happy. We were on our way to a big cut party. We left school no sooner than we got there, all twenty-five of us. Some went different ways, but we all ended up under the bridge on the railroad tracks right across from Brown High. We huddled up like our football team, all the key players in the middle. Carlos went inside his book bag and pulled out what looked to be about an ounce of cocaine. It looked like fresh snow, then a big freezer bag full of the greenest weed, no seeds, lastly a fully loaded brand new all black .38 snub nose.

"Aightt, aight. Calm down niggas. I been locked up. Don't get too close, I would hate to give one of ya'll niggas one of these hollow heads," Carlos said with a big smile.

"Let me hold that gat Carlos? You just jumped free, I ain't got no paper on me," I said. I had to get the gun from Carlos, because when he gets drunk people can get hurt.

"Nigga I ain't on probation neither. I can hold all that shit," Willy

(Killer) James said. He was already hyped.

"Nawl niggas don't start that bullshit. Dis my shit, Imma do it like I wanna do it, and dis how I'm doing it. Ok Rodney you asked first, so here you get the gat, but if I get mad at one of these niggas don't give the shit back. Willy J. you get to hold the blow, here you go, and Cat roll the grass. Now niggas! I got all dis shit where the drank at? I want Hendog niggas," Carlos said. Then started chanting Hendog! Hendog! So did everyone else.

"Oakland City in dis bitch niggas! I got what you want, you got what I need. Baby, we made for each other," Bobby Carlton sang. He came down the hill looking and walking just like JJ from Good Times. He held up two enormous bottles of Hennessy, to the cheers of the crowd. He was sweating, and it was cold as hell. That meant he had just pulled a Rayfield and ran out of somebody's Liquor store with those bottles, and so the party began. We got higher than a motherfucker and we blessed the dead. We all knew someone who had been murdered this year, and the murder rate was only rising. The latest hood hero to meet his fate was Tony Tripp. They found him and one of his bitches, in a house, throats cut, dogs didn't even bark. It's getting colder and colder in these streets, niggas doing more than just trying to eat.

"Who wanna fuck wit OC, we under the bridge, nigga somebody gotta get they back slammed out"? That was one of those twins; Vert or Bert. It was the same one Pete hit in the head with the bat. He took his shirt off, ready to rumble. There were too many brawlers in this crew for no one to take the challenge, plus this is how we grew up getting our stripes. We had to fight, or stay in the house. Everyone was pass high and drunk, and the coke wasn't helping. All but Carlos, he had the biggest nose I ever saw, but I never saw him snort coke. I see him take it and numb his mouth and teeth, but not that big nose.

"Fuck that shit you talking nigga. Who wanna fuck wit the Cat? Hold this shit Rodney, let me hit that blow Willy," Cateye Tony said. He gave me the weed, hit the coke, took his shirt off, and flexed up like Bolow. Cateye ain't never ran or backed down from no nigga. The crowd was getting hyped now. A lot of pushing and shoving, and plenty of shit talking. It was about to be some chaos.

"Hand me my hater nigga, Imma fire this bitch up," Carlos slurred. He could barely stand up. I knew better than to talk any sense into him, so I just gave it up.

Bang-bang-bang-bang-bang-bang! Carlos fired the gun with no hesitation toward a warehouse which was a little further down the tracks. He dumped the shells out. You could hear them when they hit the ground. Things had quieted down. Carlos reloaded, half of the mob headed for the hills when the gun went off. I really didn't know what to do. I was stuck, coked up, high, and drunk.

"Who wanna walk wit God niggas? Fuck all that fighting shit. Niggas don't fight no more, all they do is this. Run niggas, run fucking cowards, now that I done separated the real from the fake, let's do what real niggas do. Get wit some bitches. Cat put yo shirt back on nigga. I thought you was going to the school and get that hoe Carla," Carlos asked. He was still hyped. I thought, where did those shots go? If I was smart, I would get up and go, or would that make me a coward? We smoked a couple more joints, and took a few more bumps, and once again my mind went numb.

"Ah man, ain't no more getting high until we get some hoes," Carlos said. He was serious now.

"Aight, aight. Pimp B gotcha! We bout to go on hoe patrol! Let's get it, Cat! Ya'll niggas just chill, we'll be right back," Bobby said. He was trying to sound as cool as can be. I did a quick head count, it's 12 of us left. Chances are they won't get but one, maybe two girls, and Cat will be the one that gets them. I watched them head up the hill on their way back to the school. Then all hell broke loose.

"12-12-12! Run niggas they everywhere," Cateye yelled. Then I saw him and Bobby running back our way. My mind froze, then my heart dropped. Everyone else was already running before I remembered that 12 meant the police. They were all running the same way down the tracks, some tripping and falling over each other. They were headed the way Carlos had shot. I thought better and went the other way. I didn't even run, I couldn't anyway, I just walked, and not even that far, maybe 25 yards. I heard a helicopter overhead, so I jumped in some kudzu bushes. Took my backpack off, and thought this looks like a nice place for a nap, all things considered. I laid back deep in the kudzu and fell asleep listening to helicopters and sirens. Loud music coming from some dope boy's car awakened me. I stood up to see what I could see and passing by on the bridge was DeShawn's Monte Carlo. There wasn't a police in sight. I looked at my Sir watch. It was lunchtime, I'd been asleep for at least two hours. I dusted myself off, put my book bag back on and headed back the way I'd come. I figured all those niggas had gone to jail. I hope Carlos got that gun off him, but either way he won't be home soon and Christmas is only a week away. I was back where it all started, cups, beer cans, and two big empty liquor bottles told the story. Well, it's lunch time. So I headed up the hill. Just another Carlos adventure, I will really miss my nigga.

"Rodney," The voice was barely a whisper, but a little familiar. I stopped in my tracks and ducked down quickly.

"Rodney what the fuck you ducking foe? It's me nigga. How the fuck you get away," Carlos asked. He looked like he just jumped out of a grave. He was covered in Georgia's red clay.

"My nigga I thought you was gone boy. Where the fuck you been," I said. I was so happy to see him. I ran over and hugged him, mud and all.

"Nigga! I passed out right here, you just woke me up. I'm hungry as hell. Let's dip," Carlos said.

"Dip where nigga? Where the fuck we gonna go the chopper just stop flying? You look like you been playing in the mud. I told you not to shoot that gun Low. You made shit hot man. The cops are everywhere," I explained.

"Oh yeah, I forgot about that shit. But nigga fuck the police, I'm hungry. You can stay under dis bridge and starve if you want to. I'm headed to Mickey D's. RB you know it's on me lets go," Carlos said. That's just how Carlos is, he thinks past the bullshit fast then it's on to some new shit.

Boom boom boom.......boom.. Boom boom... boom boom boom. Somebody's car system sounds like thunder, bumping that Public Enemy.

"Let's go nigga. That's Pillhead we can catch a ride," Carlos said. We made it to the top of the hill just as the burgundy Monte Carlo boom machine was riding by.

"Ah Pill...Pill," Carlos yells to no avail.

"Man, that nigga can't hear you. I can't hear you myself," I said as the Monte Carlo went around the curve to Brown High.

"I know he didn't hear me, but I think he saw me," Carlos said. No sooner than he said it, the Monte Carlo was coming back towards us, music still bumping. He pulled up on us. The truck was beating like a gorilla was trying to bust out of it. Carlos opened the door. I got in the back. He jumped in the front and we pulled off.

"What the fuck ya'll lil niggas done this time? The police were all over the school. They done locked up bout ten niggas already. I'm riding dirty. I gotta get y'all hot boys out of here ASAP. Imma drop y'all at the Westend Station. I don't even wanna know what you've done. Just don't get caught niggas," Pillhead said. Then turned his music all the way back up. Ice T was rapping about the police being at his door at six in the morning, and something about some fresh Adidas across the bathroom floor. This song is a real banger. My inside was shaking like jello from the bass, but it felt good. One day I'll have nice things like this. Daddy says I just have to work hard. Pillhead doesn't look like he is working that hard, ain't no dirt under his nails, he seems to be enjoying himself. Nothing is what it really seems. Lil Willy used to say his only job is staying alive, and he's dead. It doesn't seem too hard to get nice things these days, but how long will you keep it? Some say, easy come easy go, but if you work hard, you will have something to show.

"Alright Lil-niggas get out, and I ain't dropped y'all nowhere. I ain't even seen you," Pillhead said as we pulled into the park and ride. We jumped out fast.

"Yeah Pill man, we got you man you ain't fuckin wit no rats, and you know that man we family. We appreciate it homie," Carlos said.

"Good looking out, Pill. Appreciate it," I said. He didn't say another word. He just pulled off, disturbing the peace.

"That's a cool mutherfucker right there Rodney, and that nigga fuckin' all the baddest bitches. I wish that was me nigga," Carlos said.

"Me too," I said. I really meant it for a minute.

"Let's go down to five points, I need some shoes and shit look at me, and nigga you always need some new shoes. I got you and I got dis and dis Merry Christmas nigga maybe we can find some hoe, hoe, hoes," Carlos said showing me a big bank roll of money and his 38. We hopped the train downtown and went to Walter's. Carlos bought us both new outfits and shoes. I got a black Adidas suit, shell toes, and a black Kango. Carlos did the same in all white. He spent $560.42, and the bank roll was still fat. We went to The Underground to that $5.00 hamburger spot, and we both ate two burgers. Then we went to the top of Five Points to find some cut. We smoked a joint and left before the smoke spread too far. We hopped the train back to the West End just in time to catch some of our classmates getting out of school. It was all the same conversation. How a lot of students cut school and went to jail over a shootout. No one said our names at all.

"Ah Rodney, you going over Willie James' house wit me, they say that's where all the cut at," Carlos asked. He'd given me all the weed and coke that was left. I had other plans.

"Man, I told you on the train who imma bout to go fuck, and you gave me all I need to fuck her wit. You need some of dis shit back? I gotta ask you one more time, let me keep the 38. I really need it Low, shit come off right, you know imma skin you down," I begged. I didn't really have a move, but if I had the gun, I would come up with one, and Lord knows Carlos didn't need it. Carlos was bad enough without a gun, with a gun it was like a murder case in his hand. The nigga with the money shouldn't be the one with the gun.

"Nawl! I don't want none of the shit, use it to buy you a gun nigga and stop playing wit yo nose. Nigga I told you dis ain't my shit. It's my daddy's. Look man, don't forget to call me on Christmas. Imma get a car and a new motorcycle. We gonna ride now for real, for real. Ah man one love nigga we bout to be out. The 71 just pulled in, see you on Christmas. Stay fly nigga," Carlos said as we gave each other dap and one of those one arm hugs.

"One love nigga, and good looking out wit these new threads and shit, imma bring you a gift on X-mas nigga even if I have to Rayfield the shit," I said. We both laughed when I said Rayfield, it meant running out the store with whatever you want, and they knew us for it. I watched Carlos walk away. He was crewed up now with some Cascade cats. They walked all the way down to the last stop in the MARTA station, 71 Cascade, talking loud, saying nothing. Carlos the loudest. I hope Carlos doesn't kill anybody. He's the nicest person I know until you try to cross him. Then you are dealing with an actual enemy, an enemy with money and power, and the heart to pull a trigger. I really love that nigga. I had to wait on the 69 Dill Avenue, but it won't take long. I'm full and fresh, I got good weed and blow on my way to see a hoe. Not just any hoe.

I THINK I LOVE HER

I'm going to see Niecy, Junebug's sister, one of Tony Tripp's hoes, and my best girlfriend. She loved to get high and freak me off real nasty. She really is a molester, but I'll never tell. She talks to me a lot. Mostly about pimp and hoe shit. She turns tricks right in her momma house when she's at work. Sometimes I'll be in the next room, watching her lil girl and her back. Junebug didn't know about us, but he knew his sister was a hoe, so maybe he did know. I didn't care if she was a hoe. Niecy's is a real hustler too, she has so much game, and I soaked it up like a sponge. When Niecy's giving me game, I'm like a dog. I never speak, but I understand. It's simple. Like she said, pussy rules the world. If you can rule pussy, you can rule the world. Now I was on my way, but I had some questions today. I've been thinking about her a lot, she's so sexy, crazy, and cool. For real, I think I love her. I want to know what really makes her do what she does. I have plans for us. I think we were meant to be together, because she doesn't charge me for sex, so she has to like me back, I think. Well, I'll see.

When I got off the 69 bus, I ran all the way home. I checked in with my daddy like I had been in school all day, he wouldn't find out I cut school until after Xmas. I told him I was going around to Junebug's house to watch music videos, and I was out.

I knocked on the door twice.

"Who is it," Neicy answered. "It's me," I yelled back. "Me who nigga? I done told you bout that shit, say a name when you knock on my doe nigga. Junebug ain't here anyway, he in Carver Holmes, and I don't want no company. Today ain't a good day

Rod they found Tony dead last night," she said.

"Tony who," I asked with the door still closed.

"My Tony, nigga! Tony Tripp! Tripp City. That Tony, the only Tony. Bye nigga. Go play," she said. I could hear her walking away.

"Niecy open the doe baby, I got something that will cheer you right up I promise," I yelled. The door opened so fast. There she was, bow legged in nothing but panties and a bra. Her red skin is so smooth, smiling at me with her gold tooth. I'm in love, or maybe lust. They both felt the same to me.

"What you got nigga show me now, before you come in"? She demanded; I pulled out the big bag of weed Carlos gave me.

"See I ain't bullshitin' and I got a bigger surprise for you, baby. I'm so sorry for your loss, so imma bout to make it snow. Hoe-hoe-hoe," I said. Then held up the big bag of coke Carlos gave me. The door opened and her tongue was in my mouth.

"Baby where you get all dis blow from? Just by eyeballing, I can see it's over a half an ounce. You been hitting licks again, boy? I done told you bout that shit! It'll get you killed. Rod watch who you stick up, nigga catch you slipping, and leave you with a shit bag, wheels for legs, or worst dead. Be careful! You ain't know made nigga, you ain't even know paid nigga," she said. We had both totted some coke, so words were flowing.

"Nawl baby! I ain't paid or made, but I'm alive. A nigga like me doing my job, just to survive. Speaking of alive, what happened to Tony Tripp? He was paid and made," I said. Niecy looked at me hard, then she smiled.

"We don't know yet, all Tracy told me is they found him and Angel duct taped, and shot in the back of their heads. Two times each, they wanted to make sure that nigga was dead. The only clue my daddy got is two bitch nigga eaters inside the front gates. One named Bitch and the other named Nigga, all he had to do is say they name at the same time (bitch-nigga) like that, and whoever they don't know is dead. She said the dogs didn't even bark, and for bitch not to bark, that bitch had to know you," she said.

"Wow! What about the girl? Who you say, Angel? Who was she? Why you think they did her," I asked.

"I'm glad they killed that bitch. She was the hoe I cut. Tony put me out of the house over that bitch. That was his bottom bitch Angel, but the bitch was too cute to play the bottom. I told that nigga that, I'm the one knocked the hoe, I should know, that bitch wasn't shit but cut bait. Imma tell you what I think, that bitch set my daddy up. You see, that bitch from up top, don't trust no nigga or hoe from New York. Dem niggas broke, but they think we the ones slow. They like roaches, they can't eat up top so they running down here in our shit. Now they gangsters down here, but I bet they weren't calling shots up top. I told Tony I stole that bitch from a heroin nigga from Brookline. He would buy more pussy than his hoes were selling down on Auburn Ave., but dis nigga was super paid. I fucked him and that hoe for 30 days, broke bread wit that nigga and everything. He thought he had him another sweet thang. I was just selling that nigga a dream, my daddy taught me that at fourteen. I rocked that nigga to sleep, made that hoe steal his bank roll, his dope, his hoe, and his piece. My Daddy was so happy, all them gifts, and I had a bitch, already hoed up and choose up. That's what a bottom bitch does! Not just get they pussy ate and look cute. That's all I ever saw that bitch do. A nigga like pimp Jean, he would've had that hoe walking from Auburn Avenue back to Decatur. Nigga don't you ever trust a lazy hoe, that's a hoe that wanna hoe when she wanna hoe, not when they daddy say so. That's why the hoe dead, cause she was a lazy cake bitch for real. If that hoe was on the track where a hoe belonged, she would still be breathing," she said. She talked most of the night, all about pimps and hoes. I really enjoyed the stories, and she's a great story teller, but a much better freak. She talked all night, but by morning she was doing things to me that I hadn't seen on Playboy. The coke had me going good, and I was trying my best to make her mine. She made me do things to her that girls I know, don't know anything about, and I loved it. I think I love her, I love a hoe! I was loving her way before this. For me, it was love at first sight, and she had always treated me so nice. So I told her.

"Niecy I love you! For real, for real. I love you," I said. She stopped sucking me.

"Nigga you a fool wit it," she replied.

"Why imma fool? Cause I'm too young for you, or what is it," I asked.

"Nigga how you gonna love a bitch, that ain't did shit foe you. What you wanna be nigga a mark, a trick, or a pimp. Cause that's what I'm looking foe. Love don't live here anymore. She pushed me out of her pussy. Now we need money nigga, me and my baby gotta eat we can't eat no love. Get out of my house lame ass trick," she went screaming like a crazy lady. I jumped up and found my clothes fast, and I was out the door. I was walking fast with my head down, feeling like a real Charlie Brown. Then I realized it was the next day, the sun was all the way up. I'm in big trouble, I spent the night with that whore. My daddy is going to kill me.

ALL NIGHTER

When I made it to the house, my daddy's car was gone. Walking up the steps, I could smell food, and it wasn't breakfast. What time was it? I walked in the door, Gospel music was playing.

"Boy, where the hell you been? You done worried yo daddy sick! Not me cause I been seen the devil in you. You like my dead cousin, you thank you slicker than slick. My daddy use to say find one slick nigga, find one dead. Don't end up dead boy too many people love you. Remember dis money done left a lot of niggas dead," momma said, then went back to reading her bible and humming her song. Too many people love me, but do you? I know she loves me but that's just something she doesn't say, is what I really believe. My daddy told me that, and he ain't never lied to me. I walked to the room I now share with Brad, my cousin. We took him in after his mother passed away. I was in a real daze, still high as the moon.

"What up, cuz? Boy, where you been? Uncle Walt bout to kill yo ass! Nigga you higher than a motherfucker! Where that shit at? Give me some nigga and please Rod," Brad begged. I just looked at him, my mind was ten plays ahead. That's how coke did me when I focused. I was thinking of a master plan. I went straight to my phone.

"Hello"? Neicy answered; on the first ring, not the whore Neicy. The queen pin Neicy.

"Hey momma, whatcha doing," I asked in the sweetest voice I could conjure.

"Man, I'm up and at it trying to cook up a meal, how you doing baby, you ok? I heard about yesterday," she said, sounding concerned.

"I'm good momma, but I need a favor," I asked.

"What you need baby," she asked like it didn't matter what it was.

"When my daddy calls, you tell him I spent the night over there," I asked. Not that it will make much difference, but maybe some.

"What you done now boy," she asked.

"I promise I ain't did nothing to break the law, I ain't even been in the Westend. I was at a kickback around the corner from my house. Got too drunk and passed out," I lied. I hate lying to people who I can tell the truth to, but sometimes you have to.

"Imma cover for ya, but you need to stop hanging out like that. Ain't shit in these streets but money and death. If you ain't gettin' know money, you just trying to die. I don't wanna see you dead Rodney get a job. I'll call you after he calls my cookies ready bye baby. Love you," she said.

"Love you too Niecy and thank you," I replied. She did love me a lot. People love me. I'm blessed. My daddy wouldn't dare touch a blessed man, that's what the cocaine was telling me, but my cousin Brad was saying something else.

"Boy Uncle Walt gonna beat yo ass. You thank that shit you just did gonna stop this shit? Nigga you crazy, but I can save ya. Just give me some of that shit," He begged on and on; I laid back on the bed and passed out to the sounds of the beggar. To awaken to the sounds of a madman.

"Get yo punk ass out my bed nigga, before I kick yo ass out! You nothing ass nigga!" Big Walt threatened; I jumped up like a Jack in the Box.

"Boy, I told you not to go to sleep. Uncle Walt gonna beat that ass, and that nigga high as hell. You need to search him....." Brad was saying; that snitching ass junky.

"Nigga you shut the fuck up, get the fuck out of here foe I put you out of my house"! Daddy snapped; Brad jump out the bed already dressed. That meant his clothes were already on and left the room without another word. My daddy was mad and everybody from here to the West End knew it.

"Now back to you nigga! Imma ask you one time. Where the fuck you been all night? You better not lie! Cause nigga I already know! I just wanna see if you have gotten so rotten you can look me in my eyes and tell a lie," he spoke clearly. But was he Bluffing? If he wasn't Bluffing, he wouldn't act this mad. Because I spend the night at Junebug's sometimes. He knocked on the door last night but we were too high to move, so he was bluffing.

"I spent the night at Niecy's I swear," I said. didn't lie but he did.

"Nigga you lying! I been over there, Junebug say he ain't seen you," he replied. He started to take his belt off. I knew he was Bluffing for real, because the only thing my daddy has ever beaten me for was lying or stealing. Anything else we talked about then, he would put me on punishments that wouldn't last, and I wasn't lying or stealing.

"I ain't lying daddy just call her and see," I pleaded just like baiting a fish, and he bit just like a big mouth bass.

"Hand me that phone. What's the number nigga"? He demand; like he knew something I didn't. I gave him the phone. "752-3947," I answered as meekly as possible. He dialed the number, while I smiled on the inside.

"Hey there! Is this Niecy? This Walt, Rod's Daddy. How you doing? I'm good! Thank you! I'm calling you cause dis boy over here, stayed out all night till the next day, and he said he was round there," he asked in his way. Then there was a long pause, while he listened to the phone.

"Ok I see! I'm just glad he wasn't hanging over on Holderness. I done told this boy that place there is a death trap. Thank you for telling him that too. Well, I gotta handle dis situation, so imma let you finish up yo cooking. Ok, you have a Merry Christmas too.

Bye, bye," he said as nicely as he could, then hung the phone up.

"Nigga you must got stupid across my forehead. That was Keisha's momma, not Niecy around the corner. You think everybody stupid but you," he said, looking me right in the eyes. I didn't flinch.

"But daddy, that's the Niecy I was talking bout. Junebug wasn't home, so I got a ride at the park to Keisha's house," I told him.

"But daddy my ass! How many times I done told you bout going on that side of town. Nigga you think I don't know that bitch Niecy is a drug dealer. I know that family and I knew them before you. All of them either sell dope or use dope, ain't no in between wit them people. Boy, you keep on throwing rocks at the penitentiary, they gonna lock yo ass up. Nigga's only get by for so long. When these crackers get tired of this shit and build a thousand more prisons. Don't end up in one smart ass. I know you been drinking and smoking, and ain't know telling what else. Don't leave this house for a month, nigga you need rehab, and imma give it to you," daddy said, then walked out the door. I was relieved and optimistic at the same time. Because my daddy's punishments don't last long, he gave me a month, the most I'll do is a week. I'll be out and about by Christmas. But going to the West End would be out of the question. That meant I wouldn't be able to go over Carlos' house on Christmas day, that's my biggest punishment. Other than that all is well, I got enough weed left to make a little money, and smoke good. I went to sleep thinking about the night before, I got high and let my feelings show, to a hoe.

THE WORST CHRISTMAS EVER

Christmas Day 1987 it had been a very long and high week for me. My cousin Brad hung around the house with me the entire time. He thought he was going to smoke all my weed up, and he almost did. Brad loves to get high like me, but unlike me he will get high off anything. We grew up close and still are, but he's still on. I'm his lil cuz shit. Like I'm still a kid, he doesn't know I got real stripes, and if I wanted, I could be a made nigga. All I gotta do is move out, simply said, but I know it will kill my daddy, and break my momma's heart. Brad thinks he's slicker than me. He grew up in Oakland City and then moved to Shamrock over on Campbellton Rd before his momma died. Where he lived compared to where I lived was a nice place, not many cop cars and ambulances. I say that to say I've seen a lot, and I never covered my eyes. Daddy was nice enough to let me walk to the park, seeing that it's Christmas. Christmas is different for me now, all I hope for are clothes, and I got those two outfits and a pair of Stan Smith Adidas. Not a lot to most, but enough for me. I had on one of my outfits, Jordache jeans, a white and green Adidas hoodie, my Stan Smith's, and a snow white fur Kango. Brad had on the same outfit, but a blue and white Nike hoodie, a blue Kango, and he had those new Air Max all white. His feet are so long it makes his shoes look funny. Brad claimed to be a Crip, but he ain't got no set. I don't believe in gang banging. All I really know about gangs is from the movie Colors. That's a good movie, the rapper Ice-T is the star, and they say he's a pimp in real life. Brad went to see that movie 25 times and now he is flagging. He tried that recruiting shit on me; I told him if I wanted to join a gang, I would go to jummah. The Muslims I know, get away with murder all the time. They make their killings clean, not drive by gang shit. They move more like the Mob. They walk up to you and give it to you right there, mask on or off, ain't nobody seen shit, but everybody heard it. Anyway, we were walking to the park to see who we could see. Black he would be there waiting. Encre got a car for Christmas, and he's not even older enough to drive by himself. I know he's going to ride through to show it off, and show niggas he's fat boy fresh like always. The weather was nice for the end of December, and the park showed that today is a good day. Grown-ups and kids were out and about, playing with their new toys. We spotted Black posted up down by the kiddy basketball court. He was fresh in his all black Adidas suit, black shell toes, and that cool ass black leather Kango.

"What up cuz," Brad yelled out, as we finished off the last few steps down the hill. We walk across the street to the kiddy court.

"Nigga I done told you bout that cuz shit. My name Black or Dwayne you dig, all that fake gang shit, keep it moving nigga. I ain't trying to get killed," Black told Brad.

"Man dis nigga thank he in L.A. I been telling him ain't no gangs in dis city," I said. Brad stopped in his tracks.

"Is you niggas crazy? Dis shit bout to be gang land. It's plenty bangers round here. What about 'Down by Law' and 'The Omega Homeboys' them gangs from Da 'A' niggas," Brad said.

"Nigga all them niggas in prison at Alto Motherfucker. Dem niggas up north gettin' fucked or trying to fuck every boy they see. No bullshit nigga, you gonna be a man or a hoe in the Toe. Rod, tell dis nigga. You got a lot of homeboys been in and out of that motherfucker," Black said, then looked at me. It was the truth. The only gang around here now are drug gangs, and the Miami Boyz. They are the only gang making the news. True! I've heard a lot of Alto prison stories, and everything I've heard has been beyond bad. I ain't heard no one say anything good about that place, and all the homeboys I know that's been there don't act the same, but I wouldn't call any names. I know Alto is not on my list of places I would like to visit.

"I don't know what them niggas doing in Alto and I don't wanna find out, but I know a few niggas that been there and back and back again. One nigga told me he misses his friends. When I asked that nigga why keep going back to that place. Come to find out he was in love with a fag man, real talk, and ya'll know the nigga he a G," I said.

"Say the nigga name Rod, say the fags name. I might have smoked a joint wit that nigga, and I don't wanna ever do that shit again. Say the nigga name," Black demanded. He was looking at me all crazy.

"I ain't saying shit else bout that dude! Let's get high, it's Christmas," I answered, then pulled out all the bud I had left.

"Yeah fuck that fags shit, let talk some G shit," Brad said when he saw the weed. Black reached down and picked up a brown paper, and pulled out a big brown bottle of no other than that Hendog. Black held the Hennessey to the sky.

"God bless the dead, all my niggas up state, and all my niggas in the Feds," Black preached. He said this same prayer before he opened a big bottle like this. I always had a different toss every time. "God before I take a sip of dis holy water, I pray this next year won't bring the same sorrow. We lost a lot of hustlers, pimps, and players. I don't know how Harris Holmes let them niggas kill Da Cow. Y'all heard what happened to Tony? They took the Trip right out of our city, him and his whore. They took two shots in the face, opposite the way, a nigga did Michael Lovelace. Coward shot him in the back, tryin' to jack. Flowers for the dead. God forgive our sins, I pray we don't wake up dead. Toast to the good a life niggas," I said. Everything I said was true. Life was getting shorter and shorter for niggas from the hood.

People I really know are dying, not dying, getting murdered. Like my partner Tic, he was killed over a bitch, and we still in high school. It makes me wonder about things that were unthinkable a few years ago, like which nigga I know gonna be murdered next, or will it be me.

"God love the dead, my momma and my daddy. Cuz pull out and let's crack that cap on the Hendog. Lil cuz, big cuz ready to get fucked up," the wannabe gangbanger said, and that we did, we smoked and drank the day away. Encre and all the other cool niggas from the hood showed up, everybody but Junebug. He'd been distant lately, but he'll hit my window sooner than later. Junebug is getting some good money with them Miami Boyz, and everybody ain't cool with that. I really don't know how I feel about it, but I know how Encre feels. We tried to get Junebug to set up the Miami Boyz that he gets his supply from. He told us he was down, but he faked that move and we haven't seen him since.

"Rodney man, you still ain't seen that nigga Junebug have you? I knew that nigga wasn't down wit that move. If it wasn't you, I would've robbed that nigga on the spot, and if I ever see him that nigga again, imma shoot him in the ass then jacked that pussy. No disrespect homie, but its hunting season on all Miami niggas, their work, and they hoe. We going hunting tonight, nigga I'm blasting on sight, my trigger finger been itching like a motherfuckering all day. It's time for some gun smoke niggas. Who wanna ride tonight,"? Encre said with a smile. We all knew how serious he was.

"Fat boy give that shit a break it's Christmas. Nigga you wanna be on the streets New Year's don't you," Black said. He ain't never been down with none of our evil doings.

"New Year's? Nigga imma make it New Year's tonight, cause imma load all my shit up like it's December 31, and imma ride dis city real slow like a hearse," Encre said. Everybody else was laughing, but me. I never heard the joke, Encre is a maniac, and times like this it pays to be on punishment.

"I wish I could ride, man I'm broke as hell, but a nigga still on lock down. If I wasn't on punishment, I would be over Carlos' house. He got a motorcycle and a car for Christmas. Nigga said he was gonna pull up, but he ain't pulled up yet. I'm high as hell. Been down here listening to lies all day. I'm bout to head home and eat again. Give me a ride up Big Boy," I asked, then I started walking over to his beat up Cutlass.

"Yeah nigga come on, I gotta ride to the Ville, anyway" Encre answered. He got off his hood and opened the driver's door.

"You coming," I asked Brad.

"Nawl nigga! I ain't on no punishment. Bye Lame," he popped back. Sometimes I hated that nigga.

"Lame these nuts nigga". I said; we jumped in the car, and Encre fishtailed out of the park, doing at least 70. Encre had the Beastie Boys Paul Revere bumping so hard it knocked his rearview mirror down. We were in front of my house in 30 seconds. Encre needed to be careful. The way he drives is insane, I don't like to ride with him, but a walker can't be choosy. Encre turns the music down.

"You want me to come back later. Maybe Big Walt will reconsider, it is Christmas," Encre asked. Maybe he would, I thought.

"Yeah, do that for me Big Boy. Because if he does, we can go over Carlos' house,". I answered.

"Cool nigga"! Was all he said; then his tires peeled off, and his music went all the way back up. Big Boy is a fool wit it. I walked up my driveway and up the steps. I could hear the phone ringing before I opened the door. When I opened the door momma and daddy were just sitting there looking wired, just letting the phone ring.

"Why y'all looking crazy? Why y'all just letting the phone ring? Don't even worry about it, I'll get it," I said.

"Boy, don't touch that phone, you need to come in here and sit down, we need to talk," daddy said. My heart started pounding like I was having a heart attack. He didn't sound mad at all. He sounded serious, somewhat sad. This scared me to my core. Had the cops been here? Has that cold summer finally caught up with me this winter?

"Whatcha wanna talk bout? I ain't did nothing. I ain't been nowhere but at the park since one O'clock till now, and it's almost six". I answered; before they even asked.

"Boy, come sit yo ass down. Ain't nobody said you did shit this time," daddy said. The phone had stopped ringing, then started right back. I sat down across from them and thought how strange is this shit.

"Well, what's this all about? I'm hungry, and somebody needs to answer the phone," I said. For some reason, I was getting nervous again. Then he said it.

"Your friend, the one you always get in trouble wit got killed earlier today," he said. I was in a little shock at first. I get in trouble with all my friends, but Black, we just get high. I stood up.

"What? Who got killed, Junebug? Man, don't tell me that! I told that boy dem Miami Boyz was gonna get him killed. That's bad, real bad, and I ain't seen him in a minute. I better go see...." I said before daddy cut me off. "Rod, it ain't Junebug," he said. That was a relief, but if not Junebug, who? "Who is it then? Just say his name...." I screamed. I was with most of my friends all day. Everybody, but....."Carlos Evans, voodoo Bob's son. He got run over, riding his brand new motorbike," he answered. My rode dog, my ride or die nigga is dead. This nigga family can raise the dead, so how can he be dead? I don't believe this.

"That's a lie," I snapped, looking my father in his eyes, hoping he would laugh, and say he was joking. His eyes told me the truth, my friend is dead.

"Rod, listen son, Carlos is dead. At least 50 people done called here looking for you to tell you the same. I'm sorry for your loss, but remember we were all born to die. We can rush our way to it, that's what these people are doing. The Devil is a lie, after he deals the cards, he tells you it's do till you die. They sacrificed this for that and that for this and that's what they get," daddy said. Why would he say that at a time like this?

"That's blasphemy!!! What do you mean that's what they get? You don't know shit. You not God," I said. Before I knew it, daddy jumped in my face like he'd been sitting on a giant spring.

"I know imma bout to kick the shit out of you, I know that nigga. Watch yo motherfuckin' mouth, you hear? I don't give a fuck if Jesus came back, and these crackers killed him again. You talk to me like that again and Imma crucify yo ass nigga," daddy yelled. Spit flew in my face, and veins popped out of his neck.

"Oh God, Jesus, forgive them both God they are lost. The devil is a lie. Help them Jesus, help them Lord. The devil is a lie. Help them Jesus, help them Lord. The devil is a lie, help them Jesus help them Lord," momma chanted with her bible in hand and rocking back and forward, like she was about to catch the Holy Ghost.

"Woman shut the fuck up! I'm trying to talk to my boy. Get out of here wit that shit," daddy growled. Momma stopped rocking and put her bible down.

"Who you telling to shut the fuck up? You long lip mother fucker, fuck you. I ain't going nowhere. You go back to hell nigga, cause you the devil nigga," momma went off. I think that's where I got my temper.

"Bitch don't make me slap the shit out of you," daddy snapped back.

"I wish you would nigga! You gonna pull back a nub nigga, and Imma feed yo hand to them damn rats in the backyard," momma threatened, but I knew it to be a promise.

"Don't make me fuck Christmas day up," daddy warned. I knew momma wouldn't stop.

"As long as you are alive, Christmas will be fucked up for me.

So die you drunk mother fucker," momma ignored the warning. That started a big curse off. I had heard it all before. If words really did hurt, the both of them would've been dead. I walked off to my room. The phone was still ringing, and momma and daddy were still cursing. I laid back on my bed and answered the phone.

"Hello? Rodney man where you been? You know bout Carlos," Willie James asked. He was crying, and that made me cry.

"Yeah, I did man, so it's really true," I asked.

"Carlos is dead. A van was backing out of a driveway ran him all the way over. The tires went across his chest. Our partner gone for real," Willy cried out.

"I gotta go, Willie," I said before I broke down and cried uncontrollably. When I closed my eyes all I could see was Carlos' smile. I covered my head with my pillow and cried. I thought about all the times we had together, and I just cried.

THE BIG GAME

I cried a hundred nights after Carlos died, and I don't think I was the only one. Brown High would never be the same, and it hadn't been. Football season was over, so school was extra boring for me. The only excitement at Brown High these days was our undefeated basketball team. We are 13-0 and tonight is the big game against our biggest rival, Booker T. Washington High School. Washington is only three miles from Brown, on the other side of Harris Holmes. Half of the kids in Harris Holmes go to Washington and half go to Brown. Brown used to be an all-white school. Washington has always been a black high school. Dr. Luther King graduated from Washington. Brown had no real beef with Washington, just on the Basketball court. Everybody knows everybody. I haven't done any hanging out lately, so I'm looking forward to the big game. I put on the Adidas suit Carlos bought for me and headed to the school bus stop. It's Friday, the night of the big game. When I got back home, daddy said I can use his car to go to the game. I probably hang out in Oakland City with Black Corey and Bob because the game didn't start until six. Bobby and I just really started back kicking it after Carlos died. I don't smoke, no reefer he got unless I see him roll it up. Word is Bobby Clayton smoking off the can, but I haven't seen him do it. My niggas on Holderness said Bobby buys coke all night on the weekends. They think he's freebasing because he comes back to back. All night, but that's his problem. I have problems of my own. Since my cousin Brad moved in, all my habits have gotten worse, and my grades. Since it's the end of football season, school is just a place to go for a few hours, eat lunch, smoke a few J's, and come home. My daddy's number one rule is to come straight home from school, and today I did. Then I was gone again. I had to make it over Keisha's house before anybody else makes it home, I'm going to get my bone on, and off. I pulled into Cascade Cabana a little after four. I didn't see Shell's car. Shell is Keisha's aunt, and one of pimp Shawn's girlfriends. Keisha doesn't live on this side anymore. Niecy got them a house out in Riverdale Ga. Keisha didn't come to school today. I beeped her from school. She called back from Shell's house. All she said was, come over as soon as possible, and that I did. I walked up the steps and knocked on the door.

"Who is it," Keisha answered.

"It's me," I replied. The door flew open. She pulled me in, closed the door, locked all six locks, and put a chair behind the door. She went to the window and peeped out.

"You by yourself, Rodney," she whispered. She is acting too paranoid.

"Yeah just me and my hooked dick. Get naked, you know I'm going to the game," I said, then unbuckled my belt.

"You ain't even heard what happened, have you," she asked.

"Bout what," I asked.

"Bout Walt! It's been all over the news. He got busted in his house, the one around the corner from ours in Riverdale Ga. Seventeen keys in the wall, and a lot of money," she said, then walked over and peeped out the window again. Walter Lee Freeman is locked up.

"Wow! What about yo momma is she ok," I asked. I buckled my belt back and walked over and peeped out the window with her. This is big! Walt Lee is a major drug supplier. He's bigger than this city state, too.

"We don't know yet the DEA took her in for questioning, they are picking up everybody," she answered. I know it's the Feds. Only the Mob can beat the Feds, even though I know that. I feel so sorry for Keisha, she just doesn't know she may not see her momma for a very long time.

"Did Momma get caught wit anything," I asked. I was really concerned about Niecy. She's a very nice lady to me, but everybody doesn't see it that way. I know the Feds don't see it that way. The Feds are a drug dealer's worst nightmare, if they ever get you gone forever.

"Nawl she didn't have nothing on her. She was at grand momma's house when they got her". She answered; her grand momma lives on Cascade PL. Her family sold dope all around that house, but I guess everyone had gotten the word.

"That's good, but I gotta tell you the truth ain't shit good bout the Feds," I told her.

"That's what I been hearing. Tell me this Rodney, what is conspiracy," she asked. The only conspiracy I know about are murder conspiracies.

"Why you ask that," I asked her hoping her momma ain't got a nigga killed.

"Cause that's what the paper said that they left. It said she charged with conspiracy to do all kinds of shit. They charged her and about fifty other people with something called the Rico Act," she said. Wow! This is some Mob shit.

"Listen Keisha this is some real deep shit. Conspiracy is like if you call and tell I to kill a nigga and I do for you, by law it's just like you did it yourself, but I don't know how it works with dope. I think she's cool as long as she didn't get caught with nothing," I lied. If the Feds know your name you are fucked in the dope game. Keisha's life is about to change, but so will half of the city. The Feds just took a big bite out of crime.

"You think they just gonna let her go"? She asked; I could tell she wanted to hear the truth, but the truth just wasn't in me.

"Man shiiiit, yo momma will be home today. The Feds just gonna try to shake her up, but you can't shake no bitch that ain't never been shook, she's from the westside Keisha," I told her how I hoped it would be. The truth is the Feds can shake mountains, and on their scale Niecy was barely a rock.

"Oh, I love you baby, you're always so positive," she said. Then she backed her ass up to me, unbuckled her skin-tight jeans. She pulled them down, her panties and all. She took one leg out and bent all the way over hands on the floor, just how I like it. Ten good strokes, I came and was gone.

I pulled up in front of Bob's house. He lived one block from the bridge, and two blocks from Brown High, his momma and grandma lived next door to each other Bob and Corey Allen was sitting out front.

"The deadly dinosaur in da mutherfuckin house," Bob jumped up and said. Deadly Dinosaur is the nickname for my daddy car. It's a big green dented up 73 Caprice Classic 454, it runs good and just needs a muffler. These niggas don't care, they just want a ride, and get high and so did I.

"What up niggas? It's bout game time! Let's get it," I yelled out my window. They both jumped up at the same time.

"Let-let-let's do-do it nigga," Corey stuttered. He did that when he got hyped. They got in the car, Bob was always in the front, he pulled out a big bottle of E&J, and we called it easy Jesus. He passed it to me first.

"Nigga, I'm driving you crack it, and pour some that shit out for my nigga I'm still mourning," I said. Carlos haunted my mind. Why my nigga?

"Yeah! I feel you pimp shit will never be the same without Carlos," Bob said. Then cracked open the bottle and poured some out the window. I was driving over the bridge as he did it.

"Hell yeah! God bless the dead". Corey added; before I made it in the parking lot, we had three joints burning and an eight ball of coke passing. Corey was fresh out of Juvenile with a fresh bomb of cocaine, and a big fresh bank roll. We parked in the back of the parking lot, windows rolled up. Soon my daddy's car was full with half of the football team. We got as high as we could get, then off we went.

The game was packed standing room only, Washington on one side, Brown on the other, the two teams in the middle. I had never seen our gym this packed, and it seemed they were all looking at me, cocaine is a helluva drug. I caught up with my crew and sat back to watch the game. We are up by 7 with two minutes left until half time. Corey tapped me on the shoulder.

"Look at Bob over there, I think he calling us," Corey said. I looked in the direction he pointed, and Bob was waving his hand in the air, and yelling something we couldn't possibly hear. Then he waved his hand for us to come over. He was on the other side of the gym by the entrance. We got up and made our way through the crowd. We got a lot of what's up from people in the stands as we passed. Bob met us halfway with trouble.

"Ah Rodney man one of them pussy ass Washington High niggas keep trying to push up on Keisha. I heard her tell the nigga that her boyfriend is here, and she told the nigga yo name," Bob said.

"What the nigga say after that, Bob," Corey asked.

"He said fuck that lame and get wit the real thang," Bob answered. Bobby is a hype man, but I ain't never seen him in not one fight. Corey and I fight all the time, it ain't nothing to us. Bob is all mouth! I feel like all his respect comes from the fact he lives across the street from Sweet Pea.

"I don't believe that shit nigga where this bad ass nigga at? He better be able to fight," Corey replied.

"I don't need you to fight my fights nigga just get my back. Where dis nigga at Bob," I asked. My heart was beating fast, and the hair on the back of my neck stood up.

"There that nigga go, still right there rapping to yo hoe. Let's go smash dis nigga"! Bob said; I looked in the direction that Bob was looking, and there was Keisha talking to this shiny black nigga

I knew from Harris Holmes, but he didn't live there when I did. His name is Corey T, and I'm about to bust my fist with his face. Keisha looked up and saw me coming and tried to walk away.

"Nigga let my arm go! I told you I got a boyfriend". She fronted; she snatched her arm away and walked away. Corey reached out and slapped her on her ass, then looked me right in the eyes and smirked. I was headed right up to him. I was about to turn that smirk to a real painful frown. Then a very familiar face jumped in front of him.

"Rodney Brown how you been boy," Monte said. He used to live on Lucile across the street from the store, until they moved to the projects, now they say Monte is becoming a shot caller. I know his entire family, his momma Shell, we have always been cool. I see his black ass brother Quan standing next to him. I smiled and gave both of them some dap, and a one arm hug.

"What's up wit dis cat standing behind you, is he wit you," I said into Monte's ear as we dapped up.

"Yeah he wit me, you know that nigga. He from the hood," Monte answered. He wasn't looking at me, he was looking behind me, so I looked too. Bob had rounded up half of the school, and all of Oakland City. I didn't see not one smiling face, nothing but thug mugs. Now all eyes on me, all I gotta do is throw the first punch, and every nigga standing near Corey will get beat to sleep. Brown High is known for putting kids that wonder on to this campus into Grady Hospital. That can't happen now. I can't let Monte and Quan get beat down, that's out of the question, its rules to this shit.

"Swing nigga what the fuck you waiting on," Bob whispered at the back of my head. This nigga really thinks I'm a gofer.

"Ah Corey, you owe me one nigga, after dis game. You gotta knuckle up tonight. I love to fight. You know how we do it, Tay," I told them. Monte bowed his head in agreement. I turned and walked away. Bob was on my heels.

"Nigga why you ain't swing? All that talk shit ain't bout shit it's time to hit. You let that nigga grab yo hoe ass in yo face, and you ain't gonna do shit? You can't hang wit me no more nigga," Bob yelled.

"Nigga shut the fuck up! You ain't gonna swing on nobody, you never have nigga. I can handle my on shit, cause nigga I ain't bout to jump no niggas from my hood. It's gonna be a fight, but one on one only. I called that nigga out, he better answer the bell cause I done rung it. Tell that nigga Corey bout this one hitter, quitter," I said. I am hyped now.

"Tha-tha-tha nigg-nigg nigga bout to get knocked the fuck out," Corey said.

"Fuck dis game let's ride niggas. I know the way they gotta go," I told them. I headed for the front door. I was thinking ahead. I know the shortcut people from Harris Holmes use, because I use it. I backed the deadly dinosaur up in a parking spot in the apartments directly behind our football field. We called this shortcut the get high cut, because this is where we gather before the school bell rang, and after. All you do is keep straight, and you will end up in Harris Holmes.

"Listen niggas ain't no jumping dis shit gonna be one on one, but Corey if I slip nigga don't let me fall, that's all," I instructed. We were sitting in the car getting high, just waiting.

"I-I got you player. Jay just hit the nigga in the nose and get it over wit quick," Corey answered. He is one of the best fighters at the school, maybe it's because he fights all the time. I don't get in fights at school anymore, and that's because I'm a member of the varsity football team. We mi fi yo (me for you and you for me), so that way we all stay out of trouble.

"Man, it's three on three, that ain't no jumping. That's as fair as fair can get nigga. I don't like that fat funny eye's looking nigga, anyway. I remember him and his black ass brother they used to go to Brown. Fuck them niggas," Bob said. He can't even fight.

"I told you Bob man, one on one. No knife, no gun. These niggas from my hood dis side of the bridge nigga. You from the other side, I got this," I told him. Just then, three heads ducked under the hole in the fence that led to the parking lot.

"Here they come," Corey announced from the back seat. The windows were fogged up, but we could see. Bob opened his door first, ain't no turning back now. Corey and I followed, we all just leaned back on the car waiting for them to walk by. I know they could see us by now, but they kept coming our way.

"Ah Corey T. it's time for that one nigga," I said as they walked up. We were face to face. I got off the car and walked up to him.

"Man, I ain't trying to fight you over no hoe. We trying to go get us some money, that's all," Corey T. answered. I could see it in his eyes. He didn't want to fight at all.

"Nigga you ain't going nowhere! You disrespected my homeboy. Go head and slap that pussy Rodney, so we can go, he ain't gonna fight," Bob said, and the drugs didn't help.

"Put yo hands up nigga, foe I slap yo ass for real. I wanna fight fuck nigga come on," I bounced around a little like a boxer and yelled.

BAM! I smashed my knuckle into his nose. I could feel it crunch. He bent over, holding it. Blood sprayed all over his fresh white Stan Smith's. I was about to shoot him with a knee.

"Ah Rodney man let that shit go man? He ain't gonna fight you," Monte said. We looked each other in the eyes. Monte's eyes glow in the dark. I don't know what color they are, but like I told Bob, Monte ain't never had no beef with me. We have been super cool all our lives, before all the coke and money, we homies. He asked me to give the nigga a pass, so I gave him a pass. I just turned and got in the car, and so did Bob and Corey. I watched as the three heads walked on the way, one bent over. I felt kind of bad for him, because he didn't fight back. It's always best to fight back, if not you will have to fight all the time.

"Man, that nigga a puuuussy," Bob said. Corey didn't say a word. We rode around and got high for a few hours, I dropped them off, and went home and went to sleep.

RUN NIGGA RUN

The next day Encre and I were riding around in his beat up Cutlass bumping some Miami bass shit called The Two Live Crew. Music was a part of our lives, but this new rap music was different. It was telling us about things we were doing. Taking us places we hadn't been, rapping about things we thought were dreams. It's a calling, like an old African chant that stayed in the slave's ears, kind of hypnotizing.

"Big Boy turn that shit down? You know I really don't dig that bottom shit," I said. Bottom is just another name for Miami. We were riding down Campbellton Road doing about 80 miles an hour. With a 1000 small bags of cocaine, $25 each, and a big fat black 357 under the seat. Encre had come up fast, but I think he's still a worker. He's trapped out of Mechanicsville working for the Perry boys, Aaron and William, they move heavyweight. I know them both, but William (Paco) Perry, I know very well. We used to be in the same classes at Brown. He's a small guy, but not a coward. I always had his back at school, but he dropped out to become a slick, young, rich, boss hustler. I haven't seen him since, but I think he blows his horn at me sometimes riding by in something new and nice behind triple tents. I keep hearing my daddy say.

'Boy, that shit is all a dream.'

'Luther king had a dream,' I replied.

"He had.... He's dead," daddy says. I think everything we see was once a dream. It had to be imagined. When I played football, I would imagine hitting the QB before I did it, and it happened. Thoughts become things.

"Change then nigga! I'm driving bout to drop you off, anyway. Time for me to hit the trap nigga. Where you wanna go," Encre asked. He is very serious about his money. The music was down very low.

"Take me to Oakland City. Imma go over here and see what's up with Bob and Corey. You know I had to break a nigga nose last night at the game," I told him. Encre made the left on Oakland Dr. He was going so fast we came up on two wheels. I hope this car won't be the death of him.

"What? Who it was," Encre asked quickly.

"A nigga out of Harris Holmes named Corey T. You know the nigga," I asked. Encre face frown up.

"Ain't he a black ass nigga," he asked back.

"Yeah black as hell," I answered.

"Yeah, I know the nigga he working for them Miami Boyz. Me and Pig was scooping out a lick over there a minute back, that nigga was running to cars for them fuck niggas on Norcross. Be Careful my nigga cause, I don't know where you been nigga, don't fight no more, that's all they do," Encre said. Then reached under the seat and pulled that fat 357, and pointed at the front window like he was about to shoot.

"Man, fuck that nigga he ain't gonna shoot. He wouldn't even fight," I answered. We were passing by Plaza Lane.

"Exactly! What was the shit about," he asked, looking a little concerned.

"Keisha," I answered. His eyes got big, then he laughed.

"That lil slut? Nigga let me hurry and get you out of my car," Encre said, still laughing, but driving faster. He rode right past Bob's house. It was a small crowd standing out in front of it.

"Stop nigga right here. Later fool," I yelled. He hit the brakes one house up.

"Nawl nigga you the fool," he replied. I jumped out, and he pulled off, music banging and tires burning. When I turn around to walk back to Bob's house. Everybody looked like they were in shock. I mean, like I'm a ghost shocked.

"Oh, lord my God! Ya'll please get that nigga away from here, he gonna get all us killed," Bob screamed like a lady in church. He ran in his house and slammed the door. What the fuck is going on? I said to myself? Latonya, Otis Lowe, Lil-Tim, and Sweet Pea were all there. I could only see the backs of everyone's heads. But they all yelled the same thing, "Run Rodney!" I stopped, I was in shock.

"You better run for it nigga! Run for it! Run," Otis Lowe said. He took his shades off. What the fuck! I still couldn't move, I'm petrified.

"Run nigga or I'll kill you myself! Boom," Pea said. He really fucks with me, we been on licks together. I trust this nigga with my life, he my G. If he says run I got to run. He just shot in the air, like he's running away a stray dog. So I ran. I ran faster than the wind.

"Run Rodney Brown, run! Those men got army guns," LaTonya screamed at my back because I was already gone. I turned the corner and headed for the bridge. I ran across Donnelly without stopping to look for the traffic. Now I was on the bridge, running two steps in front of the wind. I'm running for my life. Running to the only place my legs will go. I hear a car coming fast behind me, no music, just a big motor is all I hear. Then I realize this bridge is a death trap. I can't jump over the side, it's a hundred foot drop. The car pulled up beside me. I was still running at full speed, eyes straight ahead.

"Get in nigga," a familiar voice yelled. It was the same voice that just ran me off like a dog, and shot in the air. It was Sweet Pea, driving his black Monte Carlo. I didn't know whether to stop and get in with the killer or keep running. It looks like I got money on my head.

"Get in nigga for I run yo ass over," Sweet yelled, then pulled the car on the curb in front of me. I opened the door and jumped in. Sweet Pea had his gun in his lap. He pulled off. The tires screeched.

"Rodney, man what the fuck have you done now nigga? These niggas gonna kill you nigga. Where are you going? I gotta get yo hot ass out my shit. How much you took from that nigga," Sweet asked. I was shocked.

"Took? I ain't took shit from nobody man," I answered. Sweet Pea looked at me like a dog about to bite.

"Nigga you ain't gotta lie to me! I know ya'll niggas still doing all that petty ass robbing. That nigga Corey T. say you took five grand in blow and money, and guess who shit it was? Da Miami Boyz. Nigga they coming to kill you bout that shit. Stay away from that nigga Bob! When them niggas draw down on that nigga he went to singing like a baby. He told nigga everything but yo address, but he said you be on Dill Ave. Where you going now," Sweet Pea asked. Wow! My life changed with one punch. Now I gotta stay alive. I need to go to the safest place I know.

"Take me to the Thunderdome," I answered.

"Where," Sweet asked. He looked confused.

"The West End Park basketball court," I answered. It's the safest place for me on this Earth. Da Miami Boyz got army guns, but they don't have an army. If they come anywhere near here with some guns asking about me, they're gonna make the 6 O'clock news. What people don't know about the Westend will get you killed. Like the West End Park is considered Holy land to the Muslims, and if you disrespect it, they will kill you. Pulling up at the park with guns asking about anybody out of the hood is a death sentence.

"You know, dem Muslims down there," Sweet asked. He looked surprised.

"Not all of them, but I know the ones that count," I answered.

"You know crazy Rico"? Sweet asked; we were turning off Lawton St. on to Oak St. the park is in sight.

"Yeah, I know Rico but he ain't Muslim. Just like me, we grew up wit these niggas. I'm cool wit everybody over here, dis my hood". I told him; the closer we got to the silver dome top of the basketball court. The more Kufi's we saw. I had Sweet Pea pull right across from The Muslim store.

"Ah! Money on ya head them niggas riding in a black Bronco, so keep it on a swivel, and if I was you, I wouldn't trust none of these nigga. Don't go around spreading this kind of shit, if you do you gonna draw flies. You dig nigga," Sweet said.

"Yeah, I dig, and good looking out," I told him, then jumped out the car, and ran down the hill to the basketball court. It wasn't that cold out today, and the sun was shining brightly. There were a few people walking around the park, but the basketball court was packed. I made it through the crowd and saw Jamil (Rap) playing a game of one on one against Rico. All the Ahi's are out to see this. It's at least fifty guns and ten AK-47s in this park right now, and I know who's holding them. I know where to step, because this park is full of landmines. Now I feel safe. I look around at all the familiar faces Muslims and coffers standing side by side.

SAFE

This is where I grew up and how I grew up. I was home! A heavy hand landed on my shoulder, I almost took off running.

"Rakil! Where you been hiding at homie, and why you jumping like that," Jamil said. He's Bosha's brother and just the person I'm looking for. He's only fifteen, but he's been putting in a lot of work, wet work.

"What's up, Aki? I was just looking for you, brother. I got troubles," I whispered as I gave him a hug. He's wearing a white dashiki with a white Kufi, but he is as black as the blackest night, and shorter than a tree stump. As we hugged, I could feel the butt of a rifle under his dashiki.

"Say no more, walk with me". Jamil ordered; as we freed ourselves from the crowd, so did two other younger brothers. They followed not too far behind. Once we were away from all ears, I told him everything. He only asked one question.

"Where this nigga Corey T. live Aki," Jamil asked. He looked me in the eyes like my preacher at church.

"I ain't got it, but think I can get it." I answered.

"You want dis nigga dead or do you wanna die, Rakil," Jamil asked. His black face frowned up. I don't know if I wanted Corey T dead, but I know I don't want to die.

"Well, I don't really know if I wanna kill dis nigga Ak, niggas gonna say it was bout a bitch," I tried to compromise. I'm trying my best to save some lives, and mine, but sometimes you can't save two lives at the same time. I know Da Miami Boyz are some gangsters, and gangsters kill. The UK's I know all they do is rob, sell guns, and kill. I should've said kill first because that's what they do. Even babies and all, even the dog. But I knew them all, before their first body, before their hands became bloody.

"Fuck what a nigga says. You trying to live to see another day, just find out where this nigga stay or just find out what street he slanging. We'll just ride by and hit 'em all up. This shit I'm shooting ain't no ducking, running or hiding. This baby here goes straight through a cinder block," Jamil said. He lifted his dashiki to show me a long rifle, with a knife at the end. It was wood grain, shiny like new. Just looking at it made me feel some kind of way. An AK-47 is killing people, it's not a hunter's gun. It's a military assault rifle, and these Aki's, at this park, carry them every day all day. The park has always been protected this way ever since I can remember, even before Wayne Williams. It's just been a changing of the guards.

"Damn! Now that's a real gun, I think I need to get me one," I said. It's strange how fast my life has changed. Yesterday I didn't have a worry in this world.

"Nawl, you don't need this. Just lay low and get me that info. On Bosha, I got you Rakil. And even if they get you, I got you in death, I'll get those niggas back before you buried. You my blood cuz," Jamil said and I believed him. I had to believe him. We all we got, blood in blood out.

"Dig that Akh and dig dis. Dem Miami Boyz ridin' around in a black Bronco looking for me," I told him. He reached under his dashiki and pulled out a big black walkie talkie.

"Alert alert BOLO for a black Bronco don't approach, just report. Copy," he said into the radio.

"Copy that,"

"Copy that,"

"Copy that,"

"Copy that,"

"Copy that,"

"Copy that," the voices all repeated, very organized and very ready to kill.

"You should just hang close until it gets dark," Jamil said I stopped walking.

"Aki I gotta go up on the block and find my nigga Lee. I gotta get me some kind of money now. I can't go back home with dis heat on me. I gotta get a bank roll, I gotta get a lot of shit," I said. I had a lot on my mind, and Lee is the only coffer I can tell this to, plus I need somewhere to live.

"Ok cool, but keep dis shit between you and Lee don't trust them other cats. They are pussy's and jive, you dig, don't worry it's an Ak on Holderness Street on watch at all times. He's got a radio and he just checks in frequently. I'll be down there later," Jamil said.

"Cool Ak! Later," I said. I gave him some dap and a hug, then I headed my way. On my way to another life on Holderness St, ain't no turning back. This is not what I wanted out of life, this is what life wants out of me. Sometimes life won't let you choose, because you have already been chosen. As soon as I made it to Lucile Ave. I saw about five or six police cars, I guess that's good for me.

"Ah Rodney, where you headed," William Poon said. He's standing across the street from me in the crack. The crack is the apartments directly across from the park.

"What up Will? I'm headed up the block, I gotta find Lee you seen him," I asked. Will waved his hand in the air for me to come over. I looked both ways and crossed over to him. He was standing on the steps that lead to the rooming house I joined.

"Nigga you can't go on the block. Do you not see them cops, a nigga just got shot," Will told me. Wow! "Who got shot," I asked. I was in total fear, I didn't know what to think. Had they already jumped out over here looking for me and shot one of my homies?

"JD got shot by big Keith Postell, but he busted the nigga back, in the ass. You didn't hear the shot," Will answered. I grew up with JD. James Davis is his actual name. Keith Postell is not from Holderness. Lee told me he's Shawn's bodyguard. But he's really from Dixie Hill somewhere. He wasn't sure. I've seen him with Shawn plenty of times. He's over six feet, maybe 250lbs, a big gorilla nigga. JD is about 165lb, but he got the heart of a giant! Niggas know not to try him. I already knew all the hood politics on Holderness. Who was with whom and who sold what where. JD is a renegade. He sells what he wants, where he wants. That's my nigga!

"Why that big ole nigga shot him? Why didn't he just fight him," I asked Will. He laughed.

"Fight? Where the fuck they do that shit at? Nigga dis ain't high school rules these niggas playing by kill or be killed rules. JD was short stopping again. They warned him bout that shit, and he thought dis shit was a game, until he heard that nine go bang," Will told me. He just doesn't know how to tell the truth correctly. So I had to go see for myself.

"I don't believe you nigga all you do is cap. Now you capping on niggas lives. Is the nigga dead? where he hit at," I asked.

"Got shot, he ain't dead, he'll make it. Probably end up with a shit bag, but it's better than having wheels for legs, or being dead," Will said. This nigga wouldn't stop.

"I'm gone man, you need to stop that cap shit, Will. Shit is real for real. You dig," I told him and started walking up the block to the yellow tape. Will was on my heels fast. We made it to the corner, squeezed our way through all the on-lookers, so we could get a look down Holderness. The cops had Holderness taped off from the top all the way to the blue house (Clarence trap house), it's an alley that runs beside it. We used to play there as kids. Now I hear it's a million dollar dope hole with one way in a lot of ways out, no double traffic.

This neighborhood is a maze, and I know every turn. I spotted

Lee and Shane down on the other side of the yellow tape. They were closer to the ambulance. All the hustlers from the blue house were on that side on the tape.

"Let's go. Will," I said, then I headed to one of the many alleys that runs behind the houses of Holderness. In one minute flat, we were on the other side of the yellow tape.

"Nigga how you know bout that cut," Will asked. He'd been living here for two years. This is where I lived my best life.

"Nigga I told yo cap ass. Dis my hood, as far as you can walk. Anywhere I walk, I know somebody. All the way to Dill nigga," I told Will as I walked up behind Lee and Shane. The paramedics had loaded JD onto a stretcher, his eyes were open, and he was talking to one paramedic. He didn't look as if he was about to die.

"Ah, Lee! What happened to JD," I asked. He turned and looked at me with a big smile.

"Rodney Brown, my nigga for real! JD gonna be cool, dis just some hood shit. That nigga Postel shot first, but JD stay strapped, hit him in the ass wit one, that nigga probably still running. Watch and see dis shit ain't over. Let's bail y'all," Lee said. JD was in the ambulance now. He looked to be in a lot of pain. They say bullets are hot, a gunshot gotta burn. Just another day on Holderness. The crowd dispersed. I guess the show is over for today, or is it? You never know how things may go. We all headed to the blue house with Lee leading the way. It had to be at least 15 of us, all hood niggas, but not all Holderness niggas. If selling dope is a religion that would make the blue house the church. We all climbed the steep front steps and loaded up on to the huge front porch. This was a sizeable house and like most houses on this block, I'd played in them as a kid.

"Ah man ya'll know got damn well all ya'll niggas can't hang out right here like dis. 12 bout to be hot as hell, the jump out crew gotta be on the way. Y'all gotta make it hot somewhere else. We bout to go in the house". Shane said; then knocked on the window. Shane had really changed from a shy kid to a serious drug captain. Only two people had more rank in the blue house, Monique the house Mom and Clarence Poon the kingpin and owner. Monique looked out the window, then opened it.

"What the fuck ya'll niggas think dis is momma's daycare? Shane gets these niggas off my porch now. You lame ass fool! You trying to get us busted". Monique snapped; I really didn't like hanging in the blue house. I'm like why hang around money that I'm not getting. Now things have changed fast. I got to get some money fast. Without Shane saying a word, most of the homies started walking away. Monique left the long window open, the one everybody used to get inside, she never let us in through the door. Will and Lee had already climbed in. I walked up to the window, Shane stood in front of me.

LET'S EAT

"**W**here you going, Rod? Ain't no pool shooting today, you need to be trying to get home shit hot over here homie come back tomorrow". Shane told me; any other day I would've just turned and walked away like everyone else did. Business is business!

"Let me in nigga! I gotta get at Lee on some business". I told him; Shane frowned and looked at me hard. It was still three or four homies lined up behind me.

"What business nigga"? Shane asked; with a lot of bass.

"It ain't none yo business nigga! Yo name ain't Lee. Let my nigga in that's family. Everybody else gets the fuck on, but Twon you can come in too". Lee said; he had his head out the window giving orders. I guess they didn't tell him how the ranking went. Shane just stepped to the side without saying a word. I put one leg in the window, duck my head, and I was in. Antoine came in right behind me, followed by Shane. He slammed the window and locked it. The blue house smelled like some good reefer, and seating on the couch in the corner was Monique. She was smoking a fat joint. Inside the blue house it was very nice, fully furnished. The room we were in had a big nice drop pocket pool table in the middle of the floor, chairs and couches all around. It was a big picture of Clarence over the mantelpiece, sitting in one of those African king chairs. He was draped up and dripped out, gold and diamonds on his fingers and neck. Behind him on the wall, the name Charles Disco written in pink. I'd seen pictures taken at Charles Disco, but not one blown up big like that. Will had a pool stick already in hand, and Twon was racking the balls.

"My next imma shoot you the ten Will," Lee said. We all loved pool and loved to gamble.

"Bet nigga get out the way Twon or shoot the ten," Will said.

"Shoot fat boy, I got you anyway," Twon responded. He took ten dollars off his bank roll and put it in the corner pocket. Twon had grown into a man child, big, red with cat eyes, but he always looked dirty to me.

"Ah, Lee I need to rap at you bout something," I said. He looked at me, then nodded his head towards a door.

"Follow me to my office homie". Lee said; I walked right behind him. I could feel all the eyes on my back. Lee led us in the room and closed the door behind us. Lee dove into the big king-size bed. It was easy to see that this is Monique's room, and he let me know.

"Tell me something good my nigga. You ready to get down ain't cha. Man, look at all this shit. Dis my bitch shit nigga! No cap my bitch got bricks, well maybe a half a brick, but that's rich for a bitch. You dig"? Lee bragged; but it was true. Anybody with nine ounces of coke in this city is rich. If you know what to do with it, and by what I can see she's on her game. Everything in this room is fit for a queen, but everything is never what it seems. Maybe she's a spider spinning a good web. I used to hear Skeeter say that, but now I know what it means.

"Lee I fucked up bad. I got money on my head, nigga jumping out with army guns," I told him. Lee sat up on the bed.

"Who? Dem Muslims, nigga I told you not to get too deep with them niggas they dangerous. But my nigga Rico, he run them niggas, so don't worry he'll make it right. I can make one phone call and square all this shit up," Lee said. He reached for the phone.

"Hold on Lee, it ain't the Muslims! I told you that shit there one love. Nawl them my homies, they will never disrespect," I answered. Lee looked puzzled, so I ran it all down to him. I told him every detail of the last 48 hours of my life. Lee smiled, and I saw a bling in his eyes.

"Imma tell you like a G told me. It's time to trap or die nigga. Fuck the Miami Boyz nigga. I know the tooth fairy, we can ride on them niggas tonight. One call, that's all. Dem phony niggas pussy and jive. The Miami Boyz turned that shit into Dade county, Florida. That shit ain't Harris Homes no more we call that shit Dade County. I've been seeing Corey black ass all the time up on Northcross. He's easy to get, but he's not yo treat. Dem Miami niggas the killers, one of them niggas will give you a double tap, and by tomorrow they will be back at the bottom of the map. Rodney man, tell me the truth. How much did you hit this nigga for," Lee asked.

"Lee on all I love, I didn't take one thang from that lame. It wasn't that kind of move G. That nigga cuffin on them folks and putting the shit on me". I answered; all the truth?

"Dig that pimp, but it don't change much of shit. He cuffin, but you can't blame him. He went back to them niggas wit a broken nose and said I just got robbed. Now they wanna know where dis bad ass nigga at. That nigga trying to get you wacked. Real talk. You done fucked wit some rich niggas. Yo daddy be in the County every day. They find out who he is: a dead man. You gotta get it together, but first you need some real cheddar. It's all over wit! So fuck all that petty robbing bullshit now you part of the pulpit let's eat nigga, church! Monique," Lee said excitedly. I wasn't all the way sure, but I couldn't choose. Monique walked in the door with a trail of smoke falling like a Choo-Choo train. She closed the door behind her. She wasn't beautiful, she was cute, and she wasn't fine, she was sexy. Butter pecan skin 5'5 with a bow leg stance, diamond rings on every finger on each hand.

"What's up baby, yall trying to hit this shit," she asked, holding the fat joint out.

"Hell yeah! and dig dis too. My nigga ready to get down, so put him on for me," Lee asked, with a big smile.

"What? Not Lil-Rod, I know his family. That nigga daddy will go nuts, and he knows that shit. I ain't trying to take no losses. Why you want to put him on so bad, he all you talk about you wanna get money wit, but you don't want chance yo shit," Monique snapped.

"Listen, baby I know dis some Heavy shit to just lay on you like that. But desperate times call for desperate measures. I can't get too deep wit it but my nigga life on the line. What the fuck bitch, you want me to work my nigga? Never that hoe you gonna give him the blow". Lee preached; this nigga is in rare form. It's like watching a scene from The Mack, but Lee was just 15 and I'm 16. We are ahead of the game. Monique looked at me and rolled her eyes, then looked at Lee, and gave a smile. Then she walked to the closet and pulled out a shoebox and put it on the bed.

"Nigga I pass out bundles 25 off a 100. You dig that, dis here is a dime sack power trap. Shit simple, I front you 25 sacks, you owe me $200, you keep $50. I got three rules, don't dip in my sacks, don't cap off my sacks, and whatever you do nigga don't get caught. Any questions," Monique said. She spoke like a real boss.

"How much we gonna start wit," I asked. I didn't care, I just felt I had to ask something, because everything she just said I already knew. Don't get caught, kept ringing in my head. Right now, getting caught doesn't matter. Maybe things would work out even better. I just need a little time for things to blow over, really.

"How much Lee, you the one co-signing dis nigga," she asked Lee.

"Don't treat him like no junky, start him off wit a 50 pack," Lee answered. Monique opened the shoe box and pulled out a big zip-lock bag. It was full of small pink baggies with white powder inside. She counted out 51 sacks and put them all in a Sandwich bag. Then tossed it across the bed to me.

"I gave you a plus one, seen a J to get what you need. You can't leave the blue house front porch, if you do give me my shit first. At night you can work the back door and get all the money, these nigga round here be clubbing. What about Big Walt? I don't need no heat up here, and I gotta still see how Clarence gonna react," she said everything I needed to hear. It wasn't anyplace that I wanted to go, but what about my daddy? I'm trying to save all our lives.

"Listen Monique don't you worry bout shit but giving dis nigga some blow. I got everything else". Lee told her; and that was that. Everything went smooth, smooth like a baby's ass. I almost forgot I was on the run from the Miami Boyz. I didn't even go on the front porch. That was Lee's plan. For me to just stay in the house, roll out the back door at night, and sleep all day. Lee told everybody I was tired of being broke. I'm hiding from my daddy, so I can get some money. And money I got, more money than I'd ever seen in my life. Monday morning I counted up my bank roll $1117.00, all my own money. I'd only spent money on weed and McDonald's, that's it. I didn't shoot any craps or play tonk, gambling is an all-day everyday thing around here. This is Paradise for a young hustler, but is this really going to be my reality? I love the sound of pool balls breaking, the sound of dice hitting against the wall, the smell of weed always in the air, and most of all the sound of the back door knocking. All of it, the smell and sounds of money. This is a very addictive environment, and not just for the junkies. I'm hooked already. All I want is money. I really feel higher than I've ever felt before, and I want to get higher. Lee walked into the room.

"Get yo ass up nigga! We gotta go before Clarence gets here. It's a school day, can't hang out here until after three. We can hang at McDonald's until it's time to eat lunch, then we can hit the catwalk and eat at school," Lee said. I didn't want to go anywhere, but I had to.

"Damn man I ain't took a bath or changed my clothes since Saturday," I said as I stood up and looked down at myself.

"Nigga fuck that shit you getting money now. We gonna hit the West End Mall today pimp it was a good weekend. Believe that,"

Lee said, then pulled out a bank roll three times the size of mine.

"Man, you think it's cool for me to be walking around here like that. I ain't trying to be playing dodgeball with bullets," I said; I still didn't want to leave the blue house.

"Don't worry bout it, we gonna take all the cuts. Plus I got dis, put it on, and I got dis," Lee answered. He tossed me a black Starter hoodie. Then he pulled a Nickel-plated pistol from his Waistband.

"Fuck yeah! Let me see that jack, what kind is it," I asked. Lee passed the gat. It was a Revolver, and it looked to be a 38. I opened it up. It was empty.

"It's a 32. Just like a 38.," Lee answered.

"Where the bullets? You should've been gave me dis. You don't know nigga, I'll bring homicide," I said. Lee opened his hand six bullets.

"Here they go, but I gotta get the firing pin fix for it to shoot," he explained.

"What the fuck nigga? I can't do shit wit dis, but get killed," I snapped.

"Give it back to me then nigga! I know what to do wit it," Lee said.

"What? Throw it at a nigga"? I asked; and burst out laughing, and so did he. As he put the pin less gun in his waistband. I loved Lee like a brother, but I would be lying if I said he was the smartest nigga I ever knew. But he is the coolest. I'd sold out of everything Monique had given me and cashed out. I told her I'll be back, but I really didn't know my next move for real. Lee and I left the house around 9:30 am. We weaved our way through the alleys and the cuts, and made it to McDonald's without our feet touching a main street. We both ordered the big breakfast with OJ, it really felt good to pay for both of our meals. I couldn't wait to pull out my big bank roll. Just to see the cute girl on the cash register smile, and that she did. I played like I didn't notice. I feel different now, it's hard to describe, but it's a powerful feeling.

They say money changes people, and it does because I feel changed. I feel born again, not like a church baptism, because all I felt was water then. This feeling is so addictive. I can still hear that backdoor doorbell, I never heard a better sound in my life.

We ate our food, when we finished up Lee gave the Manager $10 so we could chill there till lunch. We didn't want any trouble with a truancy officer. At lunch we can go to school and blend in, and so we did. We walked through the cuts smoking on a joint talking about how rich we were going to get. We both wanted Cadillacs, the big long Fleetwood's. Am I dreaming, if so, don't wake me up. We made it to the school and kicked it on the catwalk with the rest of the high school hustlers. I didn't see Bob or Corey at all. We ate lunch then walked up to the smoking cut. The same cut I punch Corey T. out in. We hung out with the rest of the class cutters and smoked a few joints. I was waiting for the last bell so I could catch the school bus home. When it sounded we all walked back down to the school. Kids were everywhere, going all different ways. Lee and I went inside up to the second floor to look out the window that was over the bus parking lot.

"Rodney Brown! Imma gonna call Karen and tell bout all that trouble you in," a familiar voice said. It was Latonya, the same voice that said run, they got army guns. We have been friends for a long time, she's a Jaguarett, one of the dancers in the marching band. The Jaguaretts are the finest girls in the school. My sister Karen was a captain when she went to Brown, now she trains the squads, all the girls know her. Now she's a Bubbling Brown Sugar for Morris Brown College, marching band dance group.

"Latonya, baby be cool, I got all that shit straighten out," I said. I didn't want her to call Karen.

"I hope so! Hey Sam! Rodney just be careful," she said, then turned and walked away. She is a very fine young lady, beautiful inside and out. Everybody loves Latonya.

"Hey LaTonya! I want to fuck you, LaTonya," Lee mumbled. He didn't say the second part loud enough for her to hear. He wouldn't disrespect something so sweet. We continued to look out the window for my bus to pull in. The buses were lining up, waiting for the students to load up.

"Ah, Lee. Lee," Will screamed; from a ways down the hall. He was running towards us.

"What nigga? Why are you screaming my name like that," Lee asked him. Will ran right up to us, shaking his head and pointing his finger at me.

"Lee you better get away from this nigga! Look down there the Miami Boyz up here looking for Rodney Brown. They passing out money for you nigga," Will said. He wasn't capping this time. I looked down on the crowd and spotted them fast. Three of them. They all had on brown Dickie suits and Chuck Taylors. All three blacker than the other with gold teeth. The blackest one had a white fishing hat on and he was talking to Tara Peterson, and she was all smiles.

"Nigga fuck the Miami Boyz we Holderness St. niggas. If you scared Will, get the fuck on," Lee snapped.

"I ain't scared, they ain't looking for me. They looking for dis petty ass jack boy, that's why dis nigga been hanging around the hood. Now you wanna be a dope boy! Negro please you need go back to Dill before you get all of us killed", Will said. Will doesn't like beef at all.

"Shut up, Will. Look at that nigga in the white fisherman's hat right there," Lee said. That guy looked familiar, and we could see the Diamonds on his fingers and wrist from here.

"That's Convertible Burt, that nigga don't drive shit unless the top drops. That's the big boss he passes out weight all over dis city. If he ain't got it ain't none to be got. You know you done fucked up right"? Will explain; he was right, it was Convertible Burt I knew of him. I even saw him up close before. He's just a dope fiend away from me. My daddy is all the way in Harris Homes. One day we were parked out in front of our cousin's house. Ms. Ann's apartment is in the horseshoe. Daddy told me

195

to wait in the car, as I sat a brand new Mercedes-Benz pulled right in front of our car. I couldn't tell you what color it was, because it seemed to change colors, and it's a convertible. I've really fucked up this time. This man is a real rich nigga. I was feeling ill. I wanted to go home so bad, but that was impossible. Daddy and momma had to be worried sick, but all the spies on Holderness had sure given him the scoop.

"Fuck all dis sightseeing shit I'm gone," I said. I put my hood on and headed off.

"Where you headed, dog," Lee asked.

"I'm going to see the Ak's, I gotta buy a strap. Fuck them niggas, if I see them, imma shoot first. Then Imma go back to the blue house, imma lay low, and creep for a while. Now I gotta get me some money nigga, I ain't never getting full." I said; without even turning around. I walked up the hall like nothing was wrong. I didn't know my future. I just wanted to stay alive. One thing I knew for sure. I had graduated in more ways than one. Once I step out of this school today, I'll never step back in.

"Let's get it! Nigga I'm wit it," Lee screamed. He seems not to have a care in the world, and I think it's starting to rub off on me.

"Ah Lee you gonna let dis nigga get us killed," Will asked, as he caught up with us.

"Will stop all that cap shit! Let's go just keep yo eyes peeled if you wanna live," Lee told him. Will follows Lee's commands, and we began our way back to the hood using different cuts and alleys. We ended up in the back of Shane's momma's house. Everybody knew Shane had plenty of guns, he hung with the Tooth fairies, they sold all the guns on this side. I knocked on his back window.

"Ah Shane," I yelled but not too loud. The window slid up in seconds, and Shane's big black head came out of it.

"What's up wit yall cats," Shane asked, looking a little puzzled.

"Come outside man I need to holla at cha Boo on some business," I asked; as nicely as I could.

"What? Nigga you been rolling for a bitch for bout five days, now you trying to holla at me bout some business? Scam nigga," Shanny Boo snapped. He was closing the window.

"Nigga bring yo big dumb ass out here we need ya". Lee told him; the window slammed down, and a second later the back door opened. Big black Shane came out looking as mean as can be.

"What the fuck ya'll niggas want? For real now! What's the business," Shane asked, looking at me.

"I need a strap bad! Miami Boyz want me dead. Dem niggas got money on my head," I told him. Shane gave me a double take.

"What the fuck? The Miami Boyz? How? Why"? He asked; I ran it all down to him the way it happened.

"Wow nigga you really know how to jump all the way in the game! Money on my nigga head. Well, tell them pussy Boyz it ain't enough. What y'all wanna do? We can get a hot box and creep on them niggas tonight. I got enough gats for everybody to be double strapped, all we need is a good hot box,". Shane said. He was ready to kill, just like that. Shane had been hanging with the Muslims a lot, and I could tell.

"Let me buy a gat from you because I gotta stay strapped," I begged him.

"I'll sell you a gun, but that ain't gonna solve shit. All those niggas already strapped Rod, they hunting you. We gotta gone and bring them niggas homicide, before they bring it to you, or us now that you hanging back in the hood. Now you getting money shit really get easy. You know who do the wet work round here. $500 flat fee, any nigga you want dead we can get him dead, and I'm talking a clean kill. We tryna bust dis Ak's cherry right now anyway, we can send him on a knock and pop find out what number his momma lives in." Shane said; he was dead serious. A knock and pop means a hit man knocks on your door and shoots whoever answers in the face. Shane is another insider like me; he's seen a man breathe his last breath more than once. He knows like I know he doesn't want it to be him. Death is unknown! I don't know where we will go when we die. No one does. I do know I don't want to find out any time soon. I'll think about the afterlife when I'm dying, right now I'm living my best life. I don't want to die, and I don't want to kill anybody, but don't push me. I'll eat your face, I love revenge more than I love pussy. Shane is a killer! The kind that will help bury a body, and go to dinner after. Lee got the heart of a lion but the purr of a cat, that hasn't got to kill his first rat. As for Will... blood will never touch his hands unless you force his hand.

"Yeah Shane show you right, but got a card in play. I need a gat right now please man"! I begged;

"Ok then nigga what kind you want? Better yet what you got on it"? Shane asked;

"I want one that's gonna shoot, not too big so I can stay strapped, not too hot, I don't want a body on it before I even shoot it. I got $200 for something like that". I said;

"Dig that I'll be right back"! Shane answered; he went back inside the back door.

"Nigga if I was you, I would buy an AK." Will said. Was he capping? Sometimes it's so hard to tell? Will tell so many lies, he's like the Lil-Boy who cried wolf.

"Hell yeah I just put in an order, just waiting on the next gun show. Brand new AK-47 is $750 wit two banana clips. Then let them monkey niggas trip," Lee said. He rubbed his hands together as he talked. The back door opened up. Shane came out with a big green duffle bag on his shoulder. He put it down in front of me, then reached inside.

"Aight, check dis out Rod, I got two gats you can choose from. This a 38 Special, I gotta have $250 for it. It don't drop shells, it got a ham guaranteed not to jam, but only five shots. Now dis baby, 380. You can give me $200, it holds eight in the clip and one in the hole. You gotta keep it clean or it'll get you killed". Shane explains; He's like a real live arms dealer, well I guess he is.

"Sell me this mutherfucker right here, big Boo," Will asked, pulling out a long gun. It was some kind of rifle.

"Nigga give me my shit before you shoot somebody. My shit stayed loaded wit one in the head fool. You play too much," Shane snapped. He snatched the gun from Will and hung it over his shoulder by the scrap.

"I want the 380. How much for the rifle," I asked as I handed over $200. Shane stuffed it in his pocket, then handed over my new best friend.

"Dis 223 ain't for sale nigga dis for the hood. Dis for any nigga set tripping, but I can get you one. Now go head bust yo gun cause ain't no refunds. I got some more bullets". He said; so I pulled the trigger and let off all nine shots. Shane emptied a 30 round clip in the air. Gave me a box of bullets, smiled and went in the house. We headed to the blue house like three young men going to work.

We shot pool and rolled dice every day and every night. I didn't leave the house for anything. When Clarence came over during the daytime when I'm supposed to be in school I hid in the Attic. Today is Wednesday. I called Daddy yesterday and told him I was ok, and I would be home soon. All I could hear on the other end was a lot of cursing. He rides up and down, Holderness more than the cops. On Friday, I plan on going home to have a real face-to-face talk with him. I have another good problem, too much money and nowhere to put it, so I had to go home and hide some. I got over $10,000, 5 pairs of shoes, 7 or 8 outfits and a pistol. I can't have everything I got, all on me, all the time, living in a drug house. I haven't been hustling long, but long enough to know better than that. Everybody else in the blue house goes home every day and stash their money and valuables. On Friday, the school is having a dance after the basketball game. That's all the talk I've been hearing around the house. Everybody's going shopping for the party, including me, but I'm not going to the party. Words are the Miami Boyz are still hanging around Brown asking about me. That's bad and good, because at least they are not looking on Dill Ave. or Holderness St. I don't plan on ever stepping foot inside of Brown High again, so they can keep on looking there.

THE AMBUSH

On Friday my plan was set. After shopping at the West End Mall with Lee, Shane, Twon, and Will, Lee dropped me off at Junebug's house. He was driving Monique's Cadillac. I can't pull up at my house with all these brand new shopping bags. Plus, I was showing out a little, and it wasn't dark yet. Never know who's lurking. I'd called ahead, so I knew he was home. I got out of the car, bankroll fresh, 380 inside my Guess blue jeans. Junebug had to hear a car or was just looking out the window, because he came out the door.

"What up Lee and the Holderness St. Boyz ya'll headed to the party? I see you wanna drop dis heat off first, huh," Junebug said as he walked up to the car.

"What up Bug look like you gaining weight," Lee asked.

"Hell yeah nigga I'm getting fat, but take yo eyes off my pockets,"! Junebug said to Lee with a smile.

"Nawl, Bug man. We ain't strong arming no more we getting money on dis end nigga. Fuck yo pockets, I got pockets, I'm talking bout yo fat ass stomach. You already ugly you ain't gonna never get a bitch so you better get rich," Lee snapped.

"Aight, we gone! Let's go Bug, I gotta show you something pimp," I instructed. Junebug didn't want any trouble with the crew in that car. Things could get ugly fast, because Junebug never backs down, and he can play the dozen better than all of us. He'll make you want to fight, but he can't fight.

We went inside; I showed off all my new toys. Then we got so high we could feel the world spinning. I got the cleanest coke in town for days and the best Sesamelia for months. Niecy and her daughter Pea-Pea came home. Made me wish Junebug wasn't home, but I missed him and we had to catch up.

"Yeah, Rodney man, that's some wild shit. Don't stop now gone and get rich quick. Don't look back on them niggas planning. You know I love yo daddy like he mine, but fuck big Walt for now. Dis shit bout Rich Rod pimp. You break bread right, everything will fall just right, watch. Dis shit like going to Church, pay yo tides, if you want yo blessings. Here you go, my nigga. I told you I was gonna get it for you. Dis everything you need to know to whack that Joe. Where he lives, all the color and cars he drives. When he clocks out and when he clocks in, I got the nigga work schedule for you, my nigga," Junebug said. I took the piece of paper and looked at it. Everything I need to clock my problems out for good, now I just have to figure out the best way to do it.

"I'm digging dis! It's on point pimp! I know you ain't no Dade County dick sucker for real. You just served dis nigga ass up on a silver platter"! I bragged; Junebug was my main man, but they say money changes friends. He works for the same niggas that want me dead. I'm worth money, but I knew Junebug would never cross me for a couple bucks.

"Man! I'm so glad you getting money now. I prayed to the pimp Gods for dis shit. Pimp pimp hooray!! Real niggas get money every mutherfuckin day. You still gotta lie low and creep for a while. Get yo self-war ready, cause dig dis pimp! Dem niggas already war ready," Junebug explained. War ready? That's why Shane got a bag of guns that nigga war ready. I got to get war ready in a hurry!

"Listen niggas I don't wanna hear shit bout no murder. Give me some of that dope, Rod. Imma go in my room and get high," Niecy asked. She was really begging.

"Bitch please! That's a base head move, you might as well go on hoe cause you ain't cooking none of this good blow," Junebug snapped. It's about to get ugly in here fast.

"Who da fuck you calling a bitch? I got yo bitch buster! Dis ain't yo blow nigga! Rod don't work for you! He's his own boss! You work for the Miami Boyz nigga. You one of them Dade County dick suckers. Nigga you a fag, all you need is a wig bitch! Now like I was saying, I don't wanna hear dis shit give me my sack Rod. You know I got you," Niecy snapped back. She was up and out of her seat. Her lil girl Pea-Pea on her hip. Junebug just sat there in his seat. With that permanent Joker smile on his face. All 100 of his teeth showing. I had to defuse the situation.

"Here you go, Niecy. Now let me hold Pea-Pea". I told her. She snatched the blow, dropped Pea-Pea in my lap, and she was gone. Pea-Pea is only three, and she stays true to her name as always her Pamper was wet. Junebug and I started a game of head Tonk, $10 a hand. It didn't take long for me to get into his bank roll it's around 9:30 pm. The radio was all the latest jams, Public Enemy was on now.

"Man, fuck these cards! Let's shoot some dice! I need to get my money back! Put down nigga," Junebug demanded. He pulled the dice out of his pocket and threw them on the floor.

"Nigga I ain't shooting shit! You want yo money, back deal the cards. If not, I'm gone. I ain't gonna let you jank my money, Jack," I told him. I leaned back on the couch, Pea-Pea jumped in my arms ready to play.

"Nigga you better put that baby down and put my money down," Junebug demanded again. He stood up and reached in his back pocket.

"Fuck you! I ain't putting shit down," I answered. I looked at him like he was crazy. Then he pulled out his 22.

"You ain't gonna put my shit down nigga? Give all that shit up then," he answered.

"Nigga stop playing wit that pistol! Have you lost yo cotton picking mind, fool! You too high nigga. I'm gone," I snapped.

Junebug got a problem playing with guns, and I will not be his accident.

"Ole scary ass nigga! You know I'm just bullshitn', I ain't gonna rob yo punk ass! I took the bullet out! This shit ain't loaded! See. Bang," Junebug rebutted. Then pointed the gun in my direction and pulled the trigger. The sound was deafening. I grabbed my chest, dropped the Pea-Pea couch, and fell to the floor. I heard the gun fall to the floor beside me. Pea-Pea is crying, Niecy screaming and cursing, and I smell gun smoke. I'm lying face down on the floor, both hands under my body.

"Junebug, what the fuck you do that for boy? Why you shoot Rod? Is he dead," Niecy screamed.

"I didn't do that! It was an accident. He shot himself," Junebug lied. Wouldn't you?

"Turn him over to see if he's dead or if we can help him," Niecy demanded. Junebug reached down and tried to turn me over. I grabbed his hand.

"Nigga get yo hand out my pocket! I ain't dead nigga, but Imma bout to kill you," I said. I flipped him over on the floor and jumped on top. Now I'm sitting on his chest with my 380. Barrel pressed to his nose.

"How many times I gotta tell you bout playing wit guns nigga? I should blow yo big ass nose off. What if you would've shot Pea-Pea, you dumb fuck? You could've killed either one of us," I yelled. The bullet had to miss us by inches. At first I wasn't sure if I was hit or not, but I didn't feel any pain, or smell any blood, just gun smoke.

"Shoot that bitch right between his eyes Rod. That nigga could have killed my baby," Niecy screamed. She was standing behind me. Pea-Pea was still screaming and crying. I love Junebug, but he's just a stone-cold idiot. I stood up off of him.

"Nawl, I ain't gonna kill this idiot! He gonna end up killing himself," I said. Then I got my things and headed for the door.

"Man, I'm sorry. I thought it was empty. The rest of the bullets in my pocket. See Rod! It was an accident! Let that shit go! Ain't nobody even get hurt," Junebug pleaded. I walked out the door and slammed it behind me. I began my short walk home, but somehow it seemed so long. I'd only been gone a week, but it seemed like months. What would I say to my daddy face to face? The only thing I could think of is the truth. They say the truth will set you free, and I'm ready to be free. I made it to the driveway. The deadly dinosaur was resting in its spot. I walked up, counting each step as I went. At ten I was at the top. I walked to the door and twisted the knob. It was open, and I stepped right on in, momma and daddy eyes were glued to the small television in the corner. They both turned and looked at me at the same time. Momma fell to her knees. Even daddy looked to the heavens.

"Thank you, Jesus! Thank you, Lord! Thank you, Jesus! Thank you, Lord! Thank you, Jesus! Thank you Lord," momma sang as loud as she could.

"Thank you, Lord! Thank you, Jesus for bringing my son home safe. Thank you, Lord, for bringing Rod home safe. Lord, I pray for the families whose kids got shot down like dogs tonight on that bridge, Amen," daddy prayed. I never heard him pray like that in the open. Momma was on her knees singing to God. This is like a scene out of the Twilight Zone. That's when I read the breaking news on the TV set. It read 4 shot, 1 dead on a bridge leaving a party at Brown High. Then Monica Kaufman appeared on the television set.

"I have tragic news to report tonight. High school students leaving a party tonight at Brown high, were the victims of what early reports are saying, was a drive-by shooting. The students were trapped on a 50-foot high bridge with nowhere to run. One dead, two shot, names of the victims have not been released yet. I'll have more at 11:00pm," Monica, the news reporter said. 2 shot and1 dead on Brown High's Bridge. My body trembled and my hand started to sweat.

"Boy, we thought that was you! My God is a good God! We know you got the Devil on yo back right now but with prayer we can get him off you," daddy pleaded. I didn't hear a word he said. My mind was racing like a bullet, about to hit the target.

"I gotta use the phone! I gotta see who got killed"! I said; I walked over to the phone, hands shaking, tears already running. I knew who ever got shot, I had to know them. I also knew who ever got shot by the bullets were named for me. I picked up the phone and dialed the blue house.

"Hello," she answered on the first ring.

"Monique what's going on? Who got killed at the school," I asked.

"Rod boy, I'm so glad you didn't take yo ass to that party. Some niggas trapped Lee them on the bridge and opened fire wit an AK-47 or some kind of rifle. Lee just called me from homicide. They got him down there, said he had a damn gun. They shot Lil-Jamie in the foot, shot some nigga name Moon Pie in the ass, Kasey G got in the back and them coward niggas murdered that poor little innocent girl, blew her brains out," Monique explained. Lee is at homicide for a gun, I wonder why my crew walked that way. That's the way to OC Lee and Jamie lived the other way.

"What girl? What's her name? Tell me her name," I begged. I'm feeling kind of light-headed.

"Tonya or Latonya. Something like that. I know Lee said she from OC stayed across from Bobby," Monique answered.

"Latonya," I cried out.

"Yeah that's her. Did you know her," she asked. I hung up the phone. My God!!!!!! I dropped to my knees and put my head on the floor. All my life I've been taught to pray, so I did.

"Lord my God, please let this all be a dream. Please, Lord. Take it all back. Take back my punch! Take back the money, Lord my God take it all back. Take back the bullet that hit Latonya in the head. Put it back in the barrel, back in the chamber, back in the clip, please Lord. She didn't deserve that, but I do. I'm the sinner of sins. I'm the one that deserves to die before my life begins. Deliver me from this nightmare, make everything right, make everything fair. Amen," I prayed. I opened my eyes and lifted my head. Nothing had changed. I could still feel the money in my pocket, and the pistol on my waist. Then Latonya is still dead, in a cold place. That's not fair, they say my God is a kind man. What kind of man can see this kind man? This is a tragedy, and her blood is all over me.

"Run Rodney Brown, run! Them men got army guns," I could still hear her screaming at me. She was trying to save my life that day, and maybe she did.

FACTS

My life is at a crossroads, and I have no idea which way to go, but I know I can't stay here. I walk out of my house without saying a word. Just me, my pistol, dope and money, I had to make it to Holderness Street, so I walked from Dill Ave. I walked, and I prayed, but not how I used to pray, and not to who I used to pray to. Lee told me all the rich hustlers pray to the Pimp Gods, not that white Jesus on our momma's walls. Lee thinks all Religions are old con games.

"If we believe in God what the fuck all the guns or for. Why God kept us in slavery? Why grown men rape lil babies? I believe in the devil. Nigga God is a maybe. Round here I see way more evil than good. We living in Babylon Nigga, these bank roll in our pocket, this dope under our nuts, and that steel on your hip. Nigga we are Gods. Men have been making themselves God's since the Beginning of time, and that's what we're gonna be. But nigga you can't pray to Jesus and get all your money from the devil. That's why I pray to the Pimp Gods," Lee told me. I thought he was crazy now I get it. That's why I'm on my way to the blue house, I'm on my way to church.

I made it to Holderness around 2AM, but people were walking around like it was 12 noon. Walking around like zombies, all heads down, eyes searching the ground. Looking for dope as if it's just gonna fall from the sky. The Blue House was still up. I could hear the bass from the music and smell the reefer from here. I started up the steps before I made it to the top. I heard a Familiar voice from somewhere in the dark.

"Soft or hard how many you want," Big Will whispered. I just kept walking up and sat down on the front steps. Wil stepped from behind the big tree in the yard. He had on an all black dickie suite, with a shiny Nickel plated 357. in his hand.

"Nigga next time you better say a hootie-whoo or something. I know you done heard niggas doing drive-by on innocent kids. They left that pretty, fine ass, young girl wit her brains hanging. My God, who would do some shit like that"? Wil said; first time I ever heard him sound so real and serious.

"They don't know who did it," I asked quickly. I'd hoped that they did, and they were already dead or in jail.

"Yeah, they say they do, but they ain't got 'em yet. Dig dis! They say the killers from Mays High ain't no killers like that at Mays, Lee used to go to Mays, he knows dem niggas," Will answered. He was hyped up now.

"Was you there, Will? Did you see it," I asked. I wanted all the details I could get.

"Hell nawl nigga! I was right here, but I heard the shots. They were shooting something real big, some real war guns. Like the Muslims, and project niggas got, and we got one too. Shane ain't show it to you? But boy now it's time to strap up for real on these fools, and I no the nigga wit all the tools. I know Shahid the real Shahid. He one of Jamil bodyguards that nigga sell Grenades, grenade launchers, bulletproof vests, but all I want is that Wood grain AK-47 he selling. It got a knife on it and two 30 round bananas for any donkey that wanna act monkey," He answered. Yeah, I had a feeling Shahid will sell a lot of guns soon.

"I wonder why they got Lee at homicide," I asked.

"I don't know, man. When I got to the Bridge Lee was already in the backseat of a cop car. I heard niggas saying Lee had a gun, but he didn't shoot so he should be good, and they say them niggas was shooting at Lee and Bobby. Both of them nigga at homicide," Will answered. I hope that nigga Bobby doesn't snitch and put my name in it. I know Lee is keeping it solid. Bobby, I don't trust dude and never will again.

"Man, I'm worried bout Lee! What if they charge him for all that shit? You know what I mean? On That trying to get a mutherfucker to tell shit. Nigga believe me, somebody gotta pay for this! That sweet girl ain't did nothing to nobody! Fuck jail! Whoever did that need a AK killing! You dig," I said. I was trying hard to hold my tears, but when I saw the tears going down Wil's face. Mine soon followed.

"Rodney man, it was so much blood on the Bridge. I'm goin' in for the night, I can't focus on nothing but that," Will said. Then I headed for the front door, and I followed. A lot of blood on the Bridge, but it's going to be washed away. I can never wash the blood from my hands, they can only get more red. We climb through the window and into the house. Will and I were the only ones inside the living room; everyone else must have been out or in one bedroom. Wil took a couch, and I took a couch, and we both were soon asleep.

Bang-bang-bang-bang! The front door was shaking from somebody knocking so hard.

"Atlanta Homicide, open up now," Lee's voice said. My heart slowed back to its normal beats. Will and I jumped up and ran to the window. Lee was smiling, his vibrant smile. We opened the window and jumped out onto the front porch, the front door never opened at the Blue House.

"My nigga don't scare me like that! I thought you was a gonna boy. What the fuck happened on the bridge," I asked. I dapped Lee up and hugged him at the same time. Lee stepped back and looked at me hard. Then he looked at Wil.

"Nigga don't play crazy! You know what happened on the bridge, and why it happened," Lee answered. We both looked at Will.

"I don't wanna know why. Ain't no reason on Earth why that should've happened. Just let me know when it's time for them mutherfuckers to die! I'm hungry, bout to go get me something to eat," Will said. As he walked away. He was right, it really didn't matter why, nothing really mattered at all, but payback.

"I wanna know! Give me the business nigga"! I pleaded; and he did.

"That same cat, who noise you broke, was at the party wit some real Miami goons, mouth full of gold teeth Dickey suits and Chuck Taylors. Bob spot the niggas first. He pulled my coat. Them niggas was mean muggin us for real, and we was muggin back. You dig? Then they were gone. Leaving the party I didn't see them niggas nowhere, and I was looking for real, but when we turn to go right coming out the gym. I heard loud pipes and tires burning rubber. When we all made it good onto the bridge with no way off I heard the same pipes and tires. I was already nord, cause I knew why you weren't here. I looked back first, head light off, the barrel of a long gun hanging out the back window of that same Bronco. Then all hell broke loose. The shit was death defying. Like that nigga was shooting bombs, I ran for my life. I could feel the shoots that missed hitting the bridge. The shit was vibrating under my feet. I was running back towards the school, everybody else was running the way the truck was going. I look that nigga right in the eyes, his black ski masked face, and gold teeth gritting. No face, no case. That nigga was hitting at me, man. I had to jump over the Bridge that Kudzu shit saved my life. But fuck my life, cause man Latonya died wit her brains hanging. It was fucked up, that nigga Bob kept saying it be alright. That was a lie, and she knew it when she shook and died. What kind of God," Lee told me; he sat on the steps and cried, " No moans, no screams, just tears. It hurt me to see him cry, really it hurts me to see anyone cry. We always question God when we lose something good. When We need to question humanity. God is as real as your life makes him. My tears had turned to pain, and my pain quickly turned to hatred. The only thing that can help me is the same that's hurting me. Murder.

"Nawl man dis shit will never be alright wit me, even after we get this body back," I said.

"Yeah. Blood for blood, cuz," Lee responded.

"Nawl nigga. She deserves two for one," I answered back.

"Well, it really don't matter imma kill me a mutherfucker, and it don't matter how many I hit or who I kill. Dem niggas didn't give a fuck how many of us they bodied. How much you got on a K," Lee asked.

"I gotcha halfway right away, we gotta get that shit today," I answered.

"That's cool, we'll catch Shy at the next prayer. We can go down and wait in the park. You strapped," Lee asked.

"Hell yeah! Til death," I answered. Then we started walking towards the park. We walked in the open, no fear now, just hate.

PART-3

Eighteen months later, Latonya's killers are still free. We purged for 2 days and I still feel guilty. Have you ever cleaned your hands, blood with blood? It's like hiding a penny in mud. 18 months later, we came from Boyz to made men. Money brings bitches, bodies bring fear. Murder ain't nothing but a tattooed tear.

Our little Holderness Street click had gotten thick, but we were still the Blue House crew. That was our trap, but The alley that ran beside it, that's where all the money short stoppers hung. We name that alley dead man ally, because it leads all the way to Dead Man's Curve, and the park. Clarence Poon was a kingpin now he owned the blue house and had just opened up Poon's Car Wash on Campbellton and Delowe, Big Shane was still his right-hand man. Them two nigga's just rode around in Clarence's Convertible 74 Caprice Classic white with a black rag top. Monique still ran the Blue House, but she was losing her grip fast. The game was changing, and she wasn't keeping up. Antoine hadn't gone to school in 2 years. He still works for Monique, and I think he always will. He Graduated from JC Harris Elementary and never saw a day of high school. Big Will does nothing but sell rocks and tell lies. We call him the Cap Master. He was so tight he got more money than all of us, but you would never know it, or believe it. Pimp Shawn still on, he got cars lined up from the bottom of Holderness all the way to

Lucile. He got 50 hoes, two pagers and a briefcase phone. This cat got clothes, hoes, diamonds, and gold. I get to watch him from a Bodyguard away, and he knows my name. Pimp Shawn is everything a hustler dreams of being. He is the blueprint. He just shot a nigga name Shorty and left him for dead on the dance floor at Charles Disco. Pimp Shawn is already a living Legend. The Difference between Clarence and Pimp Shawn is Shawn works all his workers $25 off a $100. He just let them wear his Jewelry and drive his cars. When I found that out I was shocked. Clarence just fronted us whatever we bought. He let us be our own bosses, and we came up fast. Lee was buying nine and getting nine, and I was a couple re-ups behind. Lee bought a white with buck skin rag Sedan DeVille Cadillac 1978, so I didn't want to be a copycat. I bought a 1978 Caprice Box Chevy Silver with a burgundy rag. We both put trues and vogues on, and four tens in the back window put in by Shelly. We both had Jewelry, clothes, and pagers. Nothing too major, but we are getting major paid. Money has a way of making everything alright. I'm not running from anybody now, including Big Walt. He came through the hood almost everyday selling plates and getting his own re-up. We were back best friends; I guess if you can't beat them join them. My daddy is a drug dealer now, him and Wil daddy Papa Poon. Daddy made me promise that I will get my High school diploma, so Monday I'm headed to Saint Luke Academy Alternative school. They kicked me out of Brown High right after the Latonya murder. It was impossible for me to concentrate at that school, knowing the things I knew. I felt so guilty. If Homicide would have done the job correctly, they would have easily solved the case. They did not interview the students at the school. A lot of the students knew about the Miami Boyz looking for me and Bobby. The Miami Boyz came to his house with army guns, across the street from Latonya's house, not two weeks prior. Like Lee says, Bobby is a real coward, he's too scared to tell, and definitely not going to shoot. I told my daddy everything. He advised me not to say a word. I wasn't on the Bridge, and ain't nobody shot at me yet.

"Boy, you just let the police do they job on that shit. Lord knows that was a terrible thing happened to that child, and I feel for her family. But we gotta think about us and our family. The niggas that did that we gonna just pray God punish him good, but we ain't fuckin' wit dem Miami Boyz they shoot at the police," he said. I have been doing a lot of shooting myself lately. I wasn't the same person he spoke those words to over a ago.

Lee, Shane, and myself all rented rooms out of Black James' rooming house, the one on Gordon Street between the Wendy's and Willie Watkins Funeral Home. Shane still had his room downstairs, Lee and I had rooms upstairs. It was like the house was all ours, Black James only rented to niggas from the hood, but no drug dealing allowed here. Besides us, the only other person who lived there is Mississippi Tommy. Tommy buys all his Coke from Clarence, so he allows him to sell from the Blue House yard. I don't like it, but that's just the way it is. It's really about three Mississippi cats in the Westend getting money. All of them cousins or brothers or something like that. They got to work out of the yard to stay away from the sharks. Tommy thinks he is a slick, tough, country nigga. He's selling more than Clarence dope out of the yard. He's doing whatever he wants. He thinks he's faster than us because he's older, and just did a bid in Mississippi. He's one of those Buff prison looking nigga. Lee warned him once, not to get his tape pushed back. He laughed it off, but it wasn't a joke. Shootouts have become Just rock-and-roll to us! Right now it's four dope crews on Lucile and Holderness. The Outcast, they make the most money because they sell everything and they got half the corner. Shawn crew next because they got the other half of the corner, out of that bitch Tyndale apartment right there on Lucile Street. But we're up next! The blue house crew down in the hole, and still doing numbers we hustle just on Holderness, but we got dreams of having the corner all to ourselves one day. I believe everybody has that dream. The fourth crew is Rico and the Muslims. Rico sold dope mostly, but only late at night, all over Lucile and Holderness. During the day you can find him at the park shooting basketball with the Muslims, or riding around in his Jaguar with the 350 Chevy motor, looking for trouble, a car full of Kufis. Mostly we all got along great, just normal hood shit here and there. What matters most? We would shoot at any outsiders together. That's 100 guns, 200 clips, we in the Westend.

CHARLES DISCO

If you are a big baller in this city, you can ball every night. Before Shawn got shot, I only went to two clubs, Charles Disco and Montres strip club. Now we hit a different club every night, and we always see the same crews. Friday nights are special, every hustler out of our hood and every hood will be at Charles Disco, and Dem Miami Boyz. At Charles the West End just one big crew, one big family, not four.

Charles disco is legendary from state to state Atlanta to Miami, New York to Atlanta. It's been the spot even when Lil Willy was alive. This place is for all the pimps and players, money Getters and lick hitters. I'm gonna put it simple if you ain't been to Charles Disco you not a hustler in this city. This is the home of the Mr. Knockout contest and the nasty girl contest. The winners Receive $100 and a lifetime of embarrassment. We shot dice on the bathroom floor what, And the blue room for the lacers and basers, snorters and smokers.

This Friday night we pulled to Charles I'm riding with Lee in the caddy. We park up front by the front door and back in so we can get to the trunk quickly, AK-47 on deck, and I got a 22. in my Bailly shoe. We smoked a few joints and watched the hoes pass by, trying to pick out which one to try, and we had to watch every car that passed by. Looking for our enemies and looking for our crew. Clarence pulled up to the front door in his baby blue Fleetwood Cadillac Brougham Wil, Shane, Junky-T and Clarence jumped out the car. Clarence threw his keys to Junky-T. He jumped in the drivers and peeled out, everyone else headed to the front door passing the line, and we jumped out and followed suit. I heard a loud motor and it couldn't have been none other, Pimp Sean fishtailing in the parking lot, in his Vet.

"It's show time nigga's," Lee screamed out. Pimp Shawn hit that Vet so hard and pulled up so fast playing that 2 Live Crew's, 'Me So Horny.' He had serious bump in that Vet, and with the top off it's louder than the music coming from the club. Charles jumped back like afraid Shawn was about to run him over.

"Get out the way before I run your old ass over Nigga"! Shawn screamed out the roof. This nigga almost parked in the front door. He jumped out the Vet with his Baddest bitch Wanda, so many gold chains, I don't know how he keeps his head up. Shawn is the number one stunna. Out of nowhere, his crew appears right by his side. Big-Ty, Brian, Little Steve, Big-Corey, Lil Corey, and about five more of Shawn's hoes with them.

"Nigga I done told you. Do that shit one mo time, and imma give Terry White yo spot. I ain't got time for all that playing shit, gimme my gotdamn money nigga". Charles said; He one of the richest niggas in the city, and they say he has fuck every young girl in the city. Then they say Luther Vandross and Charles are very close too. I don't know, but he's rich. He stands at the door every time the club opens and collects every penny himself from every person that enters his club, just like I sell my dope.

"Come here, baby! Do you know how much I, I, I, I, I, I, I, I, loove you," Shawn sang to that nigga like Lenny Williams. Hugged him and then stuff a wad of hundreds in his top shirt pocket. Charles is a tall Big Frame man. He could be 60 or 70 hard to tell, Probably I was a handsome guy in his days.

"Shawn now you no you my mane man. Terry didn't come til 2, all he does is shoot pool, and you know that pimp, but slow it down for me, baby. You tell Margo I'm coming for them Oxtails Sunday. Now who all Westend," Charles asked. Shawn looked back.

"The line ends when Li-Steve gets in, and momma got you on

dem tails, just pull up pimp," Shawn told him. Then he and Wanda Woman went through the door. No pat down or nothing. We all made it in smoothly, but got pat down, Clarence had so much money in his pockets they let him straight through too. This is it, this shit is lit. If the blue house is my church, then this is Bethlehem, Holy Hustlers land! I love it like the Muslims love Pakistan. As we entered, we all touched the pool table that sat right in front. Just like they touch the log at The Apollo. Like Lee said, it's showtime. We touched the table for luck, and because of its history. This table has won and lost millions, for and from the biggest hustlers in the South and some from North. It's a sign to the robbers. We westside certified ride where we won't ride. Following Pimp Shawn, we all head to the main inside the big party room. The door flew open, and Public Enemy's Fight The Power is Blasting from the speakers. That's Big Shane's favorite song, and he went bananas just like Flavor Flave with his black shades on and all. We all filed in the music stopped.

"Hold up wait a minute y'all done put a pimp in it," the DJ chanted.

"Pimp Shawn just walked in, and he wit dat Westend click, and they on that Holderness St. shit. That Ak shit, shoot at the cops shit. My homies what's up pimps," the DJ shouted out. Then he put on Pimp Shawn's favorite song, Eric B and Rakim "Thinking of a Master Plan" and the club went crazy. His name is Darryl, he was the son of Willie, the funeral home director from the West End. My neighbor is the DJ at Charles Disco, the coolest club on the planet.

"Hootie-whooooooo," we all sang back. Shawn looked up at the DJ, smiled, then held up his index finger across his lips. We had to dap up 20 different crews before we made it to the bar. We all Station ourselves in between the same two crews every Friday night this our spot. Big Slick crew Me-Phi-Yo to our left. To our right Paco, Duck, Sanchez, Encre and a gang of Mechanicville niggas they 30 deep, just like those 30 building they live in. Across from us at the bar. Some of them 5th Ward Herndon home nigga Lil-Rod Tracy, Big Duke, and I and a few more. That wasn't nearly half of them nigga, but they will be here. Right beside the 5th ward nigga. A set of dem Miami Boyz, this set belongs to Big Wil, through Miami Speedy. I've been watching and studying these cats ever since my incident. The Miami Boyz were in Atlanta way before I knew what dope was. They got about ten different clicks, I know all the dangerous ones. Big Wil click certified they are not from Fort Lauderdale, they are from Dade county. Herndon homes and Techwood were infested with Miami Boyz. I looked around the club at all the rest of the money crews, Bankhead Courts Black Dave got so many nigga in his crew I can't remember all their names, but they some real niggas Miami Boy killers. Bankhead Courts is Miami Boyz free, they are holding that shit down out there. Speaking of Techwood, I can see my main man, Rabbit, ducked off in the corner with rich ass Charles, Kenny, and Vincent. Them niggas old Atlanta dope money for real. Techwood is so big and full of money, and the biggest labor pool in Atlanta is in the middle of it. Junky's get paid cash everyday all day. It will take all of Florida to stop Charles' and Kenny's money. They are standing right next to the Thomasville Heights boys Little short Moo-Moo, Frank, Big Nap, super big crew. They all good pool shark and money getting niggas. Their beef with a set of Miami I'd never heard of, but it's big beef, fire booming apartments and all. Bowen Homes's Big D and Tight, I can see them representing. Bowen Homes Is another one of Atlanta Mega Million Dollar traps. My gambling partner Fat Steve from Bowen Homes, he's up next out there. They don't have Miami Boyz out there, but they stay killing each other like crazy.

"Kil here! Get yo drink, and look that way, look who just walked right up in dis mutherfucker," Lee said. I got my drink from his hand, Then I looked towards the door. He was easy to see, almost 7 feet tall. Wearing an all white Dashiki, but no Kufi. Charles Disco has big disco balls hanging all around. They made the big diamonds around his spec lens glasses Illuminate even more.

The music stopped.

"Hold up wait a mutherfuckin 'minute! I can't believe this! Big Trav just walked up in this motherfuker! What's up my niggaaaaa"! The DJ yelled. Me So Horny started blasting from the speakers. The real Travis just stood there. Then he smiled and showed what looked to be at least 30 gold teeth. He looked like a king looking over all his peasants. His crew is 20 strong. That's at least 10 choppers and 500 gold teeth. They started their Walkthrough, and the club spread like the Red Sea. I'd never seen this nigga no where, but maybe flying by in a Benz or something. Now he's walking right towards me. Once Wil and I went to his spot on the Boulevard for some double ups, but his rocks were so big you made $50 off $10. The line was like The Mind Bender at Six Flags, too long for me. I caught a glimpse of this same tall ass cat that day, but it was from like forty Dope fiends away. This one of those nigga you often hear about but seldom see, Let my partner Shahid. I've heard a lot about this one. I think he's out of Scott projects, not sure, but he's a certified Miami Boy. What's crazy? He hunts Miami Boyz up here, they say he just robbed Miami Silk, and raped his bitch. Terry was the only boss to take him to war. You got to be war ready to fuck with a rich nigga, I know that now. Wars make Soldiers ready for war, ain't no boot camp to learn how to shoot, got to be already war ready. The way we eat, you gotta get a body count in these streets. If not.... Here come the robbers and thieves. Big-Trav war ready! He dressed to kill. That dashiki ain't for fashion, it's for AK stashing, and some of these phony niggas need an AK killing. They don't see what I see. Murder.

"Somebody gonna die tonight," Lee and I said. As he came closer, I could see clearer. He's walking right in our direction. White dashiki almost to the floor, black Bailly boots, 10 gold Cuban link chain, a big gold diamond watch, and the Diamond out Cartier's. But nothing could amount to the ring on his finger. At first I thought he had a gun in his hand. The ring is on his right middle finger. It's a gold hand rising out of the ring. A hand the size of a toddler, all five fingers, and I'm counting. That didn't blow my mind. What's amazing to me is the skinny gold pole that I could barely see. It went up at least 6 inches and placed on top as if floating in air. A diamond-encrusted basketball the size of a golf ball. I didn't get it at first, it's a hand, shooting a basketball. Can you believe this nigga? He must have been a b-baller in another life. These nigga need to tuck all their bullshit jewelry in, even Pimp Shawn with big ass gold and diamond United States map, and big gold truck rope holding it up. That shit is not enough. Nothing in here compares, Big-Trav just walked right by me. I'm Standing on two steps and still couldn't see in his eyes, he's looking up.

"Wut up Pimp Shawn? My nigga! Put down nigga 4-5-6, you know what it is. We been gettin rich! Gimme some baby," Big Trav said. They dapped and hugged. Wow, Shawn knows everybody. Lee nudged me.

"Let's dip nigga! It done got hot in here. Let's see what's happening in the blue room," Lee said. I was getting hot too, these Miami Boyz turning up the heat. So we headed to the blue room, or should I say the get high room. It goes all the way down in the Blue Room, choose your poison, weed, hard, soft, dope, you can have whatever you want. We went back out the door we came in. Pimp Gene and his pimp partner Danny are having a game of pool. I watched for a second as Pimp Gene downed the 8 ball in the corner pocket, then reached in the side pocket and pulled out a wade of cash. These are the two richest pimps in Decatur, and two of the richest in this city now. (RIP Tripp City) All Eastside niggas around the pool table Decatur on one side, East Atlanta on the other side. We knew some of these cats, they knod, we knod back. Scooby, Lil Gerald, Crawdad, Musclehead, Kiki, and there's Carver Home Sweet-Pea and Li-Boo, but more Eastlake Meadows niggas than anything. Little Dave, Jojo, Timbo, Ugly Bubble, Jack, they McAfee Decatur niggas, real rich. We walked past and into the Blue Room. It smells like Brent's spot where we cook our blow, and it's as dark as a cave.

We stood at the door to let our eyes adjust and listen for the call from the wild.

"Hootie Hoooooo,"came from way back in the corner. We went that way into this dark cave full of all the worst predators imaginable, but we fear no evil. I cocked my pocket rocket, I'd tucked in my pocket. It was so dark, I couldn't make out many faces, so I listened to all the voices. Mostly familiar voices from the same Friday night blue crew. Dim light hangs over each small table, and lines of Cocaine under almost each light.

"Lee the G and Killer Kil, what it is," Lee said; My main man, Mr. Everybody's henchmen.

"Gangsters gangsters! That's what the fuck I'm yelling," Cutie B said. My nigga from A-Z. Bobby...I love him, but I had to name him 'Can't Get Right'. This Nigga don't know if he wants to get money or get on the pipe, but he's the biggest player I know.

"Lee and Kil the two brothers from another mother what it do niggas," Black Mickey asked. He's Me-phi-yo, and we played on the same football team Brown high, we blood in blood out.

"Ah niggas, come campaign wit yo Big G. Ya'll Holderness Street. All this shit free," Kee-Kee said. He's Harris Homes' horseshoe Old G. He sat at a dirty table with a big pile of clean white cocaine. It shined like diamonds, but looked like fish scales.

"Yall niggas better gone and get yo nose right, cause tonight it's gonna be a big, I mean big ole gun gunfight. I can already smell Gunsmoke," Sweet Pea said. OC, Sweet Pea, and I looked over at him. He smiled with 5 gold teeth. I could see Otis over Pea's shoulder, macking at a hoe. I reached down like an eagle, just my hand using three fingers. Fuck a line, I ain't junky, I don't look down, I held my head back, and crumbled it so the Crumbs fell down my nostrils, I had to waste a dime on my blood red Fila suit.

"Wipe Me Down pimp," I asked Lee. He did, and I did the same for him after he dug in himself like a pig. Cocaine is a very powerful thing, for most enough just ain't never enough. For us, we think we know when enough is enough. Snorting cocaine is a westside Atlanta niggas thang. That's the hustlers drug of choice unless you from Herndon homes are the Bluff then you snort heroin like my nigga Do-Do. Now that's getting high. Heroin is a downer, it makes you numb. No more pain, not even a headache, but they have to have it every day or you will hurt like you have never hurt before. It's a physical drug, your body will ache for it. Cocaine is a mental drug, it'll make your mind ache for it. The weaker a person's mind is, the stronger it becomes. All it does for me is get me hype. I have been playing with my nose since high school. Lee's first time getting high on coke was the day after Latonya's murder. We had to ride all night. He said he wanted to stay hype. The blue room had gotten packed, and that dirty smoke was getting thicker and thicker. Wee-Wee, Todd, Lil Rod and Emmett just walked in, can't see them, but I hear their Herndon homes voices. Daddy this and daddy that, them niggas call everybody daddy. I guess it's better than calling everybody shorty, like most of Atlanta does. Herndon homes got a few dope crews. This Crew has made a name for itself. It's the same crew that saved us from the Summer Hill niggas at Cheney Stadium, R.I.P Carlos.

"Nigga lets get the fuck outta here. Dem Miama Boyz got this mutherfucker smelling like base house," Lee screamed as loud as he could. He looked right at the table full of Miami Boyz, but they didn't look back.

"Let's dip then," I said. I headed back out the door. It's two o'clock, and the line is still around the corner, Charles still standing there collecting all his cash. All the players came out tonight from far and wide. There were so many Cadillacs and Chevys in the lot, it looked like a car show. There were also so many women in short dresses you'd think the parking lot is Auburn Avenue hoe scroll. Pimp Shawn's on the pool table now, shooting a young pimp named Jarrell. All westside surrounds the pool table now, doing some side betting, campaigning, and spreading hood gossip. Who got knocked, who got robbed, who got shot, who ratting, and who fucking who's hoe. Speaking of hoes, I spotted one I want to get at. She's short, slim, and she won't stop smiling at me. She was hanging around nothing but Miami Boyz. Now she headed to the Blue Room alone.

"Ah Ms. Lady! Can I just get a dime of your time? Just ten seconds is all I ask"! I shot my shot; she was smiling the same smile. It was nice, but sneaky looking. She smiles like a wise-guy, right before he shoots you in the back of your head.

"Nigga whatcha want wit me," she snapped. She acted like I'd got on her nerves already. She's short with nice hair, a cute face, and a very slim shape.

"Maybe your heart, but your name will do," I popped back. She stared at me with a smile on her face. I could see in her eyes that she's seen a lot, and she gets higher than just pot.

"My name Smiley nigga! You so lame! Who you work for," she asked, looking me up and down. I'm Fila, fresh from head to toe. She looks like she shops at Sunshine.

"Bitch bye, you blowin my high," I snapped, then turned back to the pool table. She laughed and walked her drunk ass away.

"What that bitch talking bout," Lee asked.

"Shit! She is a li-dirt bag bitch," I answered. Lee laughed.

"Let's go get some more Henn and watch the Ms. Nasty Girl contest," Lee said. The Ms. Nasty Girl contest ain't nothing but a strip show. The girl that's good enough to win, gets a hundred bucks, and she's guaranteed an interview with one of the many pimps here, and a job at one of the many strip clubs. I'm not going to even speak on the Mr. Knockout contest, I always leave before it gets started. Who wants to see a nigga shake his ass? Nobody but a fag!

"Man, look at that bitch! She super bad," Lee said. On the small stage in the center stood a big red Stallion. Her ass looks like she is pulling a wagon, and she is wagging it. Men and women were crowded around the stage trying to stuff bills in her panties.

The ones that were standing too far back tried to throw their money on stage, but it flew in the air. We got our drink, then found a suitable spot for us to get our peek on. Wil found us, and he pulled out a big sack that Betty White. Lee and I pulled two redbones. I jumped down on Carmen, and Lee scooped up Janae. Most of our crew is back around us now. Everybody is feeling good, and we are partying like rock stars. Boogie Down Productions Love's Gonna Getcha is booming from the speakers. But I still heard him.

"It's on your head, fucknigga! You can't go back home fucknigga," one of the Miami niggas said. He's talking big shit to Big-Trav.

"Nigga you better get yo money back, cause nigga as you can see I ain't dead. Bitch boy! Trav goes where ever the fuck he want. I just left the bottom. Fuck boy call yo bitch and ask her? Better yet, fuck nigga imma call her for you," Trav said. He pulled out a big block cell phone and started dialing. I'm looking like I'm at the movies, this is some real Gangster shit.

"Hey bitch dis fuck boy KB wanna halla at cha! Here talk to yo hoe! It's her number 3057869232 I got yo bitch," Trav said. The short, black, chunky dude with all the Gold herringbone knocked the phone out of his hand. It flew through the crowd. That's when all hell broke loose. It was like a bomb went off right in front of me. A 40 nigger fight right in front of me, Miami against Miami. If you are a Vet at Charles Disco, you know what to do when rich niggas fighting. You look to the floor for jewelry. I spotted it before Lee, but he was closer than me. One big gold herringbone chain, Lee snatched it up like an eagle. Looked at me, and we were on our way out the door. We had to keep our heads low and try not to get hit by one of the many champagne bottles and glasses flying in the air. By the time we made it to the first door, all kinds of fights had broken out. We kept on moving all the way out the door.

"Pop the trunk nigga," I screamed as I ran to the back of the car.

Lee hit his remote, and the trunk popped up. There she is, My Bitch Nigga Killer, all black, all plastic with a steel blade at the tip. AK-47 number 2 for us, the first had to get shipped up north. I pulled it out, loaded it with two 30 rounds, taped together banana clips, one for me and one for Lee.

"I wanna see how that shit shoots ain't it's plastic," Will said. I see he knows which way to go.

"You gonna see if fuck boy run up," I told him. Lee jumped in, cranked the car, and turned the music up.

"And that's fo sho," I replied. We'd backed, and we weren't blocked. The big Cadillac grill is pointed towards Simpson Road. I sat on the front of the car, holding my AK like a guitar. Lee joined me with some weed, and so did Wil. We all took a hit of the blow and puffs from the weed. People poured into the parking lot, like Monsters were inside the club. Bitch were crying and screaming, running for their lives. Trav is the First Miami boy I spot coming out of the club. His white dashiki has blood on it now, I watch him and his crew disappear in between the cars. KB and his crew ran right by us.

"Nigga pass me that stick, I'm bout to make it hit," Will asked. He wasn't serious at all. He just liked to hear himself talk. That's how he got the name cap master, Wil will cap about anything, and sound so real doing it.

"Nigga please! Get yo cap ass in the car. We bout to pull before a nigga block us in," Lee demanded. Will jumped in the back seat, I slid in the front, with Lee behind the wheel. Folded the stock down on the AK, to make more room just in case I got to aim. Lee pulled off, the big grill on front jumping up and down every time he hit the gas. We made our way to the top of the lot. People were everywhere.

"Oh shit! Hit it, Lee! Look at that nigga there," Will screamed. I looked back. The back of an almost seven footer, in a white dashiki, and a blood-red Kufi. He slung out two AKs.

Bom-bom-bom-bom-bom-bom-bom-bom-bom errrrrrrrrk! He

let them both go, holding them sideways. Lee hit the gas. The death-defying sound had become oh so familiar.

"Man, that nigga just body rocked a nigga. Hit da gas! That shit knocked him down that Kudzu hill. Lee, this nigga hittin wit two sticks at the same damn time," I told Lee. We could still hear those choppers chopping when we made the right on Ashby Street.

"Man, that nigga just went off like," Will said.

"He had dem sticks hidden under his dashiki like Rap, and knock that nigga down that hill, like he gotta good aim, he ain't just shooting for the fame," I said. I've seen a lot of AKs hit but hadn't seen anybody make them hit like that. We did 90 mph all the way to Holderness St. It looked like a block party at 4 AM, we all jumped out and shot dice until sunrise. I went to bed that night thinking about that skinny girl with that cute smile. Thoughts become things.

BACK TO SCHOOL

Monday morning My first day at St Luke Academy alternative school some promises you got to keep, and this is one. Education means everything to my father, and to make him happy I will get my high school diploma. St Luke's downtown near the Civic Center Station Inside of a big old stone Catholic Church. I wanted to go to the West End Academy, but my daddy said I will just have the same old friend. I pulled up in my Chevy Alpine Bumping NWA's 'Straight Outta Compton.' I'm fresh to death. My name should be Fila. I got a different color for every day of the week. All I wear is Fila shoes, sweatsuit and Kangol, that's my everyday outfit. I get out and start my walk to the school. Oh yeah, one baby .380, $2500 in cash, a beeper, and my bookbag. I got a few mean mugs, but a lot of bitches staring. I walk in the office smelling like an entire bottle of Cool Water cologne.

"How you doing, sweetheart," I asked.

"I'm not your sweetheart, my name is Miss Mary," she said without even turning around.

"I'm so sorry Miss Mary, I didn't mean any disrespect," I replied in my proper voice. She turned to look.

"None taken! and how are you doing handsome," she replied in her very sexy grown lady voice. She walked up to the counter and looked me up and down. She's fine as wine, no more than 25 years old. I think I will like this school.

"What's your name, baby," she asked with a big smile on her face.

"Kil... no, I mean Rodney Brown. I'm sorry," I answered. She handed me a small folder.

"Tamika will you please take Mr. Kil Rodney Brown or whatever his name is, into The library so he can take his equivalents test. After you finish Mr. Brown come back in here, son you can meet The principal Smitty, I mean Mr. Smith. Any questions," Ms. Mary asked.

"Yes just one, what kind of perfume are you wearing Ms. Mary? It smells a little citrus. You making me feel like I'm in the tropics somewhere. Where's the closest beach," I said. They both burst out laughing.

"This Poison By Christian Dior baby, and you kind of slick with it. I like you already," she answered with a sexy snare, this time not a smile.

"That's a good name for it," I said. I smiled my best smile, then walked away with Tamika and the little white boy. We walked out of the office into a main hall, then into another room the size of a classroom, but full of Bookshelves and books, and three tables. We took a seat at the first table, and she put the little boy on her lap.

"I know you gotta girlfriend," Tamika said. I looked at a good for the first time. She's a nice-looking girl with a very nice shape, nice brown skin, and pretty even teeth.

"Nawl I don't! Why you say that"? I asked. I like to play slow.

"Cause I'm digging you! You got any kids? Give me yo folder. Imma do your test for you, so you'll be in all my classes," she told me. I passed her my folder, and I'm happy to do so. I'm too high to even think about taking a test.

"You got any kids," I asked. She looked at me dumbfounded.

"This my little boy right here nigga," she answered. I looked at her the same.

"That boy is white, and you black. How can this be possible," I asked.

"Nigga my baby ain't white, he mixed. His daddy White J is the only white boy that hustle out the Bluff. How many kids your cute ass got." She asked. I thought to myself, this black girl got a real white baby.

"None," I answered. The truth is, I wouldn't think of having a child in this cold, cold world.

"I ain't got none either! Meka what you doing in here wit dis boy! Girl, I'm late as hell, Smitty gonna be mad! Who is this nigga you talking to? Looks like some knew meat! How are you doing? I'm Charity," she greeted me. I turned in my chair to look at the chatty voice.

"I'm doing good lil mama," I stuttered. Unbelievable standing before me... Charity AKA Smiley. This is the same lil bitch from Charles Disco that tried me like I'm a chump. She doesn't even recognize me, but that's cool because I never forget a face.

"I'm doing better already. Tamika, I'll finish that test! I think you need to change your baby. I smell something," Charity said. This bitch is sassy and bold.

"You smelling your upper lip bitch, or that hole between your legs! You didn't come home last night freak where you been," Tamika popped back. They both laughed.

"Girl! Shell had a party at the Silver Fox last night. Baby when I say it went down it went down," she was saying.

"Kil! What up homie? I knew that was your Box in the parking lot. Boy, you at the Luke now nigga," Keyman said. He's my main man and one of Bobby's brothers. I've known him most of my life. He gets heroin money out of the Bluff, I know him from Harris Homes.

"What up Key baby? Hear you eating good! You done took the trap back, they say! Bob ain't out yet," I asked. I stood up to give him a westside hug. We always hug like we are at a funeral, because the next time we see each other it may be at our own Funeral.

"Why he calls you Kil," Charity asked.

"Cause he will bitch," Keyman snapped. He's a real comedian.

"Oliver, I know you not use profanity in my school again," a deep voice spoke from the door.

"Nawl, that ain't me Smitty! I'm on my way to class! We'll do lunch homie," Keyman said, and he was gone.

"You must be Rodney Brown," Smitty asked me. He's a tall, well groomed, very intelligent looking old man with salt-and-pepper hair.

"Yes. I am, sir," I answered while reaching out to shake his hand.

"Please sit down. I have a few ground rules to go over with you. These two, I mean three, have heard all this before. At Saint Luke's Academy St Luke Academy we do not allow alcohol, drugs, guns, Knives, or any form of weapons. We do random searches of persons and vehicles," he said.

"What that mean," I asked, but I knew the answer. I just wanted to hear it.

"That means if your car is parked on this property he can search it anytime he wants to. Why you think parking lot is so empty? You ain't gon' pop the Trunk and get the pump around here. Smitty not having it Kil," Charity chimed in and said. Smitty placed the piece of paper on the table in front of me.

"Sign here, it's saying that you agree to what I just said. Get that test finished and you all set. Ladies give Mr. Brown a tour, then get him in class for me. Thank you," Smitty said. Tamika finished my test while Charity told her what happened at the Silver Fox. When Charity and I were alone, she started asking me more questions.

"What hood you from," she asked. She really didn't remember me at all.

"I'm from the West End, Lucille and Holderness," I answered. She looks thoughtful for a second.

"You talking about where that motorcycle club at? You must work for Shawn," she asked. Everybody knows Shawn.

"Nawl baby, I work for myself. I'm trying to do some hiring. Do you want this to be your interview," I popped at her. She smiled a little more. It seems like she's always smiling.

"I don't need no job nigga. I just need me a good man," she answered. I smiled. She talked my head off about what she needs a man to do for her. Everything she's saying I've heard it all before, almost everyday it seems, now that my bank is getting bigger.

"Good luck! It's time to get this show on the road, I'm trying to learn something today," I told her. I stood up. She took my arm and pulled me back in the seat.

"I got some I can teach you," Charity said with a twinkle in her eyes.

"Like what," I asked.

"You gotta take me to lunch first! Come on, let's go, it's almost 11:30," she replied. We went to McDonald's. Then straight to the Crown Motel on MLK. She's from the Bluff. I don't want her to know where I live. We drank Remy and smoked weed all day. We made out and had a lot of pillow talk. I found out she had other brothers and sisters, most in group homes. Her mother is a smoker. She never spoke of a father at all. She had a very sad story to tell, but don't they all. Before this day, I've never met a girl that didn't have shit. Charity didn't have a thing, not even a place to stay. She lived with Tamika, on James P. Bradley in the heart of the Bluff. This young lady is hungry and homeless. 17 years old going on 70, and I think I've taken a liking to her. Over the next few weeks going to school. She and I became cool. I bought her lunch, and we kicked it a lot. Word is she digs Miami boys, so I gotta watch this bitch. All in all, we are kicking it cool, with no rules.

The lord giveth and he taketh

Back in the hood it ain't nothing but about the money. Holderness is getting crowded, it seems like more and more of them Mississippi niggas are coming to town every day. Tommy's chest has gotten bigger and bigger.

"Ah Brent! Get this Nigga out of here wit that Li-bitty ass dope. I got big thangs dropping and I need it done now," Tommy demanded. We are down in the palace, a basement in the bottom of the apartments on the corner of Lucille and Atwood, it's a coke house run by Brent, the king junky of the hood. He does most of the cocaine cooking in the hood, for a small fee. Tommy reached into his pants and pulled out at least a half a key of cocaine, and dropped it on the table in front of me.

"Move bitch, get out the way," Tommy screamed. I pulled out my 380.

"Nigga who the fuck you calling a bitch," I snapped. He put his hands in the air.

"Nawl, Kil man gone wit that shit you and me ain't got no beef. I'm just in a hurry! Player to player imma pay you for your time pimp! Here you go," Tommy pleaded, then reached in his pocket, pulling out a big bank roll. He handed over two one $100 bills, and I took them.

"My nigga! I can dig this shit now! Where you get all that blow from," I asked as I put my gun away and started gathering my shit. In my hood if you got 9 oz you're rich. Tommy has doubled that at least. If I didn't know him I would have robbed him. You need a bodyguard for that kind of blow around here. What if one of these junkies goes to tell Rico, or worst Shahid, that this country nigga got all this blow in a bass house.

"Nigga I just paid you, now go buy you some business wit that," Tommy answered. He's right, it's too much heat in here for me, anyway. I never drive when I go for my cook ups, because I don't like people knowing where I am around here. You got all kinds of robbers, murders, and a few real killers riding around here. There's a big difference between a murderer and a killer. A robber can make one bad move now he's a murderer. The killers I know, they kill you then rob you, they like killing. It's sad to say, you are predator or prey. In this hood, even predators can become prey.

I made my way back to the block, watching every car that passed carefully. We have had no real beef in a while, but I learn not to ever let my guard down. Lee and Wil were chilling on the Blue House steps when they walked up. I went, and I hid my bomb in the spot so I could watch it.

"Kil how did that shit come back? Whatcha cut off it," Lee asked. He's smoking a fat joint. He passed it to me.

"Man, I didn't have time to drop shit! That country nigga Tommy come in the Palace wit a whole brick. He dropped it on the glass table so hard that shit cracked. Then the nigga gonna say move bitch get out the way'" I told them I had to hype it up some. I got my cap game from Will.

"I need that same thang Lee. I done got these nigga going," Weenie Head asked.

"Hell nawl nigga it's my turn you gotta buy from me," Will interjected. We have rules in the yard, and one is we take turns. We all got the same blow, or do we?

"Fat boy I don't want that shit you got. That brown shit have me tweaking too much. I want that fire white! I want Clarence blow. Not Black James blow, if I did, I would go to the Mississippi boys. Kil what you got," Whinny Head asked me. Whinny Head and his brother Frank have been around since I can remember. Once basketball stars, now gone on the blow, but I still love them. They are our runners, they use the allies and cuts to bring us customers from the corner. You have to beware of the Outcast.

"I ain't got to drop yet, Whinny! Tommy gave me $200 cash for my drop. He had big thangs poppin, so I hauled ass," I answered.

"Black James selling that butter, everybody don't like that oil base shit. You can't do shit wit it but smoke it, yall know I like to bang sometimes too. Gimme what I ask for Lee. Fuck Wil imma tell CP on his fat ass anyway, selling that bullshit out his yard," Winnie said. Winnie Head is tall, dark, and skinny. We grew up across the street from each other at the bottom of Holderness.

"Nigga fuck you, and Clarence. I sell my dope where ever I want to. You keep talking shit, imma bar yo ole junky snitchin ass from up here. You be," Wil said.

Bang! One shot. It was loud with a deep recoil, but not an AK-47, more like a 357. We all looked at each other. Don't know nobody shoots guns around here in the middle of the day just for play.

"That's close, came from the corner, that sounds like a big ole pistol," Lee said. We all headed down the steps to see what was up on the block.

PIMP DOWN

"**A**hhhh-ahhhh-ahhhh-ahhh somebody please call 911. Call 911. They done shot Pimp Shawn. I think he dead," Valjean screamed as she ran from where the shot came. Pimp Shawn dead, oh my God no! That made us run to the corner, we all loved Shawn. He may be from another crew, but it's the same hood. We made it through the crowd of junkies on the corner. Everyone was looking across the street from the Outcasts at the apartment building, at Shawn's trap. Two Outcast members, Bandit and Foots, were bringing Shawn out of Tyndale's apartment. His limp body was hanging between the two of them. Shawn's yellow silk pants were red now. The scene was so surreal, and the corner was filling up fast. So many people were crying. Word travels fast, cars keep pulling up all hustler's from all over the West End. Now I hear the sirens. My nigga flat on his back on the corner, his corner, Foot's pumping his chest dear God please save him. Foot's got him, he knows what he's doing. He was in Vietnam. Another scream, a mother's scream, the same thing!

"Why lord? My baby ain't never hurt nobody," Margo screamed. The police were holding Margo back as she struggled to get to her Motionless son. The paramedics got him now and they are working vigorously. Shane walked over to us from the other side of the street, the bloody side of the street with a dazed look on his face. He had blood on his pants.

"Is he dead, Shane," I asked. Shane is crying some serious tears, his black face shining like a black sun.

"He may as well be. Some nigga out of the Bluff done shot the pimp dick off! They trying to stop the bleeding, but he hit in a bad spot," Shane confessed. Will tried to make it out of the crowd before he lost his stomach, but he didn't make it. He threw up grape soda on Rodney Smith's new shoes. Wil has a very weak stomach. Rumor Has It he throws up every time he bust a nut.

"My fault Rodney man I gotta go," Will apologized. As he continued to throw up as he walked back down Holderness. They were loading Shawn into the ambulance now. Corner now looks like a block party, police cars, and fire trucks line Lucille and Holderness. Everyone is at this party, even Jamil and around six other Aki's stood watch. In the Westend blood is an attraction, but it's not every day a boss gets hit on his own block. Tyrone Booker just pulled up in his Seville. He ran through the crowd and up to the Stretch.

"Shawn, Shawn. Say something Nigga you can't be dead," Tyrone begged. Shawn didn't say a word. He couldn't talk, he had an oxygen mask over his face. But before he made it all the way on to the ambulance, he gave the crowd a thumbs-up. That caused a lot of screaming and fainting. Some of Shawn's girlfriends were consoling each other, but his main five or six were trying to get on the ambulance. Margo pushed them back and slammed the door. The ambulance pulled off, sirens blasting. Followed by a convoy of cars, they were following the ambulance like a funeral follows a hearse.

"Yall nigga wanna ride," Shane asked as he open Tyrone Booker's Seville door.

"Yeah ya'll niggas can ride wit me if you want to," Tyrone added. Burntface Ty is the coolest cat out of Shawn's crew, and the only one getting his own money. I like him, but I didn't grow up with him.

"Nawl man. Y'all can go head. Call the Blue House when y'all know something," Lee answered.

"Cool," they said. Then jumped in the car and gave it all the gas it could take. Channel 2 News just pulled up. That pretty black lady Monica jumped out of the van with the mic in her hand, Cameraman right behind her. She's always the first on the scene, and what a scene it is. It's crazy how tragedy always brings black people together. Everybody shaking hands, giving each other a hug. People I haven't seen in years, these are the friends that come out when you are dying or dead. Like vultures, they've been waiting to see you drop. Half of these niggas, not even from our block, probably plotting the next plot.

"Let's go Kil, so we can see what they saying on the news," Lee said. We head to the blue house, I guess the sky is gray for a reason today. I pray Shawn's not dead, I pray he's just fine.

"You don't wanna go to the hospital," I asked. Lee looked at me strangely.

"For what Kil? We ain't no doctors! All them hoes running down there. The Pimp don't need us now, but If you wanna go, go, Imma stay and get this doe, everybody bout to go," Lee answered. He's right, money is about to flow. When we made it inside of the blue house, Lucille and Holderness was live on Channel 2 news.

"Breaking news 27-year-old Vershawn was robbed and shot several times in the groin right here in this apartment building on the corner of Lucille and Holderness. As you can see a very large crowd has gathered here and has become unruly. They've turned an active crime scene into a block party. Uh Excuse you," Monica tried to report until Jap The Junky jumped in front of the camera.

"That was a cold bleed blood, and to ever did it yo momma going in the mud. Long live the pimp," Jap declared. The camera quickly moved from him and stopped upon Jamil. He and his henchmen, we're talking with members of Outkast, I guess trying to get the real details. It's rare to see Jamil standing on the corner, and he looks so out of place with that dashiki on, AK probably dangling. It's like he's living in another time. I wonder how he feels about us. He protects our neighborhood and all who's in it, including the drug dealers and pimps. Outsiders have the biggest problems because they don't have a clue.

"Man, look at junky ass Jap," Will said.

"Jap done put a hit on the nigga momma live on the news. They got the camera off that nigga ass quick. Now look at Jamil the Political killer talking to a drug dealing Outcast killer. I wonder who got the most guns, the Outcast or the Muslims," Lee asked.

"Man, you know dem Muslims got more guns than the police. That who the Outcast buy their guns from, believe that. Look at em on TV, they look like buddies to me"! I said; The camera went back to Monica Kaufman.

"We'll have more on the victim on Channel 2 News at 6," she said. Then the TV went to a commercial, 3 minutes, that's all he got. Three minutes of fame, if he lives, if he dies, five more.

"Ain't know debating who got all the bodies," Will added.

"Fuck all that who got the biggest guns and shit! They done let a nigga come up on the corner and rob Shawn! I just pray to God he alright," Monique said. She was still in tears. Then the phone rang.

"Hello," Monique answered quickly. She held the phone and listened for a while.

"Thank God I'm just glad that Niggas is alive, and he's gonna live. He can buy another dick, and you say he still got one nut left? Right? Ok Shane call me back, I'll be down there when the heat dies down," Monique said. She hung the phone up, shook her head and looked at us. Lee, Wil, Antoine, Philip, Clarence, and myself, all stared back.

"He gonna make it, but one of his nuts ain't, and they had to sew his dick back on," Monique said. She put her face in her hands and began crying. I wanted to cry, but I got to be a soldier.

"Wow! nigga now that's a low blow. I wonder how Shawn let that nigga get up on him like that. In his own trap man, that's ludicrous," Lee replied. Anger was all over his face. We all loved and looked up to Shawn. He represented the entire West End.

"Man, I think that hoe Tyndale set him up. Shawn been trapping outta that hoe house for three years and ain't gave her a penny. Walking around like a real Nino Brown. They say the Nigga took that diamond mermaid ring It had to be worth 30 or 40 Grand easy. This shit real bitches will get you killed," Will added.

"Fuck all that! Who did the shit man," I asked with anger evident in my voice.

"The nigga from the Bluff They called the Nigga Square Jones. The Nigga scaffolds tickets and eat dog food," Clarence explained.

"I know that nigga," I said.

"That's right! You still fuckin that bitch from over there"? Clarence asked; and I was almost every day. I'm in the Bluff almost every day, on James P Brawley. I walk to James' store and smoke weed with Keyman and Pimpin. That's how I know Square Jones. He's at the store nodding on the boy every day, trying to keep up with that bitch Mek.

"Call her don't give her the business just see what she no, we might get lucky and get eye balls on this junky nigga quick," Clarence asked me. I picked up the phone with no hesitation.

"Hello," a familiar voice answered the phone.

"Hey how you doing today Miss Betty? By any chance is Charity there," I asked. Miss Betty is Tamika's Mother. Charity lives with Tamika; she's actually a homeless child. She was a runaway for a while, after her mother got on crack and father got on crack, brothers and sister in foster care, it's all a very sad situation. I think I have a soft spot for her, I don't like to see people I like suffer, and the sex is good.

"Yeah baby she here where else she gonna be! She waiting for you to come pick her up. Bring me some cigarettes and two Bulls, please Rodney! Smilie Rodney on the phone! Here she comes. Don't forget about me, baby," Betty begged. She is a very nice lady, and so is Tamika. She already had a baby. That didn't stop

241

Lee, he got her in love already. My daddy would go crazy if I came Home with her and that little white baby, but she's fine and cute.

"Hey, baby. What you doing," Charity asked.

"I'm gettin to the money on this end. What about you, baby," I answered.

"I just finished up all our class assignments and all the homework for this week for school, so we cool now baby. We gonna have a lot of time to cake up," She answered. It seems like that's all she wants to do is cake up. She ain't asked me for no kind of hustle yet, not even for an ounce to sell. She keeps saying she's looking for a job. I guess she thinks she's found one.

"Anyway! Imma pull up round six, we might hit the drive-in or something. Oh yeah, if you see that nigga Square Jones call me. I gave him some money for tickets. I think that nigga been ducking me, don't say shit, just beep me and put 411 in if you see him at the store," I said. Now it's time to plan up a plot.

"I gotcha baby, as soon as I see that nigga! Tamika says, "Is Lee around you now," Charity asked.

"Nawl, baby. Lee just pulled off. Imma tell 'em to call her. Ok! See ya later," I answered; Lee has a new girlfriend named Jackie Johnson. She's from Jackson, Mississippi, and she's Troy Lee's niece. She looks like a grown lady finer than a coke bottle, beauty beyond belief, and no kids. Now he's in love, and somebody got hurt.

"You played that well player," Lee said. I hung up the phone.

"Let me have that little bitch, Lee," Antoine asked. He's a man-child now, bigger than me, but not more money than me.

"Fuck dem hoes! You see where Shawn is. Yall need to be worried about watching each other's backs. A nigga done hit the corner. Who's next, the club, or one of us? Lee, you and Kil tightening this shit up around here. Monique, keep these doors locked at all times. I want that AK in the house by the front window. Everybody stay strapped up, I don't want nobody in my yard if you not in this room right now. Our threat level done doubled. I'm bout to pick Shannie Boo up, gotta see the Aki's, need more tools." He said;

"We need more soldiers, we got plenty of tools. We need niggas that's gonna shoot," Lee said. with a strange look on his face. The only shooters in the house right now are Lee and me. We got secrets we can never tell, Shane included.

"Ah Lee! I'm da nigga wit the money, not the nigga wit the gun. Yall just tell me whatcha need, and I gotcha, and keep them short stopping in straggler out of my yard," Clarence said. He's right if I had all that money I would have bodyguards.

MONEY DON'T STOP

That may be in another life, but for now I'm just a soldier, I'm gonna do what a soldier does. Follow my orders.

"Cool CP, we got this shit, man. You can go down to Grady and check on Pimp Shawn. Let that nigga know we got Bloodhounds out on that nigga already," I replied. Grady hospital will definitely put him back together again.

"Yeah, Clarence y'all go head down there, and represent the blue house. Them niggas in his crew, the ones down there playing doctors and counselors, and shit. Tell them nigga me a Kil in the Bluff, playing hide and go see nigga". Lee added;

"Dig that ya'll niggas stay safe," Clarence said. He isn't a gangster and never has been. Before he went to prison, he was halfway dope out doing nothing but stick up moves. He got caught robbing and served five years. Now he is hood rich and doesn't want to even see a gun. I don't care how much money I make, Imma always stay strapped up.

"Imma ride wit Lee and Kil," Antoine said. We both looked at him.

"Nawl hell you ain't ride wit Clarence them. We going to pick up our whores. You say you want a whore, it's plenty of dem down at Grady crying. Gone down there and be a shoulder, cause you ain't ready to be a Soldier," Lee lied. I know how he thinks, and he is not thinking about any whores.

"Whatever nigga I was born on Holderness nigga, I was born a soldier," Antoine replied truthfully! Twon is a maniac at the age of 14. Somewhere he lost his soul, traded all for a few pieces of gold. Clarence, Wil, Antoine, and Monique Walk down the steps and piled into Clarence's baby blue Fleetwood Brougham, and the taillights disappear in seconds.

"Now it's time to get all this money. You better hurry back to the Palace for your cook up. It's fixing to start rolling nigga," Lee said. He didn't have to say it twice. I got my stash and was gone. It's like the thought of money puts me in a trance.

It took me less than 30 minutes to rock everything off and be back on the Block. Lee had a line going all the way down the steps and halfway up the block. I started serving people from the back of the line, Lee was right there wasn't another dealer in sight.

"Who the fuck that is short stopping my money down there? Dem days over wit niggas"! Lee screamed; he's standing on top of the steps with the Ak hanging off his shoulder.

"It's me nigga! I'm trying to catch the lineup, you got this shit all in the streets," I yelled. It wouldn't be good if the cop turned the corner, and all his fiends lined up like homeless people at Saint Luke's soup line. I moved faster than a crew pit at NASCAR. I got the fiends out onto the street, shortened the lineup, and moved all the action to the yard.

"Nigga you gotta be out! I just made a grand walking from the palace. I ain't never seen it like this," I excitedly said. I made a $1,000 walk from Brent house to the blue house. That's $1,000 in 5 minutes, that's $500 profit in 5 minutes. I've never in my life made money that fast.

"Almost nigga, you cut my trap. You must've run back nigga," Lee said. With a big smile on his face, his pockets looked like two big camel humps. When everybody goes to Daytona, each year the money gets good, but not this fast, not half this fast. People really love Pimp Shawn, I want people to love me like that one day.

"What the fuck is this shit a thug Holiday, ain't nobody Hustlin but us," I said. Winnie is standing on the front steps playing lookout, Lee and I are sitting on The Blue House steps.

"That's cause ya'll two niggas what's up next. Ya'll niggas make ya'll own rules. Fuck that shit Lil Corey talking! Fuck closing the trap cause his boss got shot. They want to close their shop if CP got shot. That's that hate shit, that pop shit, but dem fuck niggas ain't gonna stop shit," Winnie Head said. Lee slid the AK behind the brick wall on the porch.

"Fuck dem niggas Winnie ain't nay nigga stopping my flow. I work for Lee," Lee said. He looked me in the eyes.

"Rodney man now do you still believe in Jesus and all that bible shit we grew up on. One thang I no you do no now ain't no nigga raising from the dead. It don't matter how much you pray. It's death around every corner around here. Imma tell you what I believe. I believe thoughts become things, and I'm thinking now I want this kind of money every day. I'm thinking we gonna take over all this shit, just think like me and you'll see. We gotta show these," Lee said.

"Heads up! Here come two of them Mississippi niggas, Tommy and his uncle Two Thumb Mouth," Winnie Head yelled back at us, Mouth is around 30 years old, and he really does have two thumbs on his right hand, and he's a big, shiny black, big lips, Jheri curl wearing nigga. Tommy, 25 years old, looks just like him minus the curls. Mouth lives with Pimp Shawn's sister Gale. She's the sister that drinks the hot Budweiser. I don't like out of towners, but I really don't know any like that. Only outer towners I deal with are Muslims, and they are all from up North. These are the first Mississippi niggas I ever met, and they are as country slick as they get. I don't like them, and I definitely don't trust them.

"Tell dem niggas ain't nobody here CP gone," Lee ordered.

"Get right Kil we got 3 J's headed this way," Winnie yelled. I got up and went between the houses to make my sales. I didn't like serving out in the open.

"Send 'em in the cut, Winnie. I'm ready," I answered. I stood there, dope in hand.

"How many y'all need, you better get dis shit and go, today is yo lucky day," Mississippi Tommy said. I know his voice. I came from my cut, dope in hand.

"Nigga what the fuck you doing short stopping my money! Ah ya'll it's over here or get the fuck outta this yard, take that shit out there in the street," I said. Everyone stopped and looked at me. Mouth burst out laughing.

"Nigga who done die and leave you in charge," Tommy asked.

"Ain't nobody die, but we do gotta decide, and here's a deaf decision foyer. I can blow you away or you can leave in peace," Lee threatened. With one eye closed, he was aiming the AK. The Js took off running first.

"Shit like that young nigga," Mouth asked with his hands in the air.

"Nawl, nigga that shit like dis from now on. Scram niggas," Lee said as he started walking forward. Those Mississippi boys stumbled down the steps and up the block, making threats as they left. I burst out laughing and so did Lee.

"Fuck ya'll country boys," I yelled out; Lee and I took turns selling our rocks. $5000 later we both were out, sitting on the porch smoking weed. We had to wait on CP to re-up, we were beeping him for an hour, no call back.

"Heads up y'all here come Rico and Lil George," Winnie said. A year ago, Lil George went out bad on the blow. He ain't never came back, now he works for Rico. Rico got big blow, and he didn't get it from Clarence. He may buy more keys than CP, if not he's close. I can see the top of his high top fade coming up the steps. We stood up, Lee with the AK on his shoulder again. We ain't got no beef with Rico, really this nigga like our big brother.

"Man, what da fuck ya'll done to dem country ass niggas"? Rico asked; We are standing face-to-face as Lee and I stood on the last step, but Rico is still taller than us both.

"We ain't done shit to dem niggas yet," I answered.

"What the fuck you mean Rico you checking us bout some country niggas. Fuck dem niggas! I'm sick of dem nigga! I don't need no help! Imma get rite of dem nigga," Lee snapped. Rico burst out laughing hysterically.

"Kill dem niggas then Lee! I don't give a flying fuck, but imma tell you dis cause yall my family. Dem niggas got big tabs in these streets. I no yall ain't trying to buy that. Lee for me, be easy dem niggas don't want no problems witcha G," Rico asked. Then Lil George and Rico went next door to the abandoned house and set up shop. Rico is a strange guy, but he's always been good to me and Lee. Rico is a bully, but I mean a real bully. The kind that will beat you to death, and the kind that will shoot you to death. Rico sells dope during the day, and at night he hunts under the crescent moon with the Muslims. In the West End Just because you wear a Kufi, doesn't mean you're an Aki. The sun had faded down behind the trees, fall was definitely in the air. We waited for Clarence for as long as we could.

"Let's dip Kil it's getting a little chilly out here, that nigga ain't coming back. He probably knocked one of dem crying hoes down at the hospital," Lee said. Rico walked back over to us.

"If ya'll nigga bout to go, leave me wit that chopper. Don't drive through John Holt, Terry done turn that shit into The Volcano. It was a big Shootout today old lady got caught in the crossfire. Kilt her on her front porch. You got city, state, and dem Alphabet boys over there right now. That shit ain't gonna never be the same. Terry could've got dem Miami Boyz done clean for a flat fee. TW told me he hands on wit his shit, now the nigga got clean a lot of shit off his hands, or go to prison. Pete wouldn't be in that wheelchair if he would've left the killing to the killers, y'all too, you dig," Rico preached. It's a lot going on in the city today, keeping the cops busy. Lee handed Rico the AK, with no questions, just a warning.

"If something happens, we gotta have yours," Lee said. Rico burst out laughing.

"Which one nigga? I got five. Ah! What y'all wanna do bout the Pimp? They say the nigga that did it from the Bluff on James P. Shawn crew ain't gonna do shit. Keith Postell was their muscle, but he got his own crew now, he skipped out to Dixie Hill. Now Lil Corey and Big Ty, I guess the hammers now, but them niggas wouldn't hit nail wit a slug hammer. I fuck wit Shawn, he sends me the word. We gonna load up like December 31st. He shot a pimp nut off I wanna put that nigga momma in a hearse, or his kid, wife, girlfriend, best friend, neighbors, I don't give a fuck as long as we give our friends at Watkins Funeral Home some good business," Rico said. He grabbed the rifle and checked to make sure one was in the head. Not many people would hand Rico a loaded gun. If they did nine times out of ten it would be taken, and you may get shot, or worse, killed. Lee didn't hesitate, and he didn't do it out of fear he did it out of love. Rico is our big homie, and we know for facts that we will kill for us with no hesitation. We got secrets that can never be told.

"We done put eyes out on the prize. That nigga a few beeps away," I answered. Rico looked at me and smiled that killer smile.

"Y'all know the routine, keep everything clean. Y'all need to order up a hot box. I saw car thief Tee down in the crack a minute ago," Rico said. Now he's serious. Murder is his sweetest joy next to getting pussy, and he will murder you over some pussy.

"Fuck Tee. I can get y'all a hot box," Lil George snapped. All I can say is, "man goddamn that rock cocaine." I've seen a lot of my friends get gone off that rock, but it hurt me bad to see Lil George around here sucking on that glass dick.

"Nigga you ain't gonna do shit but a nigga a case. You need to go get me some customers before I fire yo ass for the fifth time this week," Rico said. He was joking mostly. Everybody laughed but me, Lil-George was the first young dealer I knew. He had a lot of money, but he always treated me the same, so now I treat him the same. One day he may shake that shit and become the hustler he once was. The sky has gotten dark now and a full moon is overhead.

"You riding with me or riding the Caprice," Lee asked.

"Where you bout to float it to," I asked.

"I'm bout to kick up some dust through the Bluff". Lee answered;

"Let's slide, Clyde! We out y'all. Hold it down," I answered.

"Ah, y'all remember shoot first then duck, don't duck then shoot," Rico said then laughed hysterically at his own dry joke. It really wasn't a joke. Lee and I disappeared between the houses. We could still hear Rico's ridiculous laughter, the death laugh. We are not on our way to do a drive-by. We call this a drive-thru. We are about to ride through the Bluff slowly, see who doesn't wave, and see who doesn't blow. If they act like that it means they already know. We cruised up James P and down Griffin Street. Zombies were everywhere. This is truly the city of The Walking Dead. People just didn't look the same over here in the Bluff. Rocks, heroin, and AIDS have transformed this place to hell on earth. We stopped by James' store/club. I jumped out and went in. Same crowd inside, but no sign of Square Jones, just Keyman and his crew. We dapped up. I got what I came to get and was gone. We finally parked in front of Ms. Betty's house on James P.

"What that nigga Keyman say," Lee asked, then blew the horn for Tamika and Charity to come outside.

"Boi, please! You no I ain't said shit to Keyman bout that business, that nigga talk too much, don't wanna give that nigga no heads up. We just gonna chill and let that nigga thank he good, when he really dead. That nigga is one beep away from a very terrible day. You dig," I answered.

"Yeah, I dig. No pillow talk wit these hoes either," Lee said. I don't pillow talk any way it can be dangerous. It may surprise you how many niggas are robbed and killed over Pillow Talk. Charity and Tamika came, with Betty close behind. They jumped in the back, I gave Betty her goodies, and we pulled off. We headed to Atwood Street to see Iran. He looks like a real Jamaican, he can even talk that shit just like them, but he really is from D.C. I met him maybe a year ago, he's tall and dark skin with dreads down to his legs. One of my Aks turned me on to him one early morning, we've been smoking him ever since. He got some new weed called Irene. It's the hardest weed I've seen. The buds are like little rocks, hard as hell to break up. Iran and I got cool, and I turned him on to the rest of the hood and beyond. Now he's paid. He was the first for me to see smoking his weed in Philly cigars. Now it's the new thing. Everybody in the West End smokes weed, it's our religion, and we worship it. We bought some weed from Iran, then headed to our spot. The funeral home was quiet tonight but Wendy's is busy, our house is in between the two. We parked in the back, got out, and went inside. At Shane's home, I can hear Love And Happiness blast from his speakers. We went to our rooms. It has been a long day, and what about tomorrow? Will it be my blood being washed away with water hoses? We drank an entire fifth of Remy that night. I had a nightmare that it was my dick that got shot off.

GRADY MEMORIAL HOSPITAL

Two days later Pimp Shawn Shawn was still down at Grady, so the Blue house crew had to pay him a visit. Greater has the number one Trauma Center in the south, maybe in the world. One thing I know for sure, they save a lot of lies. I hate hospitals. They all smell the same, like blood and disinfectant mixed together. Will, Antoine, Lee and myself entered the ground floor at Grady. Shawn's room is on the third floor, room 357 How ironic is that. We all waited at the elevator. All of us were dressed to impress with our best jewelry on. Grady is crowded as hell as usual. The healing business is always good. The elevator popped open, and it was already packed with mostly fine nurses. We crammed in any way.

"Excuse us Ladies excuse us, ladies! Our homeboy is about to breathe his last breath. We don't bite, we only shoot. Let me squeeze in right here by you, cutie," Lee said. He's always the charming one. It worked, and we were on the elevator on our way up. We got off on the third floor and we didn't have to ask which way to go. It's a big crowd standing down the hall in front of a door, and a lot of loud talking, and it's all Westside slang. We headed that way, Lee and I leading the way. We passed a small waiting area on the right. It looked like Charles Disco, so many hoes. In the front room 357 stood all of Shawn's brothers and all of his goons.

"Ah, Shawn dem niggas from The Blue house out here. You feel like seeing these niggas," Lil Corey asked. Then Big-Ty looked out of the room.

"Hell yeah let my nigga's in here, man. What's up wit you nigga this fam right here for real. They don't need no announcing we see these cats every day. Y'all come on in and show the pimp some love man. Get the fuck outta the way, Lil Corey," Big-Ty said. Corey slid to the side without saying the word. I didn't know their chain of command, but Big-Ty was letting it be known. Sean was sitting up in bed, a big smile on his face. The room was big with two beds in it, curtains separated the two. Shawn has a roommate, but I can't see his face. Hucklebuck and Keith Postell were standing on both sides of Sean the Dixie Hills crew.

"Pimp pimp," we all said.

"Pimp down man. Pimp down! I let a sucker play me like a clown," Sean chanted. He's under snow-white sheets with colorful pillows that look like they came from home. This the first time I ever saw Sean with no Jewelry on.

"Damn Sean, man I'm sorry as hell that nigga shot your dick off. But you lucky you rich. You can buy another," Wil said. He will say anything.

"Nawl. you li-fat bitch. My dick ain't got shot. It's so big that 357. bullet went through and busted one of my nuts. Yeah, I'm lucky nigga I gotta big dick. Ain't that right nurse Reed? If it was your lil bitty dick, it would have been obliterated," Sean popped; Everyone in the room burst out laughing.

"Yes sir, Mr. Shawn and I can't wait until it's all better, so it can make me better like you said. I'll be back soon, gotta make some rounds baby," the nurse said. She then got off the bed and walked out the room. All eyes were on her fat, round ass.

"Damn Sean, I see pimping don't stop cause a nigga got popped. Not even if you get hit in the dick, and his rocks, nigga you a pimp for real. If nigga say you won't, nigga I'll say you will," Lee said. He hung around me so much he knew what I was thinking.

"Sean tell 'em you don't fuck yo hoes any way. You just eat their pussy, you douchebag fag," I cracked at him. It got a real good laugh. Then the talk got serious.

"Ah Kil you still fuckin that lil hoe Charity outta the Bluff," Big-Ty asked. The room got real quiet, all eyes were on me.

"Yeah, I got the bitch on the peep. Just waiting on the beep," I answered looking Sean in the eyes.

"I can't believe I let that junky ass nigga get the ups on me. I slipped niggas! Y'all see now slippers count, I'm missing one of my nuts. That nigga gotta die! I don't know why the fuck he ain't dead. Make me thank my crew ain't shit. I could be in my grave right now, and ain't knot a nigga dead yet. What's that telling me? I'll tell you, a pimp could've died in vain. What the fuck? I gotta say it? aight! I got 20 on his head, ten up front and ten when he dead? Here call Rico back," Sean said as he handed his mobile phone to his brother Tiger.

Beep...... beep..... Beep. My pager went off. I took a look. Betty's number with the 411.

"Say less! Here we go! Gimme the phone first, let me see if this bitch got that info," I asked. One look from Shawn, Big-Ty handed the phone over. Mobile phones had gotten a lot smaller than the big blocks we had a few years back. Sean had a nice one, the kind that flipped up. It's called a flip phone. I dialed the number back. Charity answered the first ring.

"Yeah baby. Dig that, check, check, check. Gimme bout an hour. aIght appreciate you, see you later," I said. I closed and handed the phone back.

"What she say," Lee asked.

"Close that door for me. That cat is back at the local watering hole right now. Corner of North Ave and Griffin Street. He inside of James store eating candy bars, trying to fight that dog food. Y'all know where that's at, don't you," I asked but no one answered.

"You and Lee take 'em and show 'em for me. I gotcha y'all," Sean asked.

"Then what? I don't know how this nigga quare Jones look," Lil Corey said. He had a point, but it could be solved.

"I know how that nigga look, and I'll get shorty to bring him outta that store for you, if you wit it," I said.

"Fuck that shit Sean call Rico let the killers do the killing. If you want that shit done right," Will blurted out. He doesn't have any filters. He's like a comedian, he always says what everybody else is thinking but won't say.

"Ah, Sean man really me and Kil will do that nigga just for the flat fee. Nothing up front, just ten on the back end," Lee put our bid in. That's why I love Lee, when it comes to money this nigga never gets tongue tied. Closed mouths don't get fed. Sean looked at Li-Corey.

"Hell naw nigga I got this. I just need that ID on dis nigga, is all. Y'all thank y'all the only niggas putin in work round here. I been doing dis shit don't you niggas ever forget,". Lil Corey snapped. I will say Lil Corey will bust his gun, but his partner Li-Steve is the killer.

"Yeah, yeah, yeah, let's show these younggggg niggas Lil C," Lil Steve stuttered. I've known Steve and Corey all my life, it's all love between all of us. Even Big-Ty and Big-Corey I still don't know what hood they really from, but it's still all love, because they will shoot for Lucile and Holderness.

"Let's get them niggas! Dis shit like rock-and-roll to me! I wanted to give that nigga a AK killing," Lee said.

"Y'all please don't kill me," a voice came from the other side of the curtain. Antoine snatched the curtain back fast. An older man with a face full of hair was laying flat on his back on his bed. He had a big smile on his face, and a little tent sticking up in the bed.

"Dis old man over here beating his meat," Antoine said. Then he jumped up and went to the other side of the room.

"Naw, naw, naw. That ain't it! My man Guz over there got whatcha called a gift and a curse. He was at work moving furniture. Trying to pick up a refrigerator and strain too hard. Shit made his dick hard, and it's been hard ever since, and that's been three days now. I done had six hoes to fuck him, nigga shit still won't go down," Sean explained. That got a good laugh.

"Wow, what a fuckin' roommate and I mean that shit literally'," I said, and that got a laugh too.

"Enough of this comedy show niggas it's time to go. Got my trigger finger Itching now," Lil Corey said. We all said our get wells, and a few more jokes, and we were out.

PAY BACK

In 5 minutes we were back on Holderness taking turns getting money. We had to do something while we waited on Shawn's crew. It was after dark before they showed up. They pulled a big black familiar looking van up into the blue house alley. The van is like those cop's vans with the sliding side door.

"Let's ride," Shane said. Dressed in all black, black Mac-10, and a black bandana over his nose made the match. I'm the first man in, Lee followed, then Antoine.

"Hold on now! Lil Twon too young man. I ain't killing nobody wit no damn Juvenile. Are y'all niggas crazy," Shawn's brother Jeff proclaimed. He's driving, and that's where I know this van from, it's his. Tiger is riding shotgun, in the back of the van all the seats have been taken out. Sitting in the back of the van Big-Ty, Lil Steve, Big Shane, and Lil Corey, that made eight of us. Guns laid out everywhere. Eight witnesses can make seven co-defendants. I wondered how many rats would come out of the seven co-defendants. It really doesn't matter how many, when it only takes one for a life sentence.

"Ain't enough room anyway, Twon. Come on Will," I said.

"Damn man I wish I could ride, but I ain't strapped, and ain't no more room," Will said. Before I could say a word, he was gone. We laughed and pulled off. But this is far from a joke. Murder! If caught it's hard to come back from, nearly impossible. Every move should be a calculated step. This doesn't feel right, feels like high school shit. I've ducked one life sentence, hanging with Encre. I'm not about to play dodgeball with another one. We were riding up Ashby and made a right on North Avenue. The van is so quiet all I can hear is the tires rolling over asphalt. That's not good, these niggas doing too much thinking. Now they got me in my head, but I said it out loud.

"Dis bout to be some Hat Squad shit for sure. I hope y'all can keep yo mouths close, cause one word gets us all a free ticket one-way ticket down south on a blue bird," I said.

"Man, what the fuck dis nigga here talking bout wit dis Hat Squad and blue bird shit. Just tell me which way to turn to kill dis nigga that shot my brother," Jeff asked. He is a good dude, a good working man, a family man, a man I will not commit murder with. The Hat Squad also known as The Murder Police or Homicide have made a name for themselves around this city. If you don't know who they are or how many niggas ride that blue prison bus down south down for forever every day. You don't need to be doing any killing. The Hat Squad all wear big brim hats like the old gangsters out of Chicago. To earn that hat, a detective has to solve 10 homicides. We have at least 10 homicide detectives that's way over a hundred bodies of experience. When most killers are on their first body, who has the odds. On the other hand, Latonya's murder is still unsolved.

"Bust dis right on James P. pull on up and park on the curb. Y'all niggas mask up already. What the fuck, this ain't amateur night, we ain't at the Apollo. We gotta make dis shit quick, dis van we in look like the heat, we in the heart of The Bluff twin dem trappin Keyman dope right here. Open the door, Shane, I'll be back," I said in my best Terminator voice. I put the hoodie over my head and pulled it tight. I jumped out of the van, head down, pistol in hand inside of my front hoodie pocket. I'd already planned our plot. I was supposed to give Charity a piece of paper with a number on it, to hand to Square Jones at the store. Li-Corey is to follow her there without her knowing to see who the piece of paper gets past to, then kill him. I changed my walk up, I walked with a limp all the way up to Betty's house, pulled my hoodie back and knocked on the door.

"Who is it," Tameka asked.

"Kil," I answered. I heard some moving around, and locks unlocking.

"Hey Rodney! Is Lee with you," she tried looking around me.

"Naw, he still in the trap. I just left Cueball spot on Bankhead. I stop by to smoke some of this Iring. Where shorty at," I said, then pulled out a big bag of bud.

"Come on in boy before you go to jail. Smiley! Rodney here," Tameka yells. I went in and took a seat on a sofa that had seen much better days. Charity came from the back with a smile on her face, as always.

"Hey baby what's up we bout to ride off," she asked as she sat down on my lap.

"Naw I got drop off for a minute. Will coming back in an hour, I came to burn somma dis witcha. Go get some Phillies for James store and get some OEs," I said. I gave her $20 without the paper with the number on it. She jumped up and headed for the door.

"Com'on Mek walk wit me," Charity asked. Tamika obliged, I walked them on to the front porch and watched as they talked and walked up James P. They walked right past our black van. Lil Corey was already outside of the van, and he picked up their tail as planned. But that plan wasn't the plan anymore. This is what we call a dummy mission. That's why I aborted it, but played it off at the same time. My game's loaded. I'm just waiting for them to come back. Ten minutes later Charity and Tameka were headed back my way, bags in hand, still talking and laughing. We went inside and began rolling up the weed.

"You saw that nigga square Jones up there," I asked.

"Yeah that nigga up there buying everybody drinks like he just had a baby. That nigga got a big bank roll and he flashing. You better go check that nigga bout yo money before he give it all to the hoes," Charity answered. She thinks she's smart. She's been asking me a lot of questions lately, and that's another reason tonight is not right. I don't trust this hoe, I'm just fucking this hoe.

Bump-bump-bump. A horn blew. Time for me to go.

"Damn that fat ass Will got badass timing. I'll be back later on," I said. I made my exit fast. I jumped in the van.

"Tell these niggas Kil. That nigga ain't round there. Ain't na one dem bitch's hand no nigga in there shit," Lil Corey said. All eyes were on me.

"She say the nigga done gone home. Yall niggas took too long. How long ya'll think a nigga just gonna wait to die," I asked that broke the ice in the van. Lee got a good laugh out of it.

"Just keepin' it real, it don't matter who we kill tonight. As long as somebody gets shot. Just pull round there Jeff, one ya'll get ready to slide that door open. Imma give one of these niggas a AK killing. I don't give a fuck who it is," Shane spoke up. He and pimp Shawn are closer than most, and Shane takes niggas disrespecting very serious.

"Hold da fuck up Boo man. We ain't doing no drive by in dis nigga work van. Let me out first," Lee rebutted. We think just alike.

"Naw, naw, naw. Ain't nobody gettin out dis van over here, and ain't nobody gettin shot but the nigga that shot my brother. I don't get down like that, you better go get Rico, I'm headed back to the hood. Yall gettin out where I picked ya up, you dig," Jeff interrupted. Perfect, I can't wait to get out of this van. All these guns, and all these wittinesses.

"Ya'll niggas pussy and jive! Imma let Shawn know bout you hoes. One of ya'll niggas would've ratted anyway ole Master Splinter ass niggas! Take me home, man," Shane demands. He's mad now, but not as nearly as mad he would be with a life sentence. Shane is used to riding with the Muslims, and when they ride like this, somebody momma got to cry. But they never go to jail for the bodies, because they don't do sloppy work like this shit.

CHANGE

Needless to say, a few days later Square Jones got what I knew was coming to him, a full clip. I don't know what happened to that boy and never asked. All I know is what I heard, he's gonna have wheels for legs, and that's what Charity said. The hood changed big time after Shawn's shooting. It brought us all together like a big family. After he healed up Shawn moved his trap down to the dead end on Holderness, And now we do everything together with both crews, no beef we all getting money in our hood. Lee and I both are at the West End Academy now my daddy won't stay out for us about going to school.

It's cool with us, that's where all the fast ass girls are, and no cops don't have to worry about jail for those few hours. I left St. Luke's because I came to school, with my pistol like always and RED DOG, the (run every drug dealer outta Georgia) drug task force were searching people bags at the front door. I never went back to that school again in life.

Now I'm back in the hood with my people Mr. Garrett the Principal at West End Academy would never let the Red Dogs into his school. Because he wouldn't have any students left to teach. My world, the West End, is at peace, but the rest of the city is at war. The Miami boys are not letting up, they are digging down. The city is crumbling like Rome, but we are holding our Fort down. Just too much politics in our neighborhood for anybody just to move in and take over selling drugs. Lots of old money in our hood, cocaine cowboy killers on the corner, and hungry Muslims around every block. The Muslim still patrols the neighborhood like the police, more so after the Shawn shooting.

Harris Holmes is still under siege, but the good guys are making some progress. Monta, my homeboy that used to live on Lucille Ave. He got a big break down trap on the top field. Word is he and Teddy BB declared war on Dem Miami Boyz.

John Holt Holmes is still at war, word is Terry is on an Island laughing at the feds. Miami Trav is all over America's Most Wanted. All the murders make it hard to get money, but Dent-Dent is still making big money in John Holt. He just put out the biggest and the best, he doesn't care who else is getting money around him. That's what got Terry on the run now.

From Vine City to the block and up Herndon Homes, the Miami Boys were still causing havoc. They just killed a boy over there at Eagle Holmes on Kennedy's basketball court. He went up for a layup and came down dead. It's a lot of unsolved homicides in Atlanta right now. Then they gave Herndon Homes Strong four to the face. He was sitting right there in a car parked on Cocaine Lane in the heart of Herndon home. Everybody knows them niggas out of Herndon Holmes been working for the Miami Boyz. Speedy from Miami and Marshall is fucking all of them. When you eat with the enemy, be the first to get up to take a shit. You dig. Now they have shot Herndon Homes finest Todd. I think that will change things on that side. I'm not going to even speak on Techwood, that's anybody's trap. Mechanicville Projects Mi-Phi-Yo, Big Sick click and Atlanta niggas get money over there and up through Pittsburgh. Carver Homes is still infested with Miami Boyz. Junebug caught a murder case at a dice game, he killed Lil Walt. I'll probably never see him again, and I really miss my friend.

I have to admit Atlanta is a hustler's paradise, but when you double the murder rate. Things change fast. We got a war going on with the Miami Boyz. While our Government has a war on drugs, that means us. My daddy tells me this all the time, but

I watch the news. If only to see who got killed, and I see other things, like who got busted.

WHAT HAPPENED
TO THAT BOY

December 31st 1990 was a good year. I'm putting the past behind me, because ain't nothing but money in front of me. This is my New Year's resolution: Get Rich or Die Trying. Our guns were all cocked and loaded 10 minutes before 12. We were all drunk, ready to fire up the sky.

"Speech," somebody yelled. Somebody had to toast to the year. We are 50 deep standing in the middle of Holderness Street.

"This has been a good year. I look around, and we all still here. Now it's time to reap our blessing and.....". I was saying;

"And you forgot minus one of Shawn's nuts nigga," Boom-boom-boom-boom-boom! Rico said as he pulled up in the crowd on a Ninja motorbike. Then started shooting a semi pump shotgun before the new year even began, and Lee followed with the AK-47. We shot our guns all night, shooting every street light out in sight. The year had begun, and it's sure to be plenty of smoke, and it didn't take long for a fire to start.

The sun is shining brightly for this Sunday, the third week of January right at noon. I'm where I always am, sitting on the steps down by the street that leads to the Blue House front yard. I'm the first one out today, I didn't go to the 731 last night. I was up all morning trapping by myself, so I gotta watch my pack and watch for the jump out crew too.

"What's been up, sucker," a familiar voice said. I turned around and to my surprise it was Mississippi Tommy. I was surprised to see him because I hadn't seen him in so long, not since Shawn got shot and that's been months ago. Last I heard, Wil said, this nigga ran off with a half a key of pure Peruvian flake that belongs to Black James. Ain't nobody seen Tommy since, now here he is.

"What's up Tommy you looking fresh to death. Where you get those Fila's from? You a cold motherfucker, you wearing white in the winter nigga. Where the fuck you been, T-Money? Shit put down nigga let a nigga at some that money. Imma bout to go buy some dice now. Don't you go nowhere," I said. I turned back to the street and spotted Black James car cruising by. His brake lights popped on, then quickly went off. The candy apple red 79 Impala sped off to the bottom of the dead end. I turned back to Tommy, but he was gone. The only evidence that he was ever there was a cigarette on the ground still smoking. What happened to that boy? Just as I was about to head down to Black James house to tell him who I just saw. Black James was headed my way with a black Tech Nine in his hand. You really had to be from the West End to know the black James was a drug dealer he's well-respected in the community. His wife is a teacher special ed at Brown High school, Mrs. Farrell, and they own houses and apartments all over the West End. I've known him since the days I used to work at the store. He knows my entire family. I guess that's mainly the reason he's never sold me any dope, because of my daddy. I have to give my money to Will and let him cop for me.

"Which way did that motherfucker go, Lil Rod,"? Black James asked. He was holding the TEC-9 with both hands.

"That way"! I answered quickly; and pointed up the alley behind me. Black James ran up the alleyway in the Direction I pointed. I stood there listening to hear shots, but it never rang out. A second later Black James reappeared at the bottom of the ally, still gripping his Tech Nine with both hands.

"Com here, Lil Rod! Now you listen to me, if you see that nigga there anywhere, anytime, you call me, and promise. You look at me, Lil Rod. I promise I gotcha," he said. He handed me a business card, and I couldn't wait to get into business with him. I ran to the Blue House and jumped through the window.

"Up and at it you maggots. Nothing comes to a sleeper but a dream. Yall nigga not gonna believe what just happen. Yall niggas sleeping, and Black James running Mississippi Tommy ass all over the hood with a TEC-9 sheets," I told them. Lee, Wil, Antoine, Shane, and some hoes I had never seen before all looked up from under sheets, blankets and pillows and said.

"Man, that nigga James a Real gangster. He's an old Miami boy you see all them gold teeth in his mouth don't you. Dem trophies niggas, he got bout 10 of dem motherfuckers," Will said. Everyone was up now on their way out of the window. Outside on the front porch I could see the streets had gotten busy, I wasn't the only one to witness the action. Just the thought of violence attracts black people.

"Shoot five bet five nigga I'm trying to re-up," Twon said. He was already on his knees shaking some dice.

"Yeah man fuck that nigga Tommy he gonna get what he got coming. Sooner or later all dem niggas gonna get what they got coming. Fuckin alienators infiltrators, they ain't nothing but ATL hater. Shoot 10 nigga or pass the dice, you ain't bout to crab on me," Lee said, as poetic as ever.

"My fade," Shane called. Then he dropped $20 on the ground, and that's how our day or days began, but ain't no telling how they may end, hopefully not at Willie Watkins. We shoot dice and sell hard and soft all day. Tonight is a club night, The Game Room and then Nightlite. Those clubs are off Moreland and Custer Avene. It's all the way live on Sunday nights. So around 6 we went to Greenbrier Mall and got fresh to death and went to Red Lobster on Campbellton Road. After that we all met back up at the Blue House to shoot pool and more dice. All of this is our normal Sunday routine. We've been doing the same thing since

I was Hustling and everybody knows this. The Blue House is loud and smoked up, Big Shane got the same song playing Public Enemy get up to get down nine-one-one is a joke in yo town. Is all Lucille and Holderness in the house tonight, Clarence's crew and Pimp Shawn's crew. Two bosses got a big money pool game going, and we all got big bets placed on the sides. Pimp Shawn is a better pool shooter than CP, with one or two nuts. But CP is smart and he bets big and shoots plenty of D, he's on the 8 ball now the last shot, the money shot.

"8 ball side pocket Shawn, I gotta tell you it was fun," Clarence said. Pimp Shawn put himself in front of the cue ball.

"Hold what ya got nigga, I gotta grand you can't bank out," Shawn said. Clarence moved Shawn's hand out of the way and took his shot.

"Naw nigga fuck you. Pay me," Clarence yelled. The ball hit dead inside the pocket but rimmed out. The blue house erupted in curses, cheers. Shawn won the game on the next shot. It's around 10:30-11:00 now, so everyone started to file out to their cars headed for the game room. I watch them pull off Convoy Style. I'd already planned to ride with CP in his brand new Powder blue 89 Fleetwood to the Game Room, so I went back inside. Clarence and Mississippi Stanly were starting another game pool. The only people left at the house were Clarence, Stanly, Mian Poon, Philip Poon, and myself.

"You ain't ready yet CP we can shoot pool at the game room, where all the hoes are at man," I said. CP is a Gambling fool.

"Ok, ok, ok. Dis the last game I got dis country lame. We just waiting on Philip he back there taking a shit, and imma out on dis nigga watch dis shit Kil." CP said. Boom-boom-boom-boom-booom-pow-booom-pow-boom-boom-boom-pow-pow... "Get down y'all get down get down. Everybody alright? Anybody hit? Y'all say something, man," CP asked after we heard the last of I don't know how many shots.

"I'm cool," I said. Then everyone else confirmed the same.

"Man, what the fuck going on? Somebody gotta be playing that shit came from right outside, and it didn't hit the house," Mian said. We were all hunkered down under the pool table. Maybe they weren't aiming at the house.

"Yeah, you right I think some jealous motherfucker shot my car up. Hold on y'all stay down," CP whispered. Then crawled like an army man to the window. He got on his knees and peeped out.

"I can't see shit," he said. Then someone knocked on the door. CP dove back under the table.

They knocked again. Everyone was in total silence.

"Who is it," CP answered. All eyes were on the door.

"It's Apple, man! What the fuck ya'll doing? It's cold as fuck stop playing man. Open up," Apple said. Now all eyes were on CP. He looked at me with that, you know what it is look. I pulled out my brand new 9 mm Taurus. I bought it for Christmas from the Muslim Shahid for a $50 off holiday sale. I crawled from under the pool table. Still on my knees, I use the pool table to take aim at the door. With my head, I signal for Clearance to open the door. To my relief it was Apple, and he had no gun, and he wasn't riddled with bullets. When he saw my gun he flinched, so I held it down and stood up.

"Hurry up and get in nigga! Somebody just let off a hundred rounds right out there," CP said.

"Who got shot? I just heard somebody begging for their life outside the bathroom window. They were saying why you shoot me foe? Please don't kill me, and then," Philip said. But outside next door I could hear No other than Pamela Newell screaming, cursing, and sounds of glass breaking in the street. I ran out ready to shoot, but nobody just screamed a lot of screams in the dark.

"Y'all motherfuckers done shot my brother somebody, please call 911," Pam screamed. I looked next door, and she was throwing flower pots off the porch into the middle of the street.

I ran up the alley to the back door of the Newell's house and reached for the knob.

"Kil! Help, help," a weak familiar voice said. It was coming from the other corner of the house. I headed that way. From the floodlights I saw what looked to be a big garbage bag on the ground. But it wasn't as I got closer I made him out. Laying on his stomach, his head turned sideways, looking right at me. His white T-shirt had a big red hole in the back of his shoulder, and blood was pouring out. The air smelled of gunpowder, copper, and blood, if blood has a smell. All my hairs were standing on my body, I'm on full alert.

"Oh my God, Robert! What happened, man," I shouted, hoping someone would hear. I was only speaking to Robert and the cold wind.

"Just go get help, Kil. Go get help please," Robert begged as loud as he could. My legs came to life, and I took off running down the Newell's steps and into the streets. I looked up the block. Not a soul. I looked towards the dead end. I saw a crowd standing in the middle of the street right in front of old man Skeeter's house, huddled around in a circle like their waiting on quarterback to give them the play.

"Ah, ah, I need help, man. Robert done got shot! Ah ah," I yelled as loud as I could, but no one even turned to look from only four houses away. Something real had their attention, I ran down to them, and broke through the huddle. My God! On the ground before me a body laying face down, body turned like he was headed up Holderness Street. Blood was everywhere.

"My God! Who the fuck is that," I asked. I feel like I just stepped into the Twilight Zone. Winnyhead and his brother Frank were down on the ground with the body as they turned it over. The man on the ground lying there in a pool of blood had no face and was all but decapitated.

"Oh, God! What the fuck ya'll niggas done. Get yo fuckin hands outta that man pockets! Who is that Kil? What happened,"

Mississippi Stanley screamed. He and CP were now standing behind me. I look down at the dead body being ravished by wolves. Frank had his arm up to his elbow in the man's pocket. Everything but his shoes were covered in blood, they were snow white Nike Flights like the ones I saw earlier, then it hit me.

"That's Mississippi Tommy man! Look up there, ain't that his car. What happened to that boy," I asked. Parked directly across the street from the blue house was Thomas's yellow Buick. Mississippi Stanley threw up everywhere. Frank Nitti took off running with a handful of money, and all the junkies ran behind.

"Is he dead," a voice asked from behind. I turned, and it was Rico dressed in all black like an Omen. The top of his head was steaming from sweat, like what's left of Tommy's head is steaming from blood. And yes, blood does have a smell, because I can smell it. All I smell is blood, no gunpowder, no copper, not down here, just blood.

"Yeah he dead alright, he hardly gotta head. Dis nigga is as dead as a nigga can ever die," I answered. I looked back, and Rico was gone. That's when I heard the siren, Clarence and I went on to the game room to spread the news. I don't have any empathy or sympathy. I'm just glad it wasn't me. We weigh our lives on triple beams every day. Tommy's scale wasn't leveled. He let greed outweigh his life, it's levels to this game, you gotta get away with what you can get.

AFTERMATH

After Tommy's killing, the West End turned into a crime scene. The Hat Squad was everywhere, Robert Newell got lucky, he lived with a big hole in his back. For his pain and suffering he received an ounce of hard, and his momma got a porch full of flowers. Robert knew who shot him. He talked to his shooter. Begged him for his life. All Robert was doing was taking his trash out and walked up on a hit. He wouldn't say who shot him, but it didn't take a suit and a fancy hat to figure this one out. Still no arrests were made, the cops just turned Holderness into a mini Precinct for about 2 months. No money could be made, so I moved my trap to Dill Avenue. I hustled on Athens and Dill right behind the salon. On the same street my parents lived on, and so did Encre. By now he had a few dope cases and wasn't getting money like he used to. Dill Avenue ain't no real trap, but it's about to be. I got money there for almost 2 months, just enough time for the heat to die down in the WestEnd. I left that trap to Encre, and his two workers Laddell and Titus. The money on Dill had gotten good, but I'm stone addicted to my neighborhood. Two months seemed like a lifetime. It's the first time I ever really felt homesick, so I went back. Ignoring all the warnings from my father. He begged me not to go; he felt I would surely be killed. He'd heard the rumors for years, of a clan of Muslims killing drug dealers in the WestEnd. I know the truth, because I know the Clan, so I don't have to listen to rumors. People get killed in the West End for the same things they get killed for on Bankhead, money, dope, and hoes. The time I spent on Dill Ave. made me closer to my parents again. Looking around the house at all my old baseball and football trophies, just baller dreams. That's when my life wasn't so shady. Now all my dreams are about dope-money, and dead bodies. My father tried to understand me, but now he seems to follow my path. Money can be like a disease, it can spread and take over everything, and it can definitely kill. I pick the second Friday in March to start my trap back on Holderness, and like always I'm up right before the sunrise. I tried to be the first on the block, but this morning I had some good company.

"Killer Kil what it is my nigga," Lee asked from behind the same way Tommy did the last day I seen him alive. Lee, Shane and I still lived in the rooming house, so we still kicked every day. Word is the hood is still hot, but the cops on the horses are gone now. I didn't leave Holderness because Tommy got killed. I left because I didn't want to go to jail. Any time a body hit that close, the cops will do anything to try to get a nigga to tell, like plant dope on dealers. Then we see a lot of undercover. If you catch a sale-case, you can cancel your Christmas.

"Slow motion G! You said it's been slow, but this shit is dead Lee," I explained. I'd been out for over an hour, only making $200 bucks. I used to make $2000 in that amount of time, just sitting here by myself on a slow day.

"Man Kil you know what it is! Rico done came up on some big blow man selling it all cheap down on the Muslims in across Gordon on that end on Holderness. Mac and them two brothers on that end eating. Junkies too scared to come down here. All that Muzlims killing drug dealers shit in they ears. Dem niggas playing the game wicked on us. They got the Hat Squad spent, worsted than the news people, but you see dem niggas done got greedy too. A lot of nigga been going to jail round here, ain't gonna say no names, but Don't nobody get out of Jefferson Street that fast," Lee said; with a wink

"That's real talk," I replied. I I watched one lonely feign walking our way. Not another soul in sight. I hadn't seen a cop car all morning.

"I'm tellin ya man! Hey what's up Gwen how many you need baby," Lee said as Junky Gwen came into view. Her face wet as rain, she was crying some real serious tears.

"I don't need nothing, Lee! Ya'll must've not heard yet," Gwen asked. She looked really surprised.

"Bout what," I asked. I stood up from the steps.

"They murdered Black James dis morning, shot the man 11 times all in his face, eyes, and mouth. They caught him slipping up there in dem apartments he owns over across Gordon. They left him dead in the stairwell. I pray it's the one going to heaven," Gwen answered. She cried it all out like a small child.

"My God," I screamed. I've been knowing that man all my life. I know all his kids. This is bad, very bad.

"What God nigga? I done told you bout that God shit! I tell you what, tell Mrs. Farrell, and her kids, why God would let someone shoot their husband and father 11 times in the face? That's a cold blood and you know it, and they dem niggas you grew up wit," Lee popped off. I'm still stunned, totally shocked.

"They who Gwen," I pleaded. Why did I ask when I already knew?

"Let me find out, Kil? You wearing a wire nigga, or do you just wanna hear the motherfuckers names? You ain't slow nigga! Assalamualaikum," Gwen said. She pulled her shirt down and showed me the big old bullet wound on the left side of her chest, right above her titty. Then she walked off. She had gotten it a few years back, down by the park trying to steal cars with her boyfriend Tee, from a Muslims gun no doubt. She got really lucky, but she knew better.

"You going back to Dill Kil"? Lee asked; I don't know if he's serious or not, but I'd already decided.

"Naw, I ain't going nowhere Lee, I gotta plan! They done made it hot up there now, so shit should cool down, down here now, you dig, but we bout to get our own trap house," I answered.

"I'm wit it, and I dig it," Lee replied. It's time to get our own crew, our own spot, so we can call our own shots. They made the blue house hotter than hot. The cops come to park in front for hours at a time. Murder just not good for our business, but it's a necessity in order to stay in business. Poor Black James, he had to handle his business, he had to put it on the nigga head. You can't leave a penny in these streets, it'll turn into a million. When you put on a nigga head know your killer, because a killer for money doesn't care who THEY kill.

THE FOUR HORSEMEN

We had our big money plan in full motion, Lee, Shane, Wil, and myself; The Four Horsemen. Clarence Poon is in prison for a cocaine case he's serving 18 months. The Blue House is no more, we trap from the apartment on Holderness across from Rodney's house. That's where Detroit Chuck introduced us to our first major connection. Two young cats out of California, they weren't much older than Lee and me. They were moving major weight straight from California and were soon derailed. I caught my first cocaine case April 7th of 1990 the Red Dog unit arrested me on Holderness Street with 250 cocaine rocks. Before then they had never arrested me for a felony, only for Misdemeanor gambling. They say when it rains it pours and I'm drowning. May 25th 1990, I was busted again with another 200 cocaine rocks. Now I'm out of jail on bond on two different drug charges. Dwight Thomas is my lawyer. I met him down in Brent's cook house, the Palace. He and his beautiful secretary Charlotte hang down at the palace all night. I Like Charlotte and I pray God gets her off dope, what a waste. Now I'm 10 grand in with Dwight, half blow and half cash, and he still promises me probation. That's what he promised Clarence but now Clarence is down in Reidsville, someone picking squash. Since the two murders almost everybody in the hood has gotten a case or two. All but my crew, Lee, Wil, and Shane are all case free, and I'm working on number three. It's like every time it's my turn to work the bomb I get busted. The Outcasts are not having much luck these days, they're getting raided every week. It's a real war going on against drugs and we are losing badly.

A CHARITY CASE

It's the fall of 1990 now, it's been a very hot summer, and my life will never be the same now. I found out about a month ago that Charity is pregnant. She had an abortion, well at least I gave her the money, twice. Now it's October, and she's asking me again. For money to abort the same baby.

"Ah shawty I'm cool wit it. My old man says he wants a baby, cause I know you don't," I told her. It's true, I told my daddy she was pregnant, and it's like he hit the jackpot. He felt I was on my way to prison or my grave. He wants to see Rod again. Sad to say, the old me is dead and gone. Rod died with that sweet girl on the bridge.

"Nigga you don't know what the fuck I want! I want a baby just not by yo broke, prison-bound ass nigga! Naw fuck that! Imma just put yo punk ass on child support," Charity snapped. Charity has the worst mouth I've ever heard on a woman. She's the type to beg a man for abuse, and I'm an abuser.

"Shut the fuck up bitch foe I punch out yo rabbit ass teeth. Dig dis bitch! You just trash I forgot to take out you starting to smell. I feel sorry for you and your entire family, but it ain't my fault yo momma running around in these streets sucking dicks for rocks, and you don't know where your daddy is. It ain't my fault you and your brothers and sisters are homeless! It ain't my fault you are a kuffar! You don't believe in shit bitch! Ima be rich, I don't give a fuck what you see hoe. All I see is money, when I ain't looking at you. Carla was pregnant too. Both of y'all at the same damn time. She had an abortion, and I didn't have to give her a dime. She gets her own money. Bye broke bitch, you gonna have to use a hanger to get that shit outta you," I snapped back. It's true Carla was pregnant too, and I like her. She already had two kids. It seems like every time I have sex with Carla, another one of her brothers comes over here trying to trap me. First it was Donny, now Lil Rod, and I hear another one is on the way. I had enough on my mind that I couldn't be thinking about a broke bitch and a baby. I really didn't hate Charity, she just didn't matter to me, nothing really matters to me, but staying alive and free.

Just like always, my daddy smoothed all things out between Charity and I, and we were living together on our way to having a baby. He loves Charity more than I do. I'm embracing the fact that I will now have something left on earth in case I have an early demise. I hustle round killers, people that I know have committed Malice murders and the cops ride by them every day, and lock me up for just trying to survive. You would think if you get away with something that bad you would stop, but they didn't.

Lee and I are still attending The West End Academy, I have too. I'm on probation, and my daddy. I think Lee goes for the girls and his mother. Around the end of the year, we were at school having lunch at the KFC next door. Encre, Lee, and myself, it's a lot of whispers going around about a shooting on the other end of Holderness.

"Ah Kil man who that got shot on Holderness last night," Encre asked.

"That happened on the other end. I don't know who got shot, but ain't know question who done the shooting," I answered. Encre not from the West End if he was he wouldn't be asking questions about the other side, the Clan side and we're in a Restaurant full of Muslims.

"Yall seen Lee, y'all seen Lee? Ah Lee," a voice called out. We all turned to look, Lee stood with his hand behind his back on his gun.

"Here I go," Lee answered as loud as he could, but they weren't enemies. It's MaShun and Byron from Beecher and Cascade, niggas we went to Brown with. They hurried over to our table. These are cool cats we had no beef with, it's always been all love. They had strange looks on their faces. Everybody spoke, and then.

"Y'all heard what happened to Earl," Byron asked.

"Naw what," Lee and I asked in cadence. I could feel all eyes on us in the KFC.

"We were riding on the other end of Holderness, not the dead end and we stop to Holla at some hoes. Some nigga's wearing Kufi's open fire on the car. Hit Earl in the neck, he almost died man! Who the fuck is dis nigga Shahid, ya'll gotta know him," MaShun asked. The entire restaurant went silent. It seemed like even the chicken stopped frying. These niggas just asked for the Devil in a room full of his disciples.

"Lunch over, let's go outside," I broke the silence. I didn't look at any of the faces as I passed, but I could still feel the stares. Outside, I looked both of my old friends in the eyes.

"Ya'll niggas must be trying to die? Don't ride round her asking bout that man it'll getcha killed quick. He'll turn your kids into charity cases. That nigga is a ghost man. If you got a beef with him, if you see him it's too late you already dead. Earl lucky to be alive. We drug dealers. Man, dem niggas stone-cold killer. Yall let that shit go! I got love foe all ya'll niggas, don't wanna see nothing bad happen to ya'll. I know Shy if I ask him to let it go he will. Man just lay low for a while and be cool. Whatever you do, don't say his name again around here," I explained. These niggas better start reading the newspapers.

"Ya'll act like y'all scared of this nigga Shahid! Does dis motherfucker bleed? If he got a heartbeat, I got something that can stop it. Y'all just tell that nigg......." Byron said. He always tries to go for tough, but a few bullet wounds will stop that buffoonery.

"I ain't tell that nigga shit! You better get the fuck on foe they pull up. You think dis shit a joke, some kind of movie script. Kil trying to save y'all lives. Them niggas don't shoot movies, they shoot AKs. You right he was born so he can die, but first you gotta find out who to kill. Y'all did dis shit wrong, they gonna be on the hunt for ya now. Just be careful, we gotta go to class," Lee warned. We went back to class, but I couldn't concentrate. I knew death would be coming soon.

After school, back on the block. I saw the car before they saw me, Shahid. The car stopped right beside me, Abdul, Cockeyed Casa, and Shahid got out of the car all smiles and hugs.

"Assalamualaikum Akhi? You got any beef we can eat? I'm trying to pop Cockeyed cherry, before I ride on the fool that came to the school looking for me. Where dem cats be at Kil," Shy asked. It's always a body for a body with Shahid. We call it favors. He's always grooming a new young soldier, or should I say killer. Casa is only 13 and bald-headed Assad 12. That's who he rides with, young killers.

"Naw Shy. Ain't no beef, just chicken round here. Just like dem dudes that came to the school, they came to send you an apology. They were looking for a girl that lived two streets over. It was all just a misunderstanding. You dig. Plus, we cool wit dem niggas, went to school wit dem, so if nothing else let it go for me," I asked. Shahid looked me in my eyes, then looked at Jamil.

"Kil you blood in with us. You will always have our favor. If you say, let it go, then it's gone, that's on Allah! Just tell dem cats I need all my bullets back, even the one outta dude neck"! Shahid said; the rest of the Clan just bowed their heads up and down. I'm affiliated with a lot of bad people, that I know a lot of bad things about, I got secrets I can never tell, not even to Lee. I can call a truce because I'm big enough to do it.

RIDE OR DIE

Everyone on Holderness is affiliated with the clan. Only Shane and myself are blood in kuffar on Holderness. Growing up, Rico lived right in the Muslim's den. He used to be neighbors with Jamil. Rico and Shane are best friends, they got a house together now over off Moreland Ave, and I think Shahid lives there too. When we were young Shane warned me a thousand times about Shahid. He told me not to ever get in a car with him, and if I did sit in the back and don't turn your back. I listened to Shane, and I avoided every chance of getting in the car with Shahid. Back when I first came back to the hood, on one very cold winter night, almost midnight. I was the only soul on the block when this Black two 98 Oldsmobile turned the corner. It pulled right up to the blue house ally, right in front of me. Three heads and three kufis were in there. The window rolled down.

"Ah Kil, check dis out Aki," Shahid asked. I backed up a little into the shadows of the alley. I had no idea what they may have wanted, but I had my gun on me. I walked out to the car.

"What's up Shy, Jamil, Casa y'all cool," I asked. I leaned into the car. Jamil sitting in the front seat with a pump shotgun, Shahid had a 9 mm Taurus sitting in his lap, I couldn't see if Casa was strapped, but I knew he was. They didn't look or speak to me, only Shahid.

"Where everybody at? I need ya, man! Got some big beef over in Pittsburgh,"! Shahid said. He looked hyped, like he just came out of a base house. Wow! I had to think fast.

"Dem nigga went on a lick, I let Lee use my gun," I lied. I didn't want to get in a car full of killers, and nobody saw me get in.

"Here you go Kil. You can use one of my guns," Shahid offered. Now I gotta death decision to make. It's like, I'd be damn if I do, I be damn if I don't. But without hesitation, I took the gun out of his hand.

"Ight cool, give me a minute gotta go put my pack up," I answered. I turned and ran up the blue house alley I should have kept running and never came back. Behind the blue house, I took my drugs and gun to my stash. Before I stashed my drugs, I reached in and pulled out a gram of powder. I opened it up and stuck my pinky nail inside. I scooped almost half the bag and sniffed up one side of my nose. I repeated my actions and fed the other side of my nose. I'm instantly high, I stashed my goods, whipped my nose, then headed back down the alley Shahid's gun in my right hand. His car is parked and waiting. I should just kill these niggas, the dope told my mind. My trigger finger even started itching.

"Get in Aki before the cops ride by and you looking like you are about to blast us," Shahid said. I snapped out of my cocaine daze. Black Jamil was holding the seat back for me. I jumped in and sat behind him. Cockeyed Casa sat to the left of me, black 9mm in his hand. The car pulled away from the curb. I'm riding with The Clan and a ghost is driving. Just on my count Shahid has over 10 bodies, and no jail, but every time I sell a rock I go to jail. It's a war on drug dealers, not killers. I don't know one solved murder case in my hood. The eerie part is everybody knows who's doing the killing. Now I got myself riding with them.

"Ah Kil, you bring any bud with you," Shy asked. He don't even smoke, or drink. He's a devout Muslim, very serious about his faith.

"I just gotta blunt! You smoking weed now Shy," I asked. I think cockeyed Casa turned one of his eye's my way.

"Nooo! Aki I just love how the shit smell fired up. That brother in the back may wanna hit it. Jamel and myself we on our Dean shit," Shy answered. I had no idea what he meant and didn't care. I fired up the weed and said a silent prayer, the one Mrs. Webb taught me at Sunday school. I had nothing to fear. The Lord is my shepherd. We pull to the other side of Holderness, the Muslim side of Holderness. The weed was gone, sucked up in Casa's and my lungs. We pulled up behind a car right before Darryl Mack's house near the curve. Shahid got out of the car, a few seconds later a long gray Station wagon, and a beat up black Chevy Caprice pulled right up beside our car. In the station wagon four Kufis, four long beards and the barrels of three AK-47's. I know two of the faces, the other two are older guys. The black Chevy Caprice had four head three kufis. I knew all the young faces, but one face I really knew was Roderick Fulton. Rod and I are good friends and went to school together. I had no idea he hung with the Clan, he looked at me with the same confused look I had to be looking at him with. Shahid said something into both of the cars, then got back in and we pulled away, leading the way. Ten Muslims and two kafirs, I wish I could disappear out of here right now. I have no idea who we are looking for or why. I'm just a good soldier following orders. I know what this is, so I act like a dog and lose my speech. It seemed like we all did. Shahid turned left off of Stewart Avenue onto Rockwell Street, then we made a left on Coleman Street and stopped in front of a nice brick house the front porch light was on.

"Here Kil put this on and these, and follow me. You two get points on both sides at the back of the house and we going up to knock on his door," Shahid instructed. We all followed without saying a word. I put on the black Kufi and Blues Brothers shades. I followed the devil, at the same time I made a promise to God.

CASED UP

Now I'm a made man, a shot caller, that means I don't have to shoot, and I better not get shot, that may cause a lot of bodies to drop. It's kind of funny, because I didn't ask for this. All I ask for is the money. I need to be careful about what else I ask for, because more can come with it.

I got so many drug cases I don't know which one my Lawyer, Junky Dwight Thomas just got me 90 days bootcamp for. I do know I have to turn myself in on May 21st 1991, and the baby is due in May. The judge gave me 30 days to get my life in order to do 90 days in a boot camp. Charity and I are still together. We moved in with my parents after Jackie shot Lee in both legs at the rooming house. Lee came out good considering he was shot with his own 357 Python. Not even a limp. Now they're back in love trying to have kids. I don't think I've ever been in love, maybe infatuated. I don't love Charity and never have. I don't even love myself. I have to go to bootcamp then maybe prison; I have open cases still, Junky Dwight Thomas has smoked my money dry. Now my freedom is flying away, and I can't do anything to stop it. Plus a baby girl on the way by a former homeless and still ungrateful bitch. If it wasn't for my daddy, this baby wouldn't be a thought. Who wants a baby by a prostituting, whore, with a filthy mouth? She's an embarrassment to me, but daddy loves her to death.

Speaking of death, it happened again. Shahid got word my Beecher Street homeboys were trying to get gun heavy for him. That was a very bad move. Trying to buy a lot of guns in the Westend without Shahid or a Muslim finding out is nearly Impossible. As a result of that action, Cornelius ended up with three bullets in the back of his head. Bron got shot in the jaw, he had to dive out of a two-story window head first in order to survive. Now the Ghost is on the run, talk is he sent word to the Clan, to kill a witness. Some young Muslim boy named Lil Rico but no kin to the real Rico. He's the one that set the gun deal up. I thought Muslim didn't kill Muslim, but I guess everybody kills rats. I don't have time to waste wondering how it may all play out. These days I've been thinking about what it would be like if I was a father. What if I really get to live to see it?

GOD IS GREAT

My lil girl was born on the 20th of May at around 5:13 am. She was the smallest human I ever held in my hands. I cut her umbilical cord. She cried until the doctor handed her to me, then she stopped. My heart stopped, I felt a little dizzy, light-headed, and I lost my breath. I thought to myself

"Look what God just brought from hell". She's beautiful. All of me is all I see. I looked at Charity laying there smiling at me, and I felt a crack in my heart. Poor child, she doesn't have shit but me! Nobody in her family came to see her child born. The only people at that hospital that night were my daddy, my momma, myself, and Charity didn't have a soul to call. I felt sad for her and I think I felt love for her.

I didn't leave the hospital until I turned myself in. I spent less than 24 hours with my first born baby girl. She didn't even have a name before I was on my way to turn myself in, but before I did daddy had me go by and sign that nameless Birth certificate. He tried his best with words of comfort, as he drove me to the Fulton County Courthouse to turn myself in. I didn't hear anything he was saying. My mind is dreaming of my little Sade, my sweetest taboo.

"Ask Charity to name my baby Sade," I asked daddy. He looked over at my strange.

"Boy y'all ain't naming my baby after no heroin junkie. I love her music too, but fuck that. We gonna name her after yo momma," daddy answered. Charity doesn't even like my momma, and momma hoped she died on the delivery table.

"I don't know if Charity will go for that," I said. I'm not even thinking about names anymore. I'm about to lock myself up, but now I'm thinking, not so fast! It's like daddy read my mind.

"She'll go for it boy she ain't got nowhere else to go. That girl don't want no baby. Believe it or not, Rod, I prayed you off these streets. Now God done blessed me double, I done lived to see my first grandbaby. That's a milestone in life, something you and your friends will never see. You got death all around you Rod, but you ain't dead yet. Use this little time to focus on what you want out of life, cause you ain't gonna get nothing but dead out these streets. Do I gotta walk you in there or are you gonna be a man and get this shit behind you yourself," daddy asked. He has a very sad look on his face, and his eyes are watery. He made me want to cry as we pulled in front of the Fulton County Courthouse. I looked him in the eyes.

"Daddy I promise you Imma do what I gotta do. You just do what you promise to do," I said. I opened the car door and got out.

"Take care of yourself, boy. I love you," he said. I didn't even look back.

"I love you too daddy. I love you too," I answered. I could hear his car pulling from the curve. It's a bright sunny morning, a beautiful day. Just not a good day to go to jail, and I had no plans on going. My plan is to wait until Walt is out of sight, and head to Bowen Holmes to lay up with Carmen for a few days. As I headed down the courthouse steps, Fulton County Jail prisoners in all blue headed upstairs.

"My nigga killer Kil what it is! Tell the hood I got lucky. Just got 90 days of boot camp on my way today. Be home in August, I'm going to Albers, Georgia it's a new boot camp. Love you homie," James yelled to me. JD is a Lucile Ave original, he shot Keith. Well, they shot each other. That's amazing, we're going to the same boot camp on the same day and we are from the same hood. That's a sign from God, so I turned and headed back up the steps behind them.

287

"Me too homie, I'm coming wit ya," I answered. He looked back at me and smiled.

"It's on my nigga. Let's get it," JD answered. He didn't know he just helped me make my mind up on a huge life decision.

For me boot camp was like ROTC for 90 days straight, and in school I liked ROTC. The difference was this ROTC is full of drug dealers from all over Georgia, but more from Atlanta than anywhere else. Frank Knitty from Carver Holmes had been there a month before me. JD and I went in the same day. We sleep in the same dorm. We ate at the same table. We worked on the same detail, and we got out the same day. Boot Camp was a joke to us, nothing but yelling and threatening. We are from where threats turn into death, not exercise.

DEJA VU

Now 3 months and 3 days later I'm back on the block with a pocket full of rocks. The way I see it, I have no choice. I got another court date September 13th, 1991. Now Dwight wants $10,000 to get me five years probation for the last of my cases. It seems like all the money I make goes to a junky ass lawyer, it's like I'm selling dope to stay free. Holderness has changed. After the Tommy murder, a lot of hustlers caught cases. But not my crew, Lee, Wil, Shane, and Twon were all still case free. The Outcast has been busted so many times it looks like a ghost town. The war on drugs is starting to show in my hood, and our outcome is looking grim. Here I am like I have nothing to lose, but my life.

"How many he wants Lee," I yelled from the alley behind the Outcast. Lee was posted up right across in Shane's mother's driveway. The trap had moved again.

"He need five and that one need five mo'! C'mon y'all, get it and go let's get it, let's go let's go dis ain't no peep show," Lee yelled back.

"Watch out watch out, slow down Shane nigga foe you kill somebody"! Lee screamed; I was still in the alley when I heard the tires screech to a stop, and car doors slamming.

"That pussy nigga done shot JD," Shane yelled. I ran from the alley to see what was going on. Shane's brown Nova was pulled halfway in the driveway, and I was already in the house. JD is walking around in a circle with a big hole in his left leg right below the knee.

"Who shot you JD, what the fuck happened nigga," Lee is frantic. I looked JD in his eyes, but he wasn't there. I saw an animal, a monster with blood in his eyes.

"That pussy nigga Jeff who momma stay on Cascade up by the beautiful,"! JD growled. He can't be talking about our Jeff!

"Prep Jeff," Lee and I asked at the same time. We have known Jeff for years. He used to work for William. Now since I have been gone, he and Lee have the same connection. The LA boys that Detroit Chuck brought to the hood. They got cocaine straight from California, and the cheapest in town. 18000 a kilo, and the prices out here are almost 30. We don't need this beef, we have to try to politic this.

"Yeah that nigga Prep Jeff, nigga caught me slipping in Mechanicville said some shit bout I robbed his momma house last month. I been in boot camp wit Kil for 90 days. It's on now, somebody give me a blow. I need some of that shit for my leg. Imma fire dis nigga ass back up before I go to the hospital," JD answered. Blood was running down his leg. Shane came back out with his M-1 in one and an ounce of cocaine in the other. It's just another Friday night on Holderness Street.

"Hold on, hold on niggas, I can go talk to dis nigga, and squash dis shit," Lee pleaded. JD looked up at him from the bag of coke.

"Nigga how you gonna squash dis shit? That nigga done put a hole in my leg foe nothing! Okay, make this hole disappear from my leg Lee, and I'll let the shit go! That's what I thought, so gimme that stick, and let's ride Boo," JD said. Lee looked at him like he wanted to shoot him again, and then he smiled.

"You right my dog go handle yo shit, but that ain't the same Jeff from 3 months ago. That nigga got a lotta of dope and money behind him now, so ya'll nigga's need not miss," Lee warned. Shane got behind the wheel and JD jumped in the passenger seat, gun in hand.

"Here I come, hold on," Antow yelled. He ran to the car with a pistol in his hand, ready and willing to take this ride, and he did.

Lee and I watched the headlights disappear into the night.

"Wow Kil! That's some bad ass luck for JD, when Poky hit that lick. That's why I stay strapped my brother Melo be doing a lot of foul shit, but he don't look that much like me, but yo foul ass do. I'll never get hit for another nigga shit," Lee said. We both laughed, then got back to trappin. Poky is JDs best friend, and they look a lot alike. After a few minutes we could hear the sound of an Assault rifle in the distance. Mechanicville isn't but one exit from here, on my third day out.

On my 6th day out, I'm still selling dope to stay out of prison. Back trapping out of the blue house alley. It's around 2:00 pm. All the big money hustler's not out yet, so I'm trying to get it while I can get it. Winnie Head got my traffic and Frank is the lookout. I got my pistol in my pocket, dope close at hand, one foot in prison, the other in a frying pan.

"Ah Kil! Here comes Rico," Frank yelled from the top of the block. I just sat there on the old blue house steps. Rico said nothing to me about hustling on Holderness, but for some hustlers his name means get the hell on fast. I remember right before the Black James murder Rico gave me almost two Ounces of hard for $500, real coke, and he never asked for a penny more. I got mad love for Rico, having known him since I can remember. His red S10 pulled up right in front of Mrs. Newell's house and parked not ten feet from me. He nodded his head to me. I nodded back, and that was that. Maybe two minutes went by, then....... A sky-blue Seville turned onto Holderness so fast, the two passenger wheels came up from the ground.

I heard the sound of a Glock 9mm. I didn't have a chance to run, but why would I run? That's my friend, my big homie Tyrone, shooting that gun right into Rico's truck. I sat there and watched. I didn't move or duck. When the bullets hit the truck Rico was already rolling across the seat. He came out the passenger door running like a seven foot track star, limping on one leg, he's hit. I watched like I was at the Rialto eating popcorn.

Big Ty was out of the car, running behind him. He stopped and took aim at the back of his head. The clip fell from the bottom of the gun. If I wasn't right there to witness it, I wouldn't believe it. Big Ty hurried to put it back in, but it was too late. Rico ran through Mr. Skeeter's yard, I could hear him laughing.

"What the fuck Kil I had that nigga dead! You see that shit," Ty asked. He had a black eye and a big bloody lip, I can see it's more to this story.

"Yeah! You did, you must've hit the clip button. You need to go look at your car," I told him. It was parked in the middle of the street. Just another day on Holderness Street, blood trails and bullet shells. A little later that day, I found out what all the bullets were about. Big Ty went to see Shane at his house over off Moreland. Not knowing Rico also lives there, word is Big Ty and Rico has the same girlfriend. Some bitch on Atwood, Alberna's sister. Shane says Rico slammed Big Ty on his face two times, and then he beat his fist up with Ty's face. I learned at a young age not to let a woman get me killed. Why these niggas like dipping there straws in the same drink, knowing the leading cause of death in the hood is hoes and money.

Speaking of whores, I'm trying to deal with one, Charity. She's poison, but she will never kill me, and if she thinks we will ever be together, she is highly mistaken. Rodneysha's my heart. She smiles when I hold her. I can see me all over her, it scares me, the thought of going away again. Charity left Rodneysha with my momma when she was less than a month old. She went to Miami and didn't come back until weeks later. She didn't even wait until her stitches were out. It's simple to me, my life will be better without her. She's a leech bitch is always begging, like somebody owes her something. I'm trying to pay my lawyer to stay free. She tried to get me to buy her and Rodneysha matching new Jordans. She don't give a fuck if I get life; she don't give a fuck about her own life. She just wants whatever she can get, but she's not getting it from me. She ain't with me in the trap selling rocks, or on the block popping off. She ain't never let me flip a dime. She hasn't risked her freedom for any of my crimes, she's a freeloader. Bootcamp did help me, in a way, I wasn't high for three months. I had time to identify a lot of my problems, and number one on my list Charity Grier. She doesn't know me; she doesn't know I know the Clan; she doesn't know blood is on all my money. And this bitch thinks she can eat for free, not on this campaign.

September 1st just13 days before my court date. I was standing in front of the building where Pimp Shawn was shot, on the corner of Lucile and Holderness. A brand new black BMW pulled beside me.

"What's up Kil, what it is," a voice said. I cautiously looked down inside of the window. The same Jeff Shane been shooting at almost every day, and ain't hit this nigga yet. Now look, sitting in the seat next to him is an AR-15 with a banana clip. I put both of my hands on the passenger window seal.

"Jeff! Let a pimp hold something, man. You know I just got out, nigga hit off. Gimme a survival kit," I asked. I never let these niggas know what I'm really thinking. I like to know what they are thinking. He popped open his glove box to show a big bag of cocaine and stacks of cash.

"You can get all dis, just go get that nigga Shane to walk up on dis corner. Dis 9 Os and five grand, and it's some good blow. Same shit Lee got, fish scales nigga," Jeff asked. I took my hands off the car, but I didn't step back. I looked him in his eyes. This man ain't a killer, he just doesn't want to get killed.

"Naw Jeff, you set that shit off. You shot JD when Poky was the one did the robbing. JD was in bootcamp wit me. Y'all just need to let that shit go homie. Please let that shit go," I pleaded. This situation has gotten way out of hand. Black Mickey, Lil Keith, and some of my Me-phi-yo niggas seen me at the Mall Westend and told me Jeff is looking for shooter for Shane, but I know Big Slick won't sanction that shit. When I told Shane what they said, he went and shot at Jeff again.

"I don't wanna kill that nigga, I just don't want that nigga to kill me. Here you go, you talk to that nigga, and you tell that nigga I'm my money fight my wars, so he better get his money right. I'm already war ready. That's on all I love, Kil," Jeff answered. He handed me two rubber banded stacks of cash. Then pull off burning rubber turning on Lucille headed towards the park. Shane is lucky I love him and I'm real, because big money will get you killed. I walked across Lucile to Winnie Head's momma house, Mrs. Frances. She lives next door to Shane's momma's house. Mrs. Francis' house is the first house on the corner. That's where we've been hanging since Clarence went to prison and lost the blue house. Shane and Will were in the back room sacking up rocks and sniffing blow. Shane lost his way without CP, he began snorting coke and hanging with the robbing crew. He doesn't trap anymore, he just takes. Lee and I are trying to talk to him, but Shane's a made man, he has his own plans.

"What's up gangsters," I greeted them. Neither one looked up.

"What up Kil," they both said at the same time.

"That nigga Jeff was just on the corner screaming peace, and I agree. That shit ain't even about you nigga. JD fuck wit a lot niggas let dem niggas handle that beef. That shit ain't bout no Holderness St money man. JD is a renegade, he traps anywhere he parks his car. That nigga just gotta job wit the city, he done squared up with Shane. Dis our life nigga dis how we eat, and where we stay. Don't shoot at Jeff no moe nigga if you do you better kill'em. Have you lost yo fuckin mind? That nigga gettin money man, real fuckin money. Like 20 on yo fuckin head type of money nigga," I tried to explain. Shane stood up from his chair, cocaine rimmed around his nose. He pulled his gun from behind his back and pointed it at my chest.

"You say 20 on my head? You tell dem pussy boyz it ain't enough! You and that nigga Lee ya'll thank ya'll better than me. Yall niggas ain't bust no guns foe me. I oughta shoot you in your heart nigga, but you ain't got one. Yall done turn yo backs on me foe dem LA Boyz, but when dem Miami Boyz was trying to kill you, who did you run to nigga. Now it's money over everything, but I can dig that. Just stay the fuck outta my business," Shane threatened. I had no fear, he's not gonna shoot me. We grew up together, he's just high, but what he's saying is true. My priorities have gotten different now I'm cased all up with a newborn. He lowered the gun and walked out.

"Kil that nigga has lost his everlasting mind. He pointing a gun at you wit all dis money on his head, that nigga trying to be dead. Man, dis dope got these niggas loosing they mutherfucking minds," Will said as he took a one off of his pinky nail. Almost every hustler on Holderness is playing with their nose by now, just a sign of the times. Needless to say Shane, and Twon went and shot up Jeff's trap that very same night. More wasted rounds, fifty shells on the ground. He ain't doing nothing but littering at that man, and that's so dangerous.

September 11th one day, and a wake up before my court day. My lawyer, that junkie Dwight, he's all paid up, but when I paid him the last of his ten grand. He still couldn't tell me what my outcome would be, and he didn't look too well. I'm no fool, all bets are on me going to jail. The hood is so sure Lee is throwing me a party tomorrow night, but tonight I'm trapping and Lee packing out of Shane's driveway. I'm up front in up under the street light, Lee up the driveway in the dark.

"Ah Kil man however that shit go Imma hold you down nigga, and you know Big Walt got yo lil girl. Fuck that bitch Charity! You gotta let a hoe be a hoe homie," Lee said.

"Yeah homie, I dig that shit. However that court shit goes, Imma be cool wit it. I just wanna get it over wit, so I can get on to some real money. Just keeps this connect wit these LA niggas solid, and we on to the real money, and that's real talk," I said. I'd put it all together in my head, it's a lot of money in front of us. The worst time I can get is like a 5-year sentence to serve 2 years, that will put me home in a year with good time. I will survive, but will Lee, Shane, and Wil, what will become of the hood in a year?

"I can dig it Kil, all I can tell you Imma keep it real," Lee replied. It's late now, around 11:00, we were about to take it in.

"Watch that car Kil," My lookout Whinny Head shouted. A green box Chevy pulled across the light, then stopped right in front of Shane's house. I stood in the driveway with my hands behind my back.

"Ah Rodney man come here for a minute," a voice from the inside of the car asked. I didn't recognize the car or the voice. I could only see two heads.

"Who is that? Nigga's get outta that car it's hot round here? You calling me by my govern out here nigga who is you"? I answered; I heard the sound of Lee putting one in the head of the AK.

Click-clack. The doors of the Chevy opened. I didn't recognize the driver right off, but the passenger is Chris from that Cascade crew.

"Dis Chris Kil. Don't shoot," Chris yelled back with his hands playfully in the air. This other guy had his hands in his pockets.

"I'm the nigga wit the dope tonight, not the one wit the gun. What y'all niggas want some soft? Cause we bout to dip," I said. As they walk closer to me I recognize the driver, Fathead Jimmy from Bowen Holmes.

"Naw Kil we good I'm looking for my nigga Shane," Chris answered.

"What y'all looking for Shane fo," Lee asked, standing out of the dark now with the AK pointing their way. I moved closer to Lee, I don't want to get caught in no crossfire.

"What up Big Lee everything cool homie I see that 47 piece. Dis girl was asking but Shane, so I was just," Chris said before Lee cut him off. Lee raises the AK, now I'm standing right beside him.

"Ain't no bitch asked about Shane nigga get the fuck away from here wit that game. Ain't no bitch asked about Shane. I'm telling y'all Shane ain't got shit to do wit that shit. Ya'll train to make me get in dis shit, nigga you already no I ain't gonna play witcha. Betcha I won't mess wit dis," Lee said; but they were back in the car so fast they didn't hear the other half. Lee aimed the rifle as the car backed up the hill and turned around.

"What's up wit dem fools Lee," I asked. I was a little surprised by the way he reacted.

"Shane gotta a lot of people looking for him, but a bitch ain't one. Dem nigga's hitters Kil," Lee answered.

"Chris a pussy," I said. He's no killer, and that I know.

"Naw Chris, still a little gofer! He probably just the ID man for that Bowen Holmes nigga Jimmy. Jeff been gettin money outta Bowen Holmes, he fuckin wit Fat-Steve, that nigga Jimmy be wit Fat-Steve," Lee replied. It all made real good sense to me. Shane better straighten his aim out for real.

I made it home a little past 12am, Charity the baby and I had to move in with my people. She lost the apartment in Deerfield in just 90 days, plus blew $20000 grand. She said it went on my new-born baby, but I know it went up her nose. Charity ain't nothing but a powder head prostitute, and she had the nerves to name the baby after not only, but my momma too. Rodneysha Artie Lashay Brown now that was desperation. I just pray this is not a trick, baby. All of this is my family idea, I never wanted a baby by a whore, it's embarrassing. That night I laid awake, trying to think of the best way to rid myself of what could be a lifelong problem for me. I know the best way, I just have to pick the right day.

I go to court in the morning, so tonight we're gonna party like it's 1999. Lee got kegs of beer and fifths of all the liquor you can name, and plenty of weed and cocaine. It all went down in Mrs. Francis' house, Whinney Heads momma. All the Westend G's came from both ends, from Harris Holmes to the Flatlands, all to just show respect and I love this shit. I got a 100-gun Salute like it was December 31th, I felt like this is my rebirth. At this point, I feel really loved. What level am I on? Does this make me a boss, because a lot of bosses showed up for me, or does it make me a boss because I'm about to pay the cost, and didn't fall in love with cheeses, grew four legs, and a tail out my ass. What really made my night is when Shane showed up, but he did live next door.

"Rakil, look at you now? I can just imagine how big your funeral would've been, but you still my main man," Shane said, as he stood towering over me with his arms open for a hug. I stood and gave him a big one.

"I love you nigga, and I got something for ya. That I had made just for ya," I whispered in his ear. I reached down under the couch cushion where I was seated, and pulled out a nine shot 12 gauge Mossberg shotgun.

"I always wanted one of these Kil. From my heart to this trigger you my fucking nigga, and thangs ain't gonna be the same without ya my nigga. I love you," Shane said; with his eyes full of tears. Shane had changed faster and more than any of us. He has been riding with the Aki's. They say blood makes the killer thirsty. Problem is all the real killer killers are in jail around here, if not Jeff would've been dead, and that's a fact.

"I know you do, and Big Boo dig dis. Ain't no missing wit it. Nothing but slugs give it to him like Aks did Tommy. Leave da nigga faceless," I told him. We hugged once more, and he was gone. Lee and I kicked it most of the night and into the early morning. We know the real, and that is we may ever see each other again. I'm not worried about surviving my situation, I'm praying Lee survives our situation. He's my brother, and yes, I am my brother's keeper, and so is he to me.

Flowers for the Dead, Flowers for the Dead

The next morning I woke up bright and early. Daddy had my breakfast on the table. I had to be at court by 10 am Charity was still asleep, momma feeding Rodneysha, and praying for me at the same time. I ate my food fast, I'm ready to know my faith, probation, house arrest, or prison. My lawyer has been out of the office a lot since I paid him all up. I kiss momma and Rodneysha. A couple, see you later, praying it's sooner than later.

Daddy and I didn't say much on the ride to the courthouse until we pulled up in front.

"Rod I know you think the worst will happen. Just keep in mind God knows best. Not that lawyer, judge, or prosecutor. Let God do his will, and you accept it like a man. I love you boy, you take care of yourself, and imma take care of the rest," daddy said. I hate making this man sad, I can see the tears welling up in his eyes. It made me want to cry, but I couldn't, and that hurt even more.

"I love you too old man, and I got dis don't worry," I said. I didn't even look him in the eyes, because I knew I would cry.

My daddy really loves me, and there is no greater love than a father's love. I say it because all my friends got mommas, but just a few of us have daddy's, so that's something I have always cherished.

I walked up the stone steps and didn't look back. Today is Friday September 13th. It was almost 90 degrees, and the summer wasn't trying to go away. I opened the big door and entered my fate. The air inside is so cold it gives me chills. People were walking around all on their own missions, some trying to save lives, others trying to destroy lives as I see it. Some say you do the crime, you do the time. I found courtroom D and standing outside the door was my junky ass Attorney Dwight Thomas. He's in a conversation with that fine ass white girl prosecutor Nancy Grace. I walked right past him and into the courtroom. It's full of black people like a family reunion, but it looks like we're gonna have a barbecue. I took the first seat I could find, white judge, white prosecutor, white bailiff, but all black defendants. I listened to 12 cases, all drugs 10 got prison time 2 got probation, white man's Justice black man's grief. Then the judge called my name.

"All parties involved case number Z20510 Rodney Lajuan Brown vs. The State of Georgia," the judge announced. Dwight and I stood together and walked through the little wooden gate together.

"How are you doing this morning, your honor? Dwight here. I'm representing Rodney Brown in this matter, and I'm gonna have to ask for a continuation in this case, sir," Dwight said.

"On what grounds," the judge asked. Dwight scratches the top of his head as sweat pops from his forehead. I can smell the cocaine coming from his pores, I watched his powder blue dress shirt turn navy blue with sweat in an instant. I knew that my fate was sealed.

"I need time to talk to more witnesses," Dwight answered.

"Your honor this is a drug case in which Mr. Brown was caught red-handed, what witnesses," the white prosecutor answered. All eyes were on Dwight and he's speechless.

"So I'll follow the recommendations from the state. Mr. Rodney Brown I sentence you to 5 serve 3 years, and 5 years probation to follow. Next case, please" the judge said, and that was it. I was on my way to prison, but first a stop at Rice Street, Fulton County jail...a living hell. They took me to the basement of the courthouse it's full of cages pack with nigga's. It reminded me of a slave movie. The guard picked me out a cage. He opened the door and locked me in. I sat there with the rest of the slaves for six hours. Waiting on the long chain man to come take us to Rice Street. Once we make it there, it's another 3 hours before you make it upstairs to the beds and phones, if you're lucky. I was lucky on this day I made it to my floor around 6 p.m.

"Open up six hundred southwest. Jones, Reed, and Brown, say hello to your new home, and don't stand in the red zone. Get in," Officer Whitehead said. The door slid open, and we stepped in.

"Get the fuck outta my red zone," a voice from a speaker spoke. I looked down at the 5x5 red box drawn on the floor in front of the door, that I'd become familiar with doing my time at this county jail. I step out of the box and then scan the cell block. A lot of familiar faces and voices, but nobody really stood out. It's like being at Charles Disco, but everyone is unshaved and had on county blues. I looked at the phone banks and all the phones hung from their hooks. I got to call my G, but I know by now the word is out on me. Lee and Jackie still lived together even after she shot him in both of his legs with the same bullet. Jackie is a real nut, but I love her like a sister, and I'm the one that introduced the two. I picked up the first phone and made a collect call.

"Hello," Jackie answered. Then the operator took over. Five seconds later..

"What it is G? I already know what's happening wit you. It ain't bad at all compared to what them niggas did to Shane today. They got 'em. They caught him on the corner and hit in the back twice before he could make it across the street. He died in his momma's front yard. It was fucked up homie,". Lee said, crying these words out to me.

"I ain't lying about that and I ain't lying about this. The last words from that G, was blast for me. That's what we bout to do, just watch the news nigga," Lee said. The phone went dead, and my head began to pound. I hung the phone up, and I was just about to cry.

"Phone check dad, you owe me two honey buns for that call. Didn't you see it was off the hook," a voice from behind me said. I didn't know the voice, but I knew the slang. Whoever this is they're from Herndon Homes, because for some reason they call everybody dad. I turn around quickly.

"Fuck you dad! Get it in blood nigga," I said as I looked face to face with Rufus, Wee-Wee, and my personal homeboys Lee, Beautiful Bobby. I graded Bob and cried on his shoulder as I told him what just happened to Shane.

"Kil our end is always near. Death around every corner in our hood, I'm sorry homie," Bob said.

"Flowers for the dead, flowers for the dead," Lee

LUCILE KIL

said..............................

PROLOGUE

"From The West End To Lil-Pakistan Part2" : Black Lives Don't Matter

"This shit is holy land man, it's like the Gaza Strip to these Muzlims, they will murder you for this shit. These ain't no ordinary Muzlims. They leader used to be a real gangster. He was in the Black Panthers, H Rap Brown now they call him Jamil Al-amin. He was on the FBI's most wanted list. My daddy told me a long time ago the FBI hates Jamil and they want him dead or in jail for the rest of his life. Believe me, he is the last nigga on this planet you want a war wit. These people are very militant; they train in the woods two to three times a year. They taught me how to shoot straight, and they have more guns and bullet proof vests than the police. You standing right in the middle of Li-Pakistan. I keep telling you this is holy land, one day they gonna make this place famous." I explained. I wasn't exaggerating; it was all facts.

"So why did you bring us here?" Rick asked, looking around nervously.

"Man be cool, I grew up wit these people they not gonna fuck wit us, they know where I make my money, and they know, I would never disrespect Jamil. Not because I fear Him but because I got love for him. He's a Fearless man that stands up to white people. He believes we should be more than we are, but we let the white man trick us."

"Okay, man, fuck all that civil rights shit. How long will it take you to move two bricks at 20 a block? Shit going up. I was going to give you one, and Big Wil one, but you cut him outta the pic," Rick said without hesitation.

"Give me two weeks; I've got to break one down for the block," I answered. Rick Smiled.

"I'll tell you what, you got three weeks. C'mon let's go; that cab coming back this way, look," Rick said, pointing. The brown cab circled the park all night. We headed back to the BMW. Rick's cousin stood outside the car with a black bookbag in hand, handing it to me.

"It's two bricks in the bag and a beeper; we'll be in touch," the cousin said. They both opened their doors and got inside the car, but before they pulled off, Rick rolled his window down. At the same time, the brown cab pulled up beside them.

"Assalamualaikum," a black figure inside the cab yelled out, shining the spotlight inside the car like the police do. Rick froze in his seat.

"Hell yea, I want some bacon. Gimme a ride to the top, Ahk?" I asked. I heard laughter inside the cab. The figure turned off the spotlight. Sitting behind the wheel was the little black Scarface Jamil, a Muslim brother I truly love. He saved my life more than twice.

"I'm out; y'all know how to find me," I said as I walked away.

"Keep it business; it's blood on this money, Cuz," Rick said.

"Always, nigga, on Allah!" I answered. Then the black Beemer took off, burning a little rubber. I got in the back seat of the cab. In the front passenger seat was a big, white, bald head.

"What's up, Jamil? Take me to 1177, please. Who is this white boy you got wit you?" I asked about the bald-headed guy. They both laughed.

"What up, Kil? That's Assad; you remember him, Bosha's people, Zack's brother, some sister Fatimah kids who you used to live next door to on the dead end of Holderness," Jamil explained, and I remembered him very well.

Made in the USA
Columbia, SC
24 September 2024

42213856R00167